The Latin American Short Story at its Limits
Fragmentation, Hybridity and Intermediality

LEGENDA

LEGENDA, founded in 1995 by the European Humanities Research Centre of the University of Oxford, is now a joint imprint of the Modern Humanities Research Association and Routledge. Titles range from medieval texts to contemporary cinema and form a widely comparative view of the modern humanities, including works on Arabic, Catalan, English, French, German, Greek, Italian, Portuguese, Russian, Spanish, and Yiddish literature. An Editorial Board of distinguished academic specialists works in collaboration with leading scholarly bodies such as the Society for French Studies, the British Comparative Literature Association and the Association of Hispanists of Great Britain & Ireland.

MHRA

The Modern Humanities Research Association (MHRA) encourages and promotes advanced study and research in the field of the modern humanities, especially modern European languages and literature, including English, and also cinema. It also aims to break down the barriers between scholars working in different disciplines and to maintain the unity of humanistic scholarship in the face of increasing specialization. The Association fulfils this purpose primarily through the publication of journals, bibliographies, monographs and other aids to research.

LONDON AND NEW YORK

Routledge is a global publisher of academic books, journals and online resources in the humanities and social sciences. Founded in 1836, it has published many of the greatest thinkers and scholars of the last hundred years, including adorno, einstein, Russell, Popper, Wittgenstein, Jung, Bohm, Hayek, Mcluhan, Marcuse and Sartre. Today Routledge is one of the world's leading academic publishers in the Humanities and Social Sciences. It publishes thousands of books and journals each year, serving scholars, instructors, and professional communities worldwide.

www.routledge.com

STUDIES IN HISPANIC AND LUSOPHONE CULTURES

Studies in Hispanic and Lusophone Cultures are selected and edited by the Association of Hispanists of Great Britain & Ireland. The series seeks to publish the best new research in all areas of the literature, thought, history, culture, film, and languages of Spain, Spanish America, and the Portuguese-speaking world.

The Association of Hispanists of Great Britain & Ireland is a professional association which represents a very diverse discipline, in terms of both geographical coverage and objects of study. Its website showcases new work by members, and publicises jobs, conferences and grants in the field.

www.legendabooks.com/series/shlc

STUDIES IN HISPANIC AND LUSOPHONE CULTURES

1. *Unamuno's Theory of the Novel*, by C. A. Longhurst
2. *Pessoa's Geometry of the Abyss: Modernity and the* Book of Disquiet, by Paulo de Medeiros
3. *Artifice and Invention in the Spanish Golden Age*, edited by Stephen Boyd and Terence O'Reilly
4. *The Latin American Short Story at its Limits: Fragmentation, Hybridity and Intermediality*, by Lucy Bell
5. *Spanish New York Narratives 1898–1936: Modernisation, Otherness and Nation*, by David Miranda-Barreiro
6. *The Art of Ana Clavel: Ghosts, Urinals, Dolls, Shadows and Outlaw Desires*, by Jane Elizabeth Lavery
7. *Alejo Carpentier and the Musical Text*, by Katia Chornik

The Latin American Short Story at its Limits

Fragmentation, Hybridity and Intermediality

L<small>UCY</small> B<small>ELL</small>

LONDON AND NEW YORK

2014

First published 2014 by Modern Humanities Research Association and Routledge

2 Park Square, Milton Park, Abingdon, Oxfordshire OX14 4RN
52 Vanderbilt Avenue, New York, NY 10017

Routledge is an imprint of the Taylor & Francis Group, an informa business

First issued in paperback 2020

ISBN 978-1-909662-13-1 (hbk)
ISBN 978-0-367-60175-1 (pbk)

CONTENTS

Acknowledgements   ix

Introduction:
The Latin American Short Story: Between Tradition and Modernity   1

1   Juan Rulfo, the Transculturator   27

2   Julio Cortázar, the World–Opener   66

3   Augusto Monterroso, the Microwriter   110

Conclusion:
Looking Forward: After–lives, Adaptations and Legacies   158

Bibliography   167

Index   175

For my loving and ever-supportive family,
Sheena, Roger, Katie, Tom and Joshua

ACKNOWLEDGEMENTS

This book would not have been possible without a research grant from the Arts and Humanities Research Council, which funded the doctoral project upon which this monograph is based, and a research trip to Princeton for archival research in summer 2010.

My deepest thanks go to Dr Rory O'Bryen, for all his guidance, support and motivation throughout the germinal phases of this project. Rory began supervising me at undergraduate level, and has since then been hugely inspirational, and indeed highly influential in my decision to pursue an academic path. I would also like to extend particular thanks to two fellows for their constant encouragement, advice and friendship throughout my time at Trinity Hall, Cambridge: Dr Peter Hutchinson and Dr Louise Haywood. I am also grateful to Prof. Steven Boldy, Dr Geoffrey Kantaris, Dr Joanna Page and Prof. Philip Swanson (University of Sheffield) for providing me with intellectual stimulation and academic advice in the field of Latin American Studies. Thanks to Prof. Diane Watt, Prof. Justin Edwards and Dr Dawn Marley (from the School of English and Languages at the University of Surrey) for their support in the publication of this book.

Thanks to the *Fundación Juan Rulfo*, particularly Arch. Víctor Jiménez and Dr Alberto Vital, for granting me access to materials in the Foundation, for their very generous invitation to the *Coloquio Inaugural de la Cátedra Extraordinaria Juan Rulfo* (September 2013), and for giving me permission to reproduce some of Juan Rulfo's beautiful photographs. Thanks to the staff of the *Biblioteca Nacional de la República Argentina* in Buenos Aires for helping me to consult and reproduce images from their magazine collection. Thanks to the Rare Books and Special Collections Department of Princeton University Library for their permission to consult and reproduce materials from the Augusto Monterroso Papers.

Portions of chapter 1 appeared in a different form as 'The Death of the Storyteller and the Poetics of (Un)Containment: Juan Rulfo's *El llano en llamas*', *Modern Language Review*, 107.3 (2012), 815–36, and 'Photography, Punctum and Shock: Re-Viewing Juan Rulfo's Short Stories', *Bulletin of Hispanic Studies*, 91.4 (2014), 437–52. I thank the editors of *MLR* and *BHS* for their encouragement and assistance.

An enormous thank you to my friends, who have been a constant source of emotional and intellectual support. I owe special thanks to my friends Catriona McAllister, Charlotte Lee, Hannah Mowat, Semele Assinder, Ned Allen, and Catherine Smale. Finally, I would like to thank my family for their unconditional support — particularly my father Roger Bell and cousin Jeffery Povall, who read parts of the original manuscript.

L.B., Surrey, July 2014

INTRODUCTION

The Latin American Short Story:
Between Tradition and Modernity

The Latin American Short Story and Tradition

Critics have sometimes argued that the Latin American short story is the product
of a long, oral storytelling tradition. Martha Elena Munguía Zatarain goes so
far as to propose 'la memoria de los orígenes orales en el cuento como el factor
determinante para la conformación del género'.[1] She quotes Françoise Perus, for
whom 'la persistencia y vigencia de la tradición narrativa oral en amplios sectores
de nuestros países' can go some way to explain 'la permanencia y actualidad del
cuento en la tradición narrativa.'[2] The literary tale, in this view, is constructed on
the foundations of an oral tradition; the forward-moving trajectory of the literary
short story retains a link with the oral origins of storytelling. Munguía Zatarain
pinpoints a number of (sometimes tenuous) links between the modern short story
and the oral tale: its gestural, performative quality; its ability to provide a 'puente
de comunicación artística'; the tension between constraint and creative freedom
(52).[3] The oral tale, she argues, is the 'compañera, contemporánea, de la creación
literaria' (39).

In his anthology of the Latin American short story, Roberto González Echevarría
suggests that the proliferation of short stories in Latin America

> can be explained in part by the convergence of narrative cycles from powerful
> and diverse cultural sources: the various native cultures (Aztec, Mayan, Incan);
> the several African cultures (with the Yomba prevailing); the Iberian culture,
> which includes the Portuguese, the Galician, and the Catalan, among others, as
> well as the entire European heritage reaching back through the Middle Ages,
> to classical and biblical times and to the Indo-European sources of the Western
> narrative stock.[4]

In other words, the richness of the modern short story is a partial result of the
richness of tradition; of the wealth of traditional stories that Latin America has
inherited; of its cultural heritage. On the basis that the art of storytelling entails the
retelling of old stories, González Echevarría argues that the prominence of the short
story in Latin America can be attributed to the cosmopolitan heritage that gives it
a wealth of material to re-invent. The modern Latin American short story, then, is
perceived as a product of indigenous cosmogonies, Old Testament stories, classical
mythology and even myths of Discovery propagated by the Spanish colonizers. This

vision is symptomatic of a critical position that views the *cuento* as a timeless and universal form, a position manifested by the insistence that 'everyone, everywhere, has always told stories' (5).

From an overtly Christian perspective, Lida Aronne-Amestoy reads the Latin American 'cuento epifánico' as a direct continuation of myths. Her argument is that, whereas Europe — and the short story that it produces — undergoes a 'corte de los lazos con la tradición que deja al hombre sólo frente a la nada', Latin America — and the corresponding *cuento* — 'nunca evidencia un divorcio real del mito'.[5] She links this persistence of myth in Latin America to 'el entorno primitivo y virgen (aún hoy) de nuestro continente; el exoticismo geográfico; la idiosincrasia anárquica del criollo' (79). Never divorced from archetypal models, the Latin American *cuento* is viewed in this respect not as rupture from tradition (like the European short story), but rather as a return to myth, as a spiritual — in fact Christian — attempt to achieve an integrated, whole, total experience.

Finally, in his prologue to *El cuento hispanoamericano*, Enrique Pupo-Walker argues that the short story is less a product of modernity than a continuation of tradition:

> en la prosa de ficción el cuento suele verse como la modalidad más próxima al habla cotidiana. Casi instintivamente asociamos su forma presurosa con las digresiones ilustrativas o anecdóticas que de ordinario genera la conversación. Guiados casi siempre por equivalencias de esa naturaleza, hemos asumido el cuento como la forma más accesible que nos ha legado la narrativa de creación. Certezas de ese orden han de parecernos aceptables, sobre todo, cuando verificamos las similitudes que obviamente existen entre el cuento literario, relatos tradicionales y formas diversas del apólogo.[6]

The literary *cuento*, from Pupo-Walker's perspective, is the closest literary genre to oral language. It is an inherited form that has its roots in Creation narratives, whether the Genesis or the Popol Vuh, the traditional tale or the apologue. By way of argument, he points out the traditional elements of modern stories and the modern elements of age-old stories. Recent short stories by Gabriel García Márquez, Jorge Luis Borges and Salvador Salazar Arrué are entrenched in myth. Conversely, ancient tales transcribed onto Egyptian papyruses are astoundingly modern (12), and certain brief fictions of Indian historiography (such as the tale about the black woman Juana García told by cronista Juan Rodríguez Freyle in the 1637 story *El carnero*) prefigure modern narrative forms (20). In order to highlight the timeless, universal quality of the short story, he compares stories by Horacio Quiroga, Jorge Luis Borges and Juan Rulfo to certain exempla from *El conde Lucanor* by don Juan Manuel (1335); Borges's 'El evangelio según Marcos' (1970) to 'El juramento del cautivo' (in the third night of *One Thousand and One Nights*); and points out that the Grimm brothers' tale 'The Old Man and his Grandson', in spite of its didactic aspect, has a 'capacidad revelatoria' that is akin to the modern short story. The gist of Pupo-Walker's argument is that the similarities between such disparate tales from different times, combined with the dissimilarities between modern short story writers like Anton Chekhov, James Joyce and Franz Kafka, renders the historicity of the *cuento* dubious.

Yet the twists and turns of Pupo-Walker's argument lead him to contradict this

initial viewpoint:

> En última instancia, si alguna generalización hoy nos parece viable es que el cuento literario ejemplifica — quizá idóneamente — esa ansiosa fragmentación episódica y comunicativa que ha predominado en la cultura de la modernidad. [...] Con notable exactitud el cuento ha representado la parcelación incongruente que las sociedades modernas experimentaron en el siglo pasado como consecuencia de la revolución industrial. (28)

His argument thus comes into line with that of Walter Benjamin, who in his 1937 essay 'The Storyteller', links the European short story form with the fragmentation of tradition: 'the art of storytelling is reaching its end because the epic side of truth, wisdom, is dying out'; 'familiar though his name may be to us, the storyteller in his living immediacy is by no means a present force'.[7] The decline of orality and the death of the storyteller are linked with the weakening of the structures on which the authority of wisdom is based: community, tradition and religion. The modern narrator can no longer enjoy a living, immediate relation with a 'community of listeners' because, in Benjamin's terms, 'there is no more weaving and spinning to go on while they are being listened to' (91). Displaced from the realm of living speech, modern narrative is born from a solitary process: 'the birthplace of the novel is the solitary individual, who is no longer able to express himself by giving examples of his most important concerns, is himself uncounseled, and cannot counsel others' (87). Whereas traditional stories are woven from the storyteller's personal, lived experience, the modern narrative is severed not only from listeners, but also from the teller. Cut off from others and even from himself, the modern writer is unable to provide advice, information, and counsel. It is from this situation that the genre of the short story arises:

> We have witnessed the evolution of the 'short story', which has removed itself from oral tradition and no longer permits that slow piling one on top of the other of thin, transparent layers which constitutes the most appropriate picture of the way in which the perfect narrative is revealed through the layers of a variety of retellings. (93)

The abbreviation of storytelling is connected with the dislocation of narrative from tradition, the fast pace of modern life, and the consequent fragmentation of the continuum of experience. In what follows, I shall ask a number of questions in order to gauge the extent to which Benjamin's mournful prophecies are fulfilled in the Latin American context. What is the relationship between the Latin American short story and tradition? To what extent does the Latin American short story owe its existence and richness to a narrative tradition, or to multiple narrative traditions? To what extent does its liveliness as a form derive from its detachment from those traditions?

In order to address these questions, I will delve in depth into the aesthetics of fragmentation that underpins the varied form of the Latin American short story. My argument, in brief, is that the genre constitutes itself not only as a continuation of, but also as a rupture both *from* and *in*, traditional narrative and narrative tradition. The consistencies and inconsistencies of the short story will be illuminated by the works of three writers: Juan Rulfo (b. Jalisco, Mexico, 1917), Julio Cortázar

(b. Brussels, Belgium, 1914) and Augusto Monterroso (b. Tegucigalpa, Honduras, 1921). By way of introduction, I shall begin by pinpointing the social, intellectual and literary relations between these three authors, before situating their respective theories of the short story in broader critical contexts.

Rulfo, Cortázar and Monterroso: Social, Intellectual and Literary Convergences

Though these three contemporaries were born and raised in different countries, they were connected through intellectual and social ties. In a 1975 diary entry, Monterroso reflects: 'conozco a Juan Rulfo desde hace muchos años. Lo veo todos los días durante varias horas'.[8] Their work for the *Instituto Nacional Indigenista* in the 1970s brought them together and consolidated a long friendship. Monterroso's relationship with Cortázar is attested by his trips to Managua with Cortázar and his wife Carol;[9] by the level to which he is affected by his death and his subsequent visits to his grave in Paris;[10] and by the fact that, with Alba Rojo, he would head the *Fondo Julio Cortázar de solidaridad para la lectura*, a commission in charge of sending to Nicaragua five copies of every book published by the *Editorial Muchnik*.[11] In an interview with Carlos Morales in 1995, Monterroso takes a tongue-in-cheek view of his friendship with Cortázar: when asked whether his small stature is a privilege or a disadvantage, he responds, 'me ha sido indiferente. He tenido amigos muy altos. Por ejemplo, fui muy amigo de Cortázar y cuando lo saludaba de mano siempre le decía: los extremos se tocan. (Risas).'[12] By contrast, Rulfo's tribute to Cortázar takes on a more sentimental tone:

> Lo queremos porque es bondadoso.
> Es bondadoso como ser humano y muy bueno como escritor. Tiene un corazón tan grande que Dios necesitó fabricar un cuerpo también grande para acomodar ese corazón suyo. Luego mezcló los sentimientos con el espíritu de Julio. De allí resultó que Julio no sólo fuera un hombre bueno, sino justo. Todos sabemos cuánto se ha sacrificado por la justicia. [...] Por eso lo queremos. Lo queremos tanto sus amigos, sus admiradores y sus hermanos.
> En realidad, él es nuestro hermano mayor.[13]

Rulfo's praise of Cortázar's generosity and sense of justice is a reference to his activism against Latin American dictatorships, demonstrated for example by his participation in the 1975 Russell tribunal, an investigation into Human Rights violations in Latin America, and his support for the Sandinista revolution in Nicaragua that sought to overthrow Anastasio Somoza's regime in 1979. The friendship between the 'brothers' is thus not only a social tie, but also a political one: a shared resistance to hegemonic rule; a shared socialist outlook.

The web of relations between Monterroso, Rulfo and Cortázar is reinforced by planned and coincidental encounters in intellectual, artistic contexts. In a letter to his English editor Walter Bradbury in June 1975, Monterroso notes that he and Rulfo recently went to a symposium in Poland, where they joined their friend Cortázar.[14] On another occasion, Rulfo and Monterroso meet by chance at Sants station in Barcelona, leading the latter to conjecture that 'los encuentros no deben de ser tan casuales como parecen'.[15] 'De ahí', Monterroso goes on, 'surge un obsequio: uno de los primeros ejemplares del libro de Carol Dunlop y Julio Cortázar: *Los autonautas de la cosmopista o Un viaje atemporal París-Marsella*, que ese mismo día sale a la venta'.[16] Against geographical barriers, these three authors form an intellectual triangle that in some cases echoes, and in other cases fuels, their literary connections. In this study, though, my chief concern is formal rather than biographical. My argument is that they are brought together by their aesthetics of brevity, as highlighted by their intersecting theories of the short story and Monterroso's numerous homages to his contemporaries.

To a certain extent, Monterroso shares Benjamin's view of the short story as a symptom of a break from tradition. On the one hand, Monterroso resists building an idealistic image of the traditional storyteller, implicitly rejecting the polarization of tradition and modernity, community and society that underpins Benjamin's account. In a draft of his Premio Príncipe speech on the short story, he insists: 'No cometeré la ingenuidad de hablar de la antigüedad del cuento, de sus orígenes en la noche de los tiempos; ni recurriré a la imagen del contador de cuentos de la tribu alrededor de un fuego recién inventado, ~~descubierto, o utilizado por el hombre~~'[17] (his deletion). Here, he claims that he is rejecting the myth of the storyteller, a myth that Monterroso deems a modern invention, a response to the nostalgia for more integrated, rural communities. But without conjuring this image or illusion of a tribal storyteller, he does affirm that the short story represents a departure from oral storytelling. The essay 'Breve, brevísimo' (2001) opens thus:

> En la era moderna, desde Edgar Allan Poe, Guy de Maupassant y Anton Chéjov, para mencionar tan sólo a los principales iniciadores de su modernidad en el siglo XIX, se escriben cuentos que, sin duda, ya no son lo que habían sido desde tiempo inmemorial.[18]

The modern short story, then, is a decided break from the timeless art of storytelling: the stories of Cortázar, Borges and Onetti, among others, 'ha[n] hecho a un lado las reglas tradicionales'; they are 'despojado de sus viejos asideros'; 'lejos [...] del cuento tradicional' (98). As Monterroso's language suggests, then, the short story is defined not as a continuation of the storytelling tradition, but rather as a rupture from tradition: it is stripped of, and far removed from, its old holds, moulds, and rules. One reason for this necessary rupture is laid bare in his analysis of the second of Italo Calvino's *Seis propuestas para el nuevo milenio* [Six Memos for a New Millennium] (1988): 'Rapidez' [Speed]. Changing times bring about changes in form, as Calvino's demand for speed suggests: the need for concentration will increase 'en los tiempos cada vez más congestionados que nos aguardan' (103). This is echoed in Monterroso's notes for his class on the modern short story: 'Lo que dice [Edgar Allan] Poe sobre la extensión ya no se vale. En tiempo de Poe una sesión podía ser muy larga. Hoy no: no hay tiempo.'[19] The increasing abbreviation of narrative is thus partly a result of practical factors: the lack of time. This echoes Benjamin's argument that the abbreviation of narrative results from the disappearance of the conditions for traditional storytelling, notably the availability of vast expanses of time necessitated by narrative cycles. Monterroso takes this one step further. Even Poe's restrictions on the short story — that it should not 'exceed in length what might be perused in an hour'[20] — have to be altered in order to account for the ever-increasing pace of life.

Yet Monterroso's essay 'Breve, brevísimo' also displays certain internal contradictions: the discontinuity, or the break that the short story constitutes, stands
in a dialectical relationship with continuity: 'generación va, y generación viene,
pero el cuento [...] siempre permanece' (99). The story, in whatever guise it might
appear, constitutes the link between generations: it not only stems from, but also
creates, the continuity of experience. This dialectic of continuity and rupture is also
apparent in his comments on Calvino's *Seis propuestas*. On the one hand, as the title
suggests, Calvino's memos are a call for new forms of literature that mark a break
from the last millennium. On the other hand, Monterroso suggests that Calvino
'anhelaba tan sólo que nuestra literatura [...] siga siendo en el futuro como lo ha
venido siendo durante los últimos veinticinco siglos' (102). And, as he points out,
short forms (fables, epigrams and proverbs) 'constituyen una antigua y gran riqueza
de nuestra tradición literaria' (104). The twists and turns in Monterroso's argument
display some of the complexities and contradictions inherent in the short story: it is
at once timeless and situated in a particular historical time; age old and new; rooted
in tradition and uprooted by modernity.

In spite of this hesitation, however, Monterroso insistently relates the short story
to the experience of modernity and to the fragmentation of human experience that
it brings about. In his notes for a course on the short story, Monterroso sees the
defining point of literary modernity as 'cuando el escritor ya no tiene la verdad, ya
no es profeta. Al contrario, se ve a sí mismo como alguien sin verdad que busca la
verdad sin encontrarla' (his emphasis).[21] The modern writer is devoid of counsel and
wisdom, which rely on the existence of truth and the ability to communicate it. In
his notes 'Lo moderno II', he echoes Benjamin's argument:

> (1) El autor, el poeta, ya no es aquel que lo sabe todo y que puede dar
> soluciones a los problemas de la gente.
> (2) Los protagonistas ya no son héroes, personajes ejemplares. Así, el escritor
> se encuentra solo, desamparado.[22]

The modern writer is no longer an authoritative, Benjaminian storyteller able to
provide practical advice, solutions to concrete problems; he is stripped of power,
authority and wisdom. As Monterroso puts it himself elsewhere, 'El escritor no
domina la situación.'[23] Since the author is alone, cut off from human relations, there
is no possibility of direct communication, no way of passing his experience on to
his fellow men. The terms used here by Monterroso to describe the modern writer
reflect those of Benjamin: 'uncounseled', 'isolated', 'solitary'.

Both Benjamin and Monterroso pinpoint Miguel de Cervantes's *Don Quijote*
as the first display of literary modernity, because of the internal contradictions of
the eponymous hero. For Benjamin, Cervantes's novel 'teaches how the spiritual
greatness, the boldness, the helpfulness of one of the noblest of men, Don Quixote,
are completely devoid of counsel and do not contain the slightest scintilla of wisdom'
(87–88). Similarly, for Monterroso, Don Quijote 'está lleno de contradicciones: es
loco-cuerdo, ridículo y sublime, iracundo y compasionero, agudo e ingenuo, etc.
etc. El lector no sabe ya como va a ser en la página siguiente.'[24] What we are
'taught' in *Don Quijote*, then, is in fact the impossibility of the kind of 'teaching'
offered by the traditional storyteller, wisdom that stems from accumulated exper-

ience passed on from one generation to the next. For Benjamin and Monterroso alike, continuity and stability are replaced in Cervantes's work by discontinuity and instability, internal and external fragmentation, doubt and perplexity.

Cortázar's 'Algunos aspectos del cuento' stands in a more complex relationship with Benjamin's 'The Storyteller'. Whereas Benjamin reflects nostalgically on the decay of a tradition, Cortázar celebrates the revolutionary possibilities of the aesthetics of the short story. Cortázar's lecture given in La Havana in 1962, though centred on a literary concern with the short story, is in broader terms a response to a post-revolutionary demand for openness and communication, to 'el deseo que se ve en ustedes de actuar, de expresarse, de comunicarse como nunca habían podido hacerlo antes'.[25] The question of new forms of expression, of how to 'escribir revolucionariamente' (529), lies at the centre of his lecture, and therefore at the heart of the modern short story that it seeks to theorize. Form, rather than content, is what for Cortázar determines a revolutionary piece of writing.

For him, the short story is decidedly distinct from the oral storytelling tradition. Hence he criticizes the contemporary tendency according to which Argentina's

> larga tradición de cuentos orales, que los gauchos se transmiten de noche en torno al fogón, que los padres siguen contando a sus hijos, [...] de golpe pasan por la pluma de un escritor regionalista y, en una abrumadora mayoría de casos, se convierten en pésimos cuentos. (525)

His argument stands against those who believe that writing a good story merely consists in writing down a traditional tale, preserving its oral qualities: its tone, its regional, rural linguistic turns, or its grammatical inaccuracies. Here he shares Borges's scorn — famously expressed in his 1951 lecture 'El escritor argentino y la tradición' — for 'color local', and with that, a similarly aggressive cosmopolitanism.[26] For Cortázar, the crucial difference between the 'dreadful' stories of those who attempt to translate oral tales directly into written form, and the stories written by literary masters on the same theme (Horacio Quiroga, Benito Lynch, Ricardo Güiraldes), lies in their *craft*: the labour that turns the theme into literary form, into art. In this regard, he is echoed by Monterroso, who notes that 'escribir como se habla puede ser tan malo como hablar como se escribe. Escribir es un acto artificial, y en esto consiste su interés, o su gracia.'[27] Monterroso and Cortázar alike uphold the merits of artifice, constructedness and craft, seeing the short story's rupture from the string of *gaucho* tales as a positive, necessary change. Furthermore, Cortázar erects his defence of the short story against the 'estrecho criterio de muchos que confunden literatura con pedagogía, literatura con enseñanza, literatura con adoctrinamiento ideológico' (529) — in other words, against the nostalgia for a storyteller who shares knowledge, educates and teaches, a role that rests on the belief in the communicability and communality of experience.

The short story, for Cortázar, is related less to the traditional *cuento* than to the modern art of the photograph. Just as the short story writer departs from the notion of the limit, the photographer's art consists in

> recortar un fragmento de la realidad, fijándolo determinados límites, pero de manera tal que ese recorte actúe como una explosión que abre de par en par

> una realidad mucho más amplia, como una visión dinámica que trasciende
> espiritualmente el campo abarcado por la cámara. (513)

The short story, like the photograph, produces a sudden opening onto a far wider
reality. In both cases, it is the finite nature of the object that produces infinite
potential. Fragmentation is therefore not a negative, but rather a positive quality
that seems to produce a short circuit between physical limitations and spiritual
transcendence. For Cortázar, then, the inherently fragmentary nature of the short
story constitutes not an end, but a beginning; not the closure of a tradition, but the
formation of a genre which opens up a new field of vision, a realm of possibilities
that are linked to the technology of photography.

Photographic synecdoche leads to a temporal paradox. This is shown in
Cortázar's answer to his own question '¿*Por qué* perduran en la memoria?': 'son
aglutinantes de una realidad infinitamente más vasta que la de su mera anécdota,
y por eso han influido en nosotros con una fuerza que no haría sospechar la
modestia de su contenido aparente, la brevedad de su texto' (519–20). Because the
short story exceeds its own boundaries, its brevity is dialectically intertwined with
permanence. Its inexhaustibility lies in its suspension of information, in its delay
of the revelation that means that it can forever be read and re-read. Monterroso
pays tribute to this aspect of Cortázar's own writing in a diary fragment written
originally for *El sábado*, prompted by a reminder regarding his contribution to the
testimonial collection *Queremos tanto a Julio*: 'Los años han pasado y bastante de la
moda [Cortázar] también, pero lo real cortazariano permanece como una de las
grandes contribuciones a la modernidad [...] de nuestra literatura'.[28] Monterroso
elevates Cortázar's literary works through a temporal paradox, a dialectical interplay
between ephemerality and permanence, novelty and durability — a paradox that,
as we shall see, unites the three authors in my corpus.

Another point of intersection is Monterroso's course on the short story at Stanford
University, which includes a session on Julio Cortázar, focusing on two famous
stories ('El perseguidor' and 'Continuidad de los parques') and two theoretical essays
('Algunos aspectos del cuento' and 'Del cuento breve y sus alrededores'). From his
essays, Monterroso clips out the following quotations:

> El cuento: 'hermano misterioso de la poesía.'
> 'Hay muy pocos cuentos verdaderamente grandes.'
> 'La novela gana siempre por puntos, mientras que el cuento <u>debe</u> ganar por
> knock-out.' (his emphasis)[29]

The final quotation, which revolves around a boxing image — a concept that will
be explored in depth in the first chapter, and that echoes Monterroso's own belief
that 'hoy no: no hay tiempo' — is illustrated in a drawing by Monterroso (see
Fig. 1), labelled 'ganar por knock-out' on the reverse side. These sporadic, scattered
interactions offer clues regarding the aesthetic connections between these two
authors.

To close our triangle of authors, we must return to Rulfo. Though he did
not develop any sustained theory of the short story in the way that Cortázar and
Monterroso did, he does highlight the value of the genre in his later reflections on
literature: 'el cuentista se parece un poco al poeta, al buen poeta. El poeta tiene que

FIG. 1: Augusto Monterroso, Drawing, 'Ganar por knock-out'.
Series 3: Drawings and Photographs; 1941–93; Augusto Monterroso Papers,
Box 41–47; Manuscripts Division, Department of Rare Books and Special Collections,
Princeton University Library

ir frenando al caballo y no desbocarse'.[30] He thus shares Cortázar's view, included by Monterroso in his Stanford course, of the short story as the 'hermano misterioso de la poesía',[31] and of the imperative of containment. An implicit dialogue is also established between Rulfo and Monterroso in the latter's 'El zorro es más sabio', from *La oveja negra y demás fábulas* (1969). Rulfo is without doubt the fable's hero, the cunning fox that published two successful books, which were translated into many languages and received critical attention from the most eminent North American critics. When encouraged to publish more by writers and critics, the fox thinks to himself, '"En realidad lo que éstos quieren es que yo publique un libro malo; pero como soy el Zorro, no lo voy a hacer"./ Y no lo hizo'.[32] As Monterroso hints, the whole of Rulfo's published corpus amounts to one collection of short stories, *El Llano en llamas* (1953), and one fragmentary novel, *Pedro Páramo* (1955). Interestingly, this is also the last story in Monterroso's own second collection. This self-reflexive fable on a shared aesthetics of withdrawal is therefore a simultaneous reference to Rulfo's work and a self-reference to Monterroso's own principles — a correspondence bolstered by Monterroso's notes for his essay on Rulfo, where he asserts that he only tried to imitate Rulfo in his abstinence from publication.[33]

As I have begun to show, by relating the ideas of Rulfo, Cortázar and Monterroso to those of Benjamin, their respective theories of brevity cannot be understood in isolation from broader socio-cultural contexts. Before turning to examine each individual author, two necessary detours must be taken: first through European and North American theories of the short story; second through Latin American cultural theories, most notably those of Beatriz Sarlo, Jesús Martín-Barbero and Néstor García Canclini. Together, these theories will provide intersecting frameworks within and beyond which I shall examine the complexities and paradoxes of the Latin American short story.

Between Technology and Art: Situating the Short Story's Limits

In the European and North American contexts, the short story has been widely theorized in terms of its relation to historical, social, and economic developments, as well as its formal properties. On the one hand, the short story is viewed as a practical response to the demands of the publishing industry, and to the changing conditions of reading due to the increasing pace of everyday life. On the other hand, it is related to aesthetico-philosophical developments, particularly Romantic or anti-Realist movements, and corresponding shifting modes of perception.

Frederick Lewis Pattee attributes the growth of the genre in nineteenth-century North America to that of the magazine publishing industry. 'Shortened fiction in America', he affirms, 'has resulted from international copyright conditions and from the attendant multiplication of magazines', of which he identifies *Atlantic Souvenir, The Token, The Legendary*, among many others.[34] He goes so far as to claim that the evolution of the genre was less an aesthetic response to the need for brevity — a fulfilment of the rules set out by Edgar Allan Poe in his 1847 review of Hawthorne's *Twice-Told Tales* — than a commercial, practical response to magazines' demand for shortness. Its different styles through the decades of the nineteenth century, whether sentimental, realist, or fantastic, are merely symptoms of changing fashions and consumer demands. This fleetingness, if not fickleness, leads him to take a disparaging view of the short story: 'we forget the short story just as we forget the "movie" that we saw yesterday. It has made no deep impress; it has simply titillated us for the moment, and made us eager for another sensation' (447). He therefore views the short story as a negative by-product of publishing conditions, and as a form that lives and dies in magazine format. Interestingly, he also establishes a link — albeit a negative one — between the short story and the emerging medium of cinema; a connection whose significance I shall explore in the body of this study.

Andrew Levy adopts a different stance in his exploration of the culture and commerce of the North American short story. On the one hand, he shares with Pattee the view that the short story is the literary genre 'best suited to a mercantile culture.'[35] This is because it is a short piece of prose that can be read and digested quickly, and then discarded: 'from the time of Poe, the short story has been designed as a culturally disposable artifact' (2). On the other hand, he argues that, 'just because the short story may be a disposable product [...] does not mean that it is trash. Our ability to appreciate short stories', he goes on to say, 'is hampered by the alienation of time that is essential to most of our presuppositions about what constitutes great art' (2). The presupposition to which he is referring here is durability, the assumption that the artwork cannot merely be rooted in a particular moment, the immediate present, but rather must be atemporal. Since the short story is present–oriented, Levy suggests, it has been rejected as inferior, unartistic. The short story's temporality, Levy suggests, calls for a different reader and a reconfiguration of the artwork.

In the British context, Stuart Sillars explores the apparition, between 1891 and 1900, of a new type of monthly magazine whose main content was short fiction, the first example of which is *The Strand Magazine*. Whereas its predecessors (Charles Dickens's *Household Words* and *All the Year Round* among others) were composed of serial parts of longer fiction, these monthlies published single stories or self-contained episodes with shared characters.[36] They enjoyed huge popularity, opening up the world of literature to a vast readership, a 'largely overlooked group of the reading public' (71). The social implication of this development is clear: the democratization of culture thanks to the increased availability and accessibility of the artwork. But this is not the focus of Sillars's essay: his concern is the importance of *images* in these illustrated short stories. One explanation, again, is a practical one. The image constitutes an aid for the reader, since 'these short stories were read in a short time, and very often in railway trains: the reading process has become a consequence of shifts in patterns of balance between living and working' (71). Conditions of day-to-day life, related to modes of transport, therefore have a profound effect on patterns of reading and spans of attentiveness, shifting the primacy from text to image.

Whether on the side of producers or consumers, then, the short story is closely related to technological developments. From the perspective of production, we might highlight the rise of mechanical reproduction and the explosion of the magazine industry; from that of consumption, changing modes of transport (rail travel) and communication (the moving picture, the image).

On the other hand, critics have located the short story in its own aesthetic territory, contrasting it with other art forms and genres, most notably the realist novel. Nadine Gordimer begins her essay on the short story by asking the following question: 'why is it that while the death of the novel is good for post-mortem at least once a year, the short story lives on unmolested?'[37] She approaches this problem by addressing the essential feature of the genre, its brevity: against the totalizing attempts of the novel, 'the short story recognizes that full comprehension in the reader [...] is something of limited duration' (265); it is 'a fragmented and restless form, a matter of hit and miss' that suits modern consciousness (265). Hence she attributes the obduracy of the genre, paradoxically, to its temporal core, to its brief instant of illumination, to its momentary form of contact which she relates to the flash of fireflies.

Mary Rohrberger, who anchors her understanding of the modern short story in Romanticism, characterizes the genre and the movement in opposition to realism: 'men began to assert that there is more to the world than that which can be discovered through the senses, that there is what might be called an underworld, no less real.'[38] The realm of the short story is one which exceeds ordinary reality: the strange, the supernatural, the terrifying, the inexplicable, the transcendent. The short story writer is interested less in capturing reality than in questioning, challenging and fragmenting it.

From a different angle, Charles May asserts that the short story is more 'realistic' than the novel if 'we feel that beneath the everyday or immanent there is something that exceeds us, if our view is a religious one in its most basic sense'.[39] Its location outside the realm of the familiar, the normal, the everyday, is closely connected to its formal compactness: the tightly spun web or centrifugal force of the narrative draws the reader in to a point of intensity, of heightened experience. Far from being a merely contingent response to changing cultural conditions, then, the short story is for May (who quotes Borges) 'essential', because it takes the reader to a point of rupture from the inauthenticity of everyday reality. May thus opposes the form of the short story to that of the novel:

> My thesis is that long fiction, by its very length, demands both a subject matter and a set of artistic conventions that primarily derive from and in turn establish the primacy of 'experience' conceptually created and considered; whereas short fiction, by its very length, demands both a subject matter and a set of artistic conventions that derive from and establish the primacy of 'an experience' directly and emotionally created and encountered.[40]

For May, then, the differences between the novel and the short story are not merely formal and temporal, but also epistemological and ontological, corresponding as they do with different views of the nature of knowledge and experience.

It is along the same lines that Terry Eagleton contrasts the short story with the realist novel: 'a chronically naturalizing mode, it is hard for it to cope with the ineffable or unfathomable, given those built in mechanisms which offer to transmute all of this into the assuringly familiar.'[41] The 'mechanisms' to which he refers are temporal ones, the structures of chronology and causality that underpin the novelistic genre. By isolating moments from logical sequences of events, on the contrary, the short story produces effects of defamiliarization in order to force the reader to question the normality of that which was formerly taken for granted.

Yet these two critical perspectives leave unanswered many questions regarding the link between aesthetic practices and social processes. How can the practicalities of the short story form be squared with its aesthetic properties? What is the relationship between text and context, production and consumption, art and market? How do the requirements of readers and publishers affect modes of writing? How can the artistic form be reconciled with the format in which it is presented? Do the contingent circumstances of its formation undermine, or in fact paradoxically corroborate, its 'essential' qualities? How is the literary technique of the short story related to the technologies alongside — and *from* — which it was born?

Benjamin arguably presents the most illuminating and suggestive connections between the different strands of the genre. When one examines his essay 'The Storyteller' in relation to 'On Some Motifs in Baudelaire' (1939) and 'The Work of Art in the Age of Mechanical Reproduction' (1936), deep, complex connections become apparent between the abbreviation of art and narrative on the one hand, and the emergence and explosion of technological, mechanical media on the other: among others, journalism, photography and cinema. All in turn are linked to broader social processes of fragmentation, rupture and severance. A crucial difference must be noted between the theories of literary critics May, Eagleton, Rohrberger and Gordimer and those of Benjamin. Whereas the former are based on the contrast between the genre of the short story and that of the novel, the latter are constructed on the contrast between the short story and the oral tale. As I shall argue, Benjamin's theories are a fruitful point of departure for an exploration of a complex genre which in fact has much in common with its sister form, the novel: the isolation of the author from the audience, the intensification of self-consciousness and the fragmentation of experience.

In 'The Storyteller', Benjamin implicitly links the abbreviated narrative of the short story with a 'new form of communication', the information provided by newspapers (88). He describes the contrast between the narratives of modern journalism and traditional storytelling thus:

> the value of information does not survive the moment in which it was new. It lives only at that moment; it has to surrender to it completely explain itself to it without losing any time. A story is different. It does not expend itself. It preserves and concentrates its strength and is capable of releasing it even after a long time. (90)

Benjamin thus sets up a binary contrast between modern, ephemeral and traditional, lasting forms of communication. The fragmentary attributes of the newspaper article — its freshness, brevity and disconnection from the surrounding items — prevent it from entering into the fabric of tradition. Information, based on events rooted in specific temporal contexts, is as momentary as the experience that it captures. Storytelling is thus replaced by impermanent forms deriving from, and producing, temporal experiences and isolated sensations.

In his now well-known essay 'The Work of Art in the Age of Mechanical Reproduction', Benjamin adopts a far more positive position on the rupture from tradition, celebrating the shift entailed by processes of mechanical reproduction that free the artwork from the aura:

> The technique of reproduction detaches the reproduced object from the domain of tradition. By making many reproductions it substitutes a plurality of copies for a unique existence. And in permitting the reproduction to meet the beholder or listener in his own particular situation, it reactivates the object reproduced. These two processes lead to a tremendous shattering of tradition which is the obverse of the contemporary crisis and renewal of mankind.[42]

The two processes to which he refers here, reproduction and reactivation, are forms of liberation rather than symptoms of decay, permitting the release of the artwork from the shackles of tradition and authority. This account contrasts that of 'The Storyteller', where Benjamin praises the 'incomparable aura' of the storyteller (109), who leaves his mark on the story like the potter leaves his print on the pot: severed from its origins, freed from its subservience to cultural heritage and from the aura of uniqueness, the short story that displaces the oral tale is able to enter into new relations; to be reactivated in different contexts by different viewers or readers. The short story's relation with the industry, commerce and market of the publishing industry, as explored in different contexts by Pattee, Levy and Sillars, is therefore one of revolutionary potential and democratic promise.

'On Some Motifs' complicates the situation of the short story further, tying its technique of brevity with the experience of shock resulting from the mechanization of everyday life and the crowds of big cities. In this essay, Benjamin expands the argument of 'The Storyteller', arguing that modernity entails a change in the very structure of experience, from *Erfahrung* to *Erlebnis* — that is to say, from accumulated experience, handed down continuously from one generation to the next, to isolated experiences, impressions and sensations that 'remain in the sphere of a certain hour in one's life'.[43] Connecting Baudelaire with Poe in this context, he argues that lyric poetry 'can have as its basis an experience for which the shock experience has become the norm' (164). The creative process for Baudelaire, Benjamin explains, consists of a 'duel in which the artist, just before being beaten, screams in fright' (165). Hence it is best captured in the image of the fencing match. Though Benjamin does not expand on the importance of the duel in Poe's short fiction, the implication is that the short story and lyric poetry are both connected to a broader social phenomenon, the new *sensorium* of the urban masses that conditions modern perception.

In turn, the day-to-day experience of shock is connected, if not confused, by Benjamin with the technology of photography:

> Of the countless movements of switching, inserting, pressing, and the like, the 'snapping' of the photographer has had the greatest consequences. A touch of the finger now sufficed to fix an event for an unlimited period of time. The camera gave the moment a posthumous shock, as it were. (176–77)

A material dimension is therefore added to the phenomenological experience of shock, which brings us back to the practices of mechanical reproduction explored in 'The Work of Art': the photograph, by reproducing the instant, disembeds the isolated *Erlebnis* from a shared, linear *Erfahrung*, creating a rupture in the spatio-temporal continuum. The image used by Gordimer to represent the art of the short story, the 'light of the flash', is therefore a pertinent one: it implies the camera flash, the spark of light that illuminates a particular situation for a split second. The short story's partiality and fleetingness are therefore not only connected generally to the hit-and-miss character of modernity as Gordimer argues, but also to the specific medium of photography that corroborates the temporal dislocations of modern experience.[44]

Taking Benjamin's theories as a point of departure, this study will examine the short story's formal, spatio-temporal limits in relation to two other, inter-related limits: the historical limit of an oral narrative tradition, the point at which rural communities are dispersed by urbanization and the flesh-and-blood storyteller is displaced by the print industry; the cultural limit between art and technology, literature and photography, short story form and newspaper format. The literary genre of the short story — with its techniques of abbreviation, defamiliarization, directness, 'knock-out' and intensity — will be linked with intersecting technological forms: mechanical reproduction, cinematic montage, photographic representation, long-distance communication and accelerated transport. These interrelated processes, which are inscribed internally within the forms and plots of the stories, lead to a complexity in terminology. In different theoretical contexts, the notions of fragmentation, rupture and shock will take on nuanced meanings, relating to processes that are — often simultaneously — spatial and temporal, material and spiritual, historical and phenomenological, artistic and technological, formal and practical.

The short story's fragmentation will be related to Benjamin's historical sense of a shattering of tradition and a crumbling of communities. This cultural, social predicament is in turn related to literary, formal processes which, as Monterroso and Benjamin both point out, manifest themselves not only through the internal fragmentation of characters, exemplified by Don Quijote, but also through that of plot and form. Rupture implies more active processes of detachment, whether the formal severance of the part from the whole, a deliberate tearing of literary narrative from an oral tradition, or a wrenching of the artwork from the artist. Here too, formal techniques are related to social shifts and technological developments, notably the explosion of the print industry and mechanical reproduction. Shock refers both to the mechanical power to shock and to the psychic reception of that shock. For Benjamin, it is the norm of modern existence, related as it is to the mechanization of everyday life. For Cortázar, it is the technique of a great short story, which wins not on points, but by 'knock-out'. My purpose is not to evade or suppress, but rather to face and grapple with, these nuances and complexities, which as we shall see are fundamental to the complex form of the short story.

The Latin American Short Story: A Hybrid Form for a Hybrid Culture

In order to understand the configurations of the fragment in the Latin American short story, several crucial, interrelated questions still need to be addressed. To what extent does the Latin American short story share the practical and aesthetic features of the European short story? Is its productivity as a genre owed to its origins in oral storytelling, to its rupture from that very tradition, or to the combination of these seemingly opposing trends? How is the formation of the genre affected by Latin America's particular experience of modernity?

As outlined above, some critics have seen the genre in terms of its embeddedness in an oral tradition. This perspective, though, overlooks the material conditions that gave birth to the modern genre: a print culture which, as Stephen Hart points out, is part of 'an ongoing historical process which rearticulates the oral continuum of culture in written form'.[45] Esteban Echeverría's *El matadero* (1871), often regarded as the first Latin American short story, was published in the *Revista del Río de la Plata*.[46] Indeed, it was in periodicals and literary reviews that most short story writers first saw their work published thereafter — whether Horacio Quiroga in *La nación* and *Caras y caretas*, Juan Rulfo in *Pan* and *América*, Julio Cortázar in *Los Anales de Buenos Aires* and *Confirmado*, or Augusto Monterroso in *Acento* and *El Imparcial*. The layout of these journals, the demands of their editors, and the consequent spatial restrictions, partly explain the brevity of the form. Quiroga, for example, states: 'Luis Pardo, entonces Jefe de Redacción de *Caras y Caretas*, fue quien exigió el cuento breve hasta un grado inaudito de severidad. El cuento no debía pasar entonces de una página, incluyendo la ilustración correspondiente.'[47]

The short story genre cannot be separated from the changing face of the printing industry in twentieth-century Latin America. Though Hart does not deal directly with the genre in '*El oficio de escribir*', the broader object of his study is surely relevant: he examines how modern, technological developments, and the exponential growth of the mass media, have resulted in paradigm shifts in the literary culture of Spanish America. At the beginning of the twentieth century, Hart affirms, the growth in newspaper sales was such that the literary print culture of the book industry was 'subsumed within a new paradigm of cultural transmission derived from newspaper print' (387). This paradigm shift was particularly acute in periods of Revolution. For example, it was during the turmoil of the Mexican Revolution (1910–17) that newspaper sales rocketed because of the huge growth in the anti-authoritarian press. *La sátira* is but one example. This print explosion of dailies and literary reviews — notable not only in Mexico, but all over Latin America — unleashed a process of democratization, the growth of what Habermas designates as the 'public sphere', an arena away from the monastic cell, the pulpit, or the viceregal court where opinions could be transmitted and shared. The Latin American short story, like its European and North American counterparts, must be viewed in relation to this shift from the book culture of the lettered city to the newspaper culture of the modern metropolis.

Aníbal González makes a case for the strong relationship between the complex phenomena of journalism and literary fiction in Latin America. As he notes, many of Spanish America's authors — particularly the modernists José Martí, Rubén Darío and José Enrique Rodó — depended on journalism not only as a source of income, but also as place to publish their writings.[48] This, he argues, had a profound impact on literary output, producing contaminations that he explores through various genres of narrative prose, focusing particularly on the novel, but including the short story, the essay, the *crónica* and a particular form developed by Ricardo Palma, the *tradición*. Rodó, in his essay 'Cómo ha de ser un diario' (1914), points out that good journalistic writing is based on the 'Spencerian theory of style', which 'reduces the secret of good literary form to an economy of attention' (104). Yet it was not just the style, but the inherent immediacy of journalism, that constituted a challenge to narrative fiction: 'How could [it] compete with a medium such as the newspaper, which offered its readers — through the technological wizardry of the telegraph and the transatlantic cable — detailed, factual and gripping accounts of events that were taking place on the other side of the globe?' (102) For González, it is the avant-garde of the first two decades of the twentieth century — from the French poet Guillaume Apollinaire's *Calligrammes* (1916) to the Chilean poet Vicente Huidobro's *Poemas árticos* (1918) — that responds most creatively to this impasse. As he points out, many of the characteristics of those works are shared or derived from journalism: the demolition of the author, the spatialization of language, the passion for novelty, action and colour, and the penchant for brevity and synthesis (103).

In the specific context of Buenos Aires in the 1920s and 30s, Beatriz Sarlo asks how Argentine intellectuals responded to the huge upheavals in the shifting urban landscape, the modernization of communication media, and the impact of these on cultural customs. She registers the shifts in the profile of the reading public and the consolidation of a local editorial market, which led to the invasion of the middle classes into a domain previously reserved for the *señores* of the upper classes. The consequence was a huge growth in output. The journal *Claridad*, for example, increased its print runs from 10,000 to 25,000 in the 1930s, at once responding to, and creating, a new readership.[49] Sarlo's affirmation of the democratization of culture resulting from processes of distribution and consumption — which she documents with particular clarity in relation to the work of Roberto Arlt — echoes Benjamin's celebration of mechanical reproduction in his essay written in the same decade: the 1930s. Her characterization of the emerging newspaper format echoes Sillars's description of the short stories in *The Strand Magazine*: '[El mundo] proporciona un material configurado sobre la base de artículos breves, que pueden ser consumidos por entero durante los viajes al trabajo, en la plataforma del tranvía o los vagones de tren y subterráneo. El diario, por su formato tabloid, no exige la comodidad de la casa o del bufete' (20). Similarly, the journal *Crítica* is characterized by speed, rhythm, graphic materials, articles in colour: 'la incorporación de narraciones, artículos de color, notas de costumbres, historietas, cartoons e ilustraciones, le dan muy rápidamente a *El Mundo* un perfil que conservará durante toda la década del treinta' (20). The style of the newspapers echoes the speed of the international cables, the velocity of the production and reproduction of the news, and the rapid pace of consumption.

The paradigm shift is therefore not limited to that of two different types of writing: literary and journalistic. As Sarlo highlights, *nuevo periodismo* promotes an intensely visual experience of 'reading', maximizing on colour, illustrations and cartoon art. Similarly, Stephen Hart opens his article by dismantling el *oficio de escribir* with the following assertion: 'The exponential growth of the mass media in Spanish America during the twentieth century — particularly in the areas of radio, TV, and the film industry — has led to new forms of interpenetration between book-based culture and other types of cultural transmission' (387). As Hart points out, paradigm shifts in literary print culture are such that the book is displaced by other modes of mass-cultural production. Monterroso, in his draft of the piece 'De qué vive y de qué muere el escritor en América Latina', highlights the relevance of this shift in the context of Latin America:

> si calculan en un setenta por ciento el número de personas que no saben leer en América Latina, podrán formarse una idea ya no de nuestro atraso y nuestra miseria, bien conocidos por todos, sino de la locura que significa allá entregarse al ejercicio de las letras, con el cual uno está dirigiéndose generalmente al vacío, a seres inexistentes como lectores, dando curiosos saltos sin siquiera la esperanza de obtener una respuesta [...] a menos que el escritor invada los campos de la política o la sociología, o acuda a la televisión, al cine, o al radio, hasta por fin hacerse notar por estos otros medios dudosamente literarios.[50]

The problem of communication in the Latin American context is therefore not only a literary, self-conscious awareness of the deficiencies of language, but also a very practical problem: that of the absence of an addressee. As Jesús Martín-Barbero argues, it is a fact that the majority of Latin Americans experience modernity not through the book, but rather through the mass media, 'no siguiendo el proyecto ilustrado, sino desde los formatos y los géneros de las industrias culturales de la radio, el cinema y la televisión'.[51] Similarly, Carlos Monsiváis, commenting on the urban inhabitant in Mexico — 'un país que cuenta con 22 millones de analfabetas reales y funcionales' — confirms that 'lo más común es que lea la prensa deportiva, publicaciones amarillistas e historietas'.[52] To illustrate his point, he notes that before its economic crisis in 1982, Mexico was the country that proportionally consumed most comics in the world (over a hundred million per month in total). In addition, newspapers' treatment of sport and crime brings a shared sense of community to urban populations. The prominence of football fanaticism and crime-centred sensationalism in the national press allows the individual to connect with a collective through 'catarsis elementales, la estética del shock (morbo teatralizado o genuino)' (141).

These cultural conditions arguably have a huge impact on the literary text. In form if not in practice, the short story often tries to occupy the same domain as the mass media, though it perhaps fails to compete with mass forms, or, from a different perspective, resists the dictates of the culture industry. As I shall demonstrate, there is a strong, complex relationship between its aesthetics of shock and the techniques of the popular press; between its literary principles and the visual arts, from photography to comic strips; between its fragmentary form and the heterogeneous media that surround its production. The invasion of literature by other media is a response to a social situation, a profound uncertainty regarding the relevance or power of the written word, as well as a liberating movement that breaks down the exclusive walls of the lettered city.

The short story must thus be considered not only as an heir of an age-old tradition of oral storytelling, but also as a bastard child of the emerging media. As Sarlo insists in relation to Buenos Aires, both Mexico and Argentina must be regarded as '*cultura[s] de mezcla*, donde coexisten elementos defensivos y residuales junto a los programas renovadores'.[53] The short story is a product of a hybrid culture, a complex configuration of residual traces and signs of emergence. In this sense, my work is located in a crucial field of research in Latin American studies; namely, that of transculturation.

The term 'transculturation' was coined by the Cuban anthropologist Fernando Ortiz in his 1940 work *Contrapunteo cubano del tabaco y del azúcar*. In the second chapter of this book, he develops the neologism as a means of characterizing a historical process of cultural clashes and negotiations. Cuba's history, for Ortiz, is 'una intensísima, complejísima e incesante *transculturación* de varias masas humanas, todas ellas en pasos de transición.'[54] The term marks a shift away from the notion of acculturation, which implies a unidirectional relation between a hegemonic culture and a subordinate culture, whereby the former is the donor and the latter, the receiver. Transculturation, conversely, refers to creative processes of cultural contact that result in dynamic forms of selection, interaction, and mutual transformation. Economic exchanges are bound up with racial and cultural exchanges in an overflowing concoction: 'los mismos fenómenos económicos, los más básicos de la vida social, en Cuba se confunden casi siempre con las expresiones de las diversas culturas' (257). Ortiz presents the tobacco and sugar industries as the paradigmatic examples of these interactions.

Ángel Rama extends the anthropological research on transculturation to literary studies in his *Transculturación narrativa en América Latina* (1982). Transculturation, for Rama, constitutes a 'tarea selectiva sobre la tradición': four processes, 'pérdidas, selecciones, redescubrimientos e incorporaciones', lead to 'una reestructuración general del sistema cultural, que es la función creadora más alta que se cumple en un proceso transculturante'.[55] The unity of modernity as a continuous line of technological, industrial progress is fragmented in Latin America by a number of variables: the different periods, intensities and durations of its insertion, its varying adaptability to local circumstances, the resistances that it faces, and so on. His aim is therefore to 'registrar los exitosos esfuerzos de componer un discurso literario a partir de fuertes tradiciones propias mediante plásticas transculturaciones que no se rinden a la modernización sino que la utilizan para fines propios' (75). Rama's guiding notion is that literature has a particular ability to turn *mestizaje* from an abstract, theoretical concept into living forces, modes of narration and forms of perception. Arguedas's *Los ríos profundos* (1968) is a key example, mixing as it does elements of indigenous song, popular poetry and literary narrative. It is referred to by Rama as 'la novela-ópera de los pobres', because it is a Lévi-Straussian *bricolage*, built from the left-overs of two great cultures, Incan and Spanish (267).

García Canclini's concept of hybridity is in many ways an offshoot of the notion of transculturation. As he insists in a recent article, for the full potential of the concept of hybridization to be released, 'debemos situar[la] en otra red de conceptos: por ejemplo, contradicción, mestizaje, sincretismo, transculturación y creolización'.[56] In *Culturas híbridas: estrategias para entrar y salir de la modernidad*, García Canclini examines the sociocultural hybrids in which the traditional and the modern are entangled. He argues against the Manichean compartmentalization that underpins modern ideologies, from nineteenth-century liberalism to developmentalism, which imagined that modernization (whether scientific, industrial or technological) would put an end to traditional forms of production (whether myths, handicrafts or books). His argument is that, 'del lado popular, hay que preocuparse menos por lo que se extingue que por lo que se transforma'.[57] Rather than a process of substitution (of the ancient and the traditional by the new and the modern), we have one of hybridization and transformation, which in turn leads to what he terms 'la *heterogeneidad multitemporal* de la cultura moderna [hispanoamericana]' (47). Contamination and cross-fertilization undermine the possibility of choosing between local tradition and global modernity.

García Canclini's analysis in *Las culturas populares en el capitalismo* is especially useful in the context of this study. According to him, indigenous handicrafts and festivals are inscribed both *historically*, 'en un proceso que viene desde las socie-dades precolombinas', and *structurally*, 'en la lógica actual del capitalismo'.[58] Their simultaneous insertion into two different cultures corresponds with the mutual dependence of Latin America's coexisting socio-economic structures: 'Ni las culturas indígenas pueden existir con la autonomía pretendida por ciertos antropólogos o folcloristas, ni son tampoco meros apéndices, atípicos de un capitalismo que todo lo devora' (104). Adopting a single perspective, García Canclini argues, misses the complex meaning of popular events and artefacts in the capitalist era, where traditional cultural forms are transmitted and transformed by modern media. Loudspeakers and video recorders, he notes, have become an integral part of ritualistic ceremonies in Patamban (86). Indigenous pyramids have taken on aspects of mass entertainment and technological development, with sound and light shows (97). The tourist industry has turned the Day of the Dead ceremony in Janitzio into a spectacle emptied of its religious meaning: droves of tourists are attracted to the festivities by newspapers and television; the illumination provided by candles is combined with that of the camera flashes (180); the music is diffused over loudspeakers; the entire event is made into an episode of mass communication through photographs (for which the locals pose and charge), cinema and television (182).

It is in the context of this hybridization that I shall situate the short story, nego-tiating between two readings. The Rama-inspired studies of the Latin American short story are arguably symptoms of what García Canclini sees as 'la tentación folclorista de ver sólo el aspecto *étnico*, considerar las [artes populares] apenas como supervivencia crepuscular de culturas en extinción' (104). Focusing on the modern tale from the exclusive point of view of its indigenous roots negates the impact of contemporary developments on the social meaning of the texts, its transformation through dominant modes of production, reproduction and consumption. On the contrary, the Anglo-American studies of the short story by Pattee, Levy and Sillars run the risk of 'aislar la explicación económica, estudiarlas como cualquier otro objeto regido por la lógica mercantil' (104). My work seeks to fulfil a mediating function befitting its subject matter, producing encounters between seemingly opposing schools of thought just as the short story draws its strength from popular sources and market forces, declining cultures and booming media.

One of the implications of García Canclini's research on the hybridization of Latin American society is a cross-disciplinary approach. 'Esta mirada que se multiplica en tantos fragmentos y cruces,' he explains, 'no persigue la trama de un orden único que las separaciones disciplinarios habrían encontrado'.[59] He therefore employs the tools of three different research fields: art history and literary criticism, concerned principally with the 'culto'; anthropology and folklore, which deal with the popular; communication and media studies, which specialize in mass culture (17). Given the cultural, historical circumstances of Latin America — its heterogeneity and uneven rates of development — it is difficult and even dangerous to isolate these areas of study, viewing high-brow, popular and mass media as black-and-white categories. In what follows, I shall situate my argument at the intersection of these three areas, producing revealing encounters between my own and others' literary criticism of the short story, existing studies of popular traditions (centring on Rama-influenced criticism of the short story, and borrowing from theories by Claude Lévi-Strauss), and reflections and works on emerging media and mass communication (by García Canclini, Monsiváis, Martín-Barbero, Benjamin and Marshall McLuhan).

Martín-Barbero's approach in his work on popular and mass culture furnishes a useful critical framework. Based on the premise that communication is the site of intersection of multiple conflicting and integrating forces, he turns away from a concept of the media towards one of 'mediations', which refer to 'the articulation of different tempos of development with the plurality of cultural matrices'.[60] Approaching Latin American culture from the receiving end, the *pueblo*, he argues that the mass media cannot be reduced to alienating devices or tools of domination, since they are in fact adopted creatively as intermediaries between cultural poles: the state and the masses, the rural and the urban, tradition and modernity.

Examples he gives include the cinema, the radio and the press. Mexican cinema in the 1930s and 1940s bridged a rural past and an urban present, at once preserving and subverting popular legends, myths and traditions, and drawing on the popular art of melodrama (166–67). The mediation of film reproduced a deformed version of the collective lived experience upheld by the Revolution. A source of learning, solace and comfort (166), film might also be seen as a mechanized form — or deformation — of the traditional storyteller. The success of Argentinian radio from the 1920s is attributed by Martín-Barbero less to the technical, commercial development of the medium itself than to the mediation established with a cultural tradition (169–70): on the side of production, radio theatre was born from a mixture of circus theatre and popular drama; on the side of reception, it takes the place of collective reading. A third case is that of the Chilean press, where new journalistic styles emerged in the 1920s, with local slang, graphic descriptions of crimes, and a scandalous tone. Rather than seeing the sensationalist press as a bourgeois tool of manipulation or a commercial exploitation of crime, he insists on the '*cultural* connection between the melodramatic aesthetic and the forms of survival and revenge in the matrix pervading popular cultures' (178).

Crucial to Martín-Barbero's argument is the reclaiming of 'lo popular' from the folklorist view that associates it with a bygone era, with rural, peasant culture. As Martín-Barbero argues, popular culture is to be found 'not just in memories of the past, but in its conflictive and creative presence in the present' (209) — notably in urban, mass cultural forms. Rather than insisting on the 'distinción esencial entre el cuento literario y el relato popular', as Eva Valcárcel does,[61] my contention is that the *cuento literario* is permeated by multiple elements of the urban popular imagination: film, sensationalist newspapers, radio, cartoons, graffiti, and so on; the emerging languages that forge, and are forged by, the collective identities of the *pueblo*. In this respect, the genre lies at the heart of the 'cultural matrices' identified by Martín-Barbero: 'the combinations of contemporaneity, profound anachronisms and conflicting rhythms of time that make up cultural modernity' (231). In what follows, I shall seek to grapple with the contradictions and complexities of the short story form, bringing together different readings of the genre — ethnic and economic, local and global, historical and structural — to demonstrate that the tales constitute *mestizajes* of ancient myths and contemporary economic demands, oral communicational forms and emerging technological media.

The short stories of Rulfo, Cortázar and Monterroso, as we shall see, are not only products of transculturation but also *processes* of transculturation, *mediations* between constructed cultural binaries: respectively, between rural communities and urban culture, oral communication and literary forms, indigenous rituals and Christian symbols; between Paris and Buenos Aires, Roman times and modern times, ritualistic sacrifice and motorcycle accident; between agrarian modes of production and industrial methods of reproduction, classical satire and modern cartoon, wild animals and urban pets. As I shall argue, the short story genre functions as a channel or tunnel, and as a vessel or container, of hybrid cultural experiences and experiential forms. In all cases, the reader plays an active role, participating by filling in the vessels, moving through the channels or reconfiguring the fragments.

Chapter 1 focuses on Juan Rulfo's short story collection, *El Llano en llamas* (1953). Orality and myth have been the loci around which Rulfo's critics have tended to gravitate: Rama, Walter Mignolo, Evodio Escalante read Rulfo's work as return to the oral storytelling tradition; Raymond Bartra, Carlos Fuentes and Joseph Sommers see it as deeply, even dangerously, entrenched in mythical narrative structures. Borrowing from the terms of Raymond Williams's *Marxism and Literature* (1977), I argue that these residual cultural forms in fact stand in a dialectical relationship with emergent forms — notably, the interconnected literary devices of suspension and suggestion, and the technological device of photography. The stories not only build from the foundations of oral, mythical narratives, but also create ruptures from those and inhabit a temporality that undercuts mythical cyclicality. It is this narrative transculturation that gives them their power as short stories.

I begin by examining the fragmentation of rural communities, tradition and religion that constitutes the socio-historical backdrop against which these stories are set. My contention is that the death of the storyteller, prophesied by Walter

Benjamin in 1937, is staged within his stories. Yet it is in, and from, the ruins of traditional narrative that Rulfo forges new techniques, as I demonstrate through his treatment of different tropes: the body, the corpse, and the ruin. Fragmentation is not only a negative symptom of decay, but also a deliberate artistic technique, which potentiates new meanings, stories and relations. Bringing together Cortázar's theory of the short story as 'knock-out', Benjamin's notion of the shock experience, and Barthes's theory of the photographic *punctum*, I argue that Rulfo's fragmentary aesthetics are inextricable from the temporality of the instant, which was brought to the fore of modern experience by the art and technology of photography.

Chapter 2 re-evaluates the relationship between Cortázar's short stories and the rest of his artistic corpus. Arguing against those critics who have situated his 'closed' short stories in formal opposition to his 'open', multimedial works, I question the theorization of the short story as a self-contained genre. Cortázar's short stories, I argue, display a constant, self-conscious attempt to transgress their own linguistic, literary, narrative boundaries, in order to produce what the author himself calls 'new forms of contact', in order to become intermediaries. Their aesthetic immediacy is paradoxically achieved through multiple media and mediations.

Focusing first on *Todos los fuegos el fuego* (1966), I identify a series of connections between the spatio-temporal limits of the narratives and the borders with other media. Close readings of 'La isla a mediodía', 'Todos los fuegos el fuego' and 'El otro cielo' enable me to point to the different modes that underpin the stories' form and structure, from photography and cinema to sensationalist journalism and telephony. From this perspective, his short stories enclose and foreshadow the logic of his later, collaborative collage works, particularly *Buenos Aires Buenos Aires* (1968) and *Fantomas contra vampiros multinacionales* (1975), which combine literary forms with photographs, comic strips, and more. I argue that the modern media that characterize, and indeed create, Cortázar's urban settings function as mediators that allow characters — and complicit readers — to move between different realities, to transgress spatial and temporal boundaries. I then turn to *Queremos tanto a Glenda* (1982), where Cortázar embraces new modes of resistance and rebellion by opening up the literary *cuento* to different popular forms of expression, from testimony to graffiti. Aesthetic concerns and techniques become intermingled with ethical, political questions regarding the place of a writer in a country where the majority of the population is illiterate; the relationship between culture and revolution; the possibility of communicating and commemorating violence. By framing the short stories 'Recortes de prensa' and 'Graffiti' with some of his political writings from the early 1980s, I bring to the fore the political rhetoric that underlies his experiments with popular media.

Chapter 3 examines the dialectical tensions that underlie and structure Monterroso's fragmentary fiction, which help to gain a better understanding of the complex, often contradictory relations between genres, authors and critical strands: between short fiction, novels and collage works; between Rulfo and Cortázar; between divergent interpretations of the short story genre. These contradictions, I argue, are inextricable from the paradoxes of fragmentary form upon which Monterroso plays in his fiction.

I begin by examining the transcultural facets of his collage work *Movimiento perpetuo* (1972) through the central figure of the fly. The opening essay, 'Las moscas', indicates a contradictory relationship with tradition: one of attachment and severance, unity and fragmentation, transmission and intransmissibility. I unpack these contradictions by exploring the relationship between Monterroso's fly collection and Benjamin's shifting attitudes to the art of collecting, from the essay 'Unpacking my Library' to his *Arcades Project*. In turn, the fly quotations that invade the collection act as mediators between different countries, time periods and genres. Together, they constitute a Lévi-Straussian *bricolage*, a combination and reconfiguration of fragments from pre-existing signifying codes.

Finally, I turn back to look at Monterroso's first short story collection, *Obras completas (y otros cuentos)* (1959), whose hybridity foreshadows that of the fly collection. Each story self-consciously depicts the ways in which cultural objects are exchanged, negotiated and contested, creating a network of relations between different spatialities and temporalities. It is not just at the level of plot, though, but also at the level of form, that cultural hybridization takes place. Implicitly or explicitly, the short stories incorporate different media, from drawings and cartoons to journalism, photography and radio. On the one hand, the individual media are employed to fragment reality into isolated elements that are recomposed into new configurations. On the other hand, the interplay between different, sometimes dissonant, media produces encounters or clashes between cultural forms and, by extension, between the cultures to which they belong. In this respect, the short stories constitute hybrid structures that are inextricable from Latin America's multitemporal, multispatial heterogeneity.

Notes to the Introduction

1. Martha Elena Munguía Zatarain, *Elementos de poética histórica: el cuento hispanoamericano* (Mexico City: El Colegio de México, 2002), p. 11.
2. Françoise Perus, 'Algunas consideraciones histórico-teóricos para el estudio del cuento', *Plural*, 189 (1987), 37–39 (p. 38).
3. The idea is that the traditional storyteller and modern short story writer are both guided by constraints (the old tales that the storyteller repeats and the 'rules' of the genre of the short story that the modern writer 'follows'). Yet they also enjoy freedom, which is associated with the improvisational element in storytelling and the ability to play within and against the short story genre.
4. Roberto González Echevarría, 'Introduction', *The Oxford Book of Latin American Short Stories*, ed. by Echevarría (New York: Oxford University Press, 1997), pp. 3–22 (p. 4).
5. Lida Aronne-Amestoy, *América en la encrucijada de mito y razón: introducción al cuento epifánico latinoamericano* (Buenos Aires: F. García Cambeiro, 1976), p. 82, 79.
6. Enrique Pupo-Walker, *El cuento hispanoamericano* (Madrid: Editorial Castalia, 1995), p. 13.
7. Walter Benjamin, 'The Storyteller: Reflections of the Works of Nikolai Leskov', in *Illuminations*, trans. by Harry Zohn (Glasgow: Fontana, 1982), pp. 83–109 (p. 87, 83).
8. Augusto Monterroso Papers, Subseries 1F, Box 20, Folder 43, personal journal entries. All further references to this archive will employ the abbreviation AMP.
9. Augusto Monterroso, 'Para lo alegre o lo triste', in *La letra e*, in *Tríptico: Movimiento perpetuo; La palabra mágica; La letra e* (Mexico City: Fondo de Cultura Económica, 1995), p. 295. All further references to *La letra e* are from this edition.
10. Notebook, 1984, in AMP, Subseries 1A, Box 1.

11. Clipping from *Excelsior*, in AMP, Subseries 1B, Box 9, Folder 5.

12. Interview with Carlos Morales in *Semanario Universidad*, 30 June 1995, n 1160, p. 12, in AMP, Box 51, Folder 9.

13. Sergio Ramírez and Hugo Niño, *Queremos tanto a Julio: 20 autores para Cortázar* (Managua: Nueva Nicaragua, 1986), p. 127.

14. AMP, Subseries 1B, Box 14, Folder 5.

15. Fragments removed from *La letra e*, in AMP, Subseries 1B, Box 10, Folder 4.

16. Fragments removed from *La letra e*, in AMP, Subseries 1B, Box 10, Folder 4.

17. Notebook, Notes for his *Premio Príncipe* speech, in AMP, Subseries 1A, Box 2.

18. Augusto Monterroso, *Literatura y vida* (Madrid: Alfaguara, 2004), p. 97.

19. AMP, Subseries 1A, Box 2, Folder 10.

20. Edgar Allan Poe, 'Review of *Twice-Told Tales*', in Charles May, *The New Short Story Theories* (Athens: Ohio University Press, 1994), pp. 59–72 (p. 60).

21. 'Curso de cuento', UNAM, notebook [n.d.], in AMP, Subseries 1A, Box 2.

22. AMP, Subseries 1A, Box 2, Folder 6.

23. 'Curso de cuento', UNAM, notebook [n.d.], in AMP, Subseries 1A, Box 2.

24. 'Curso de cuento', AMP.

25. Julio Cortázar, 'Algunos aspectos del cuento', in *Obra crítica 2* (Buenos Aires: Suma de Letras Argentina, 2004), pp. 505–34 (pp. 527–28).

26. Jorge Luis Borges, 'El escritor argentino y la tradición' (1951), in *Discusión* (Madrid: Alianza, 1997), pp. 188–203 (p. 196).

27. Notebook [n.d.], in AMP, Subseries 1A, Box 2.

28. Monterroso, *La letra e*, p. 239.

29. AMP, Subseries 4D: Teaching Materials, Box 51, Folder 3.

30. Rulfo, 'El desafío de la creación' (1986), in *Toda la obra*, ed. by Claude Fell (Paris: Colección archivos, 1992), pp. 383–85 (p. 385).

31. Cortázar, 'Algunos aspectos' (p. 510).

32. Augusto Monterroso, *La oveja negra y demás fábulas* (Mexico City: Ediciones Era, 1990), p. 97.

33. AMP, Box 19, Folder 6: Works in Progress.

34. Frederick Lewis Pattee, 'The Present Stage of the Short Story', *English Journal*, 12 (1923), 439–49 (p. 441).

35. Andrew Levy, *The Culture and Commerce of the American Short Story* (Cambridge: Cambridge University Press, 1993), p. 1.

36. Stuart Sillars, 'The Illustrated Short Story', in *The Art of Brevity*, ed. by Winther, Lothe and Skei, pp. 70–80.

37. Nadine Gordimer, 'The Flash of Fireflies', in *The New Short Story Theories*, ed. by Charles May (Athens: Ohio University Press, 1994), pp. 263–67 (p. 263).

38. Mary Rohrberger, *Hawthorne and the Modern Short Story* (The Hague; Paris: Mouton, 1966), p. 11.

39. Charles May, 'Why Short Stories are Essential and Why They Are Seldom Read' in *The Art of Brevity*, ed. by Winther, Lothe and Skei, pp. 14–25 (p. 24).

40. Charles May, *The Short Story: The Reality of Artifice* (New York: Routledge, 2002), p. 133.

41. Terry Eagleton, *Heathcliff and the Great Hunger* (London: Verso, 1995), p. 150.

42. Benjamin, 'The Work of Art in the Age of Mechanical Reproduction', in *Illuminations*, pp. 219–53 (p. 223).

43. Benjamin, 'On Some Motifs in Baudelaire', in *Illuminations*, pp. 157–202 (p. 165).

44. Two critics have sensed the significance of this connection: Jane Marjorie Rabb, in *The Short Story and Photography, 1880's–1980's: A Critical Anthology* (Albuquerque: University of New Mexico Press, 1998), anthologizes short stories relating to photography by authors like Arthur Conan Doyle, Thomas Hardy and Italo Calvino; Daniel Balderston, in 'The Twentieth-Century Short Story in Spanish America' (in *The Cambridge History of Latin American Literature*, ed. by Roberto González Echevarría (Cambridge; New York: Cambridge University Press, 1996), pp. 465–96), traces the theme and motif of photography through stories by Cortázar, Virgilio Piñera, Silvina Ocampo and Juan Carlos Onetti.

45. Stephen Hart, ' "El oficio de escribir": Some Notes on Literary Print Culture in Spanish America in the Twentieth Century', *Neophilogus*, 83 (1999), 387–409 (p. 400).

46. Esteban Echeverría, *El matadero*, in *Revista del Río de la Plata, periódico mensual de historia y literatura de América* (Buenos Aires), 1 (1871), 556–85.

47. Horacio Quiroga, 'La crisis del cuento nacional' (1928), in *Cuento terciario y otros cuentos*, vol. xii (Montevideo: Claudio Garcia, 1945), pp. 35–40.

48. Aníbal González, *Journalism and the Development of Spanish American Narrative* (Cambridge: Cambridge University Press, 1993), p. 83.

49. Beatriz Sarlo, *Una modernidad periférica: Buenos Aires, 1920 y 1930* (Buenos Aires: Ediciones Nueva Visión, 1999), p. 19.

50. AMP, Subseries 1E, Box 18, Folder 3, pp. 2–3.

51. Jesús Martín-Barbero's entry on *medios de comunicación* in *Diccionario de estudios culturales latinoamericanos*, ed. by Mónica Szurmuk and Robert McKee Irwin (Mexico City: Siglo XXI, 2009), p. 169.

52. Carlos Monsiváis, 'La cultura popular en el ámbito urbano: el caso de México', in *Posmodernidad en la periferia: enfoques latinoamericanos de la nueva teoría cultural*, ed. by Hermann Herlinghaus and Monika Walter (Berlin: Langer Verlag, 1994), pp. 134–58 (p. 139).

53. Sarlo, *Una modernidad periférica*, p. 28.

54. Fernando Ortiz, *Contrapunteo cubano del tabaco y azúcar (Advertencia de sus contrastes agrarios, económicos, históricos y sociales, su etnografía y su transculturación)* (Madrid: Cátedra, 2002), p. 260.

55. Ángel Rama, *Transculturación narrativa en América Latina* (Mexico City: Siglo XXI, 2004), p. 39.

56. Néstor García Canclini, 'Noticias recientes sobre la hibridación', *TRANS/Revista transcultural de música*, 7 (2003), <http://www.sibetrans.com/trans/a209/noticias-recientes-sobre-la-hibridacion> [accessed 6 April 2014].

57. Néstor García Canclini, *Culturas híbridas: estrategias para entrar y salir de la modernidad* (Buenos Aires: Editorial Sudamericana, 1995), p. 17.

58. Néstor García Canclini, *Las culturas populares en el capitalismo* (Mexico City: Nueva Imagen, 1986), p. 104.

59. García Canclini, *Culturas híbridas*, p. 25.

60. Martín-Barbero, *Communication*, p. 189.

61. Eva Valcárcel López, 'El cuento: aproximación teórica', in *El cuento hispanoamericano del siglo XX : teoría y práctica*, ed. by Eva Valcárcel López (A Coruña: Universidade da Coruña, Servicio de Publicaciones, 1997), pp. 21–29 (p. 21).

CHAPTER 1

Juan Rulfo, the Transculturator

Introduction: Re-Viewing *El Llano en llamas*

Inspired perhaps by Ángel Rama's highly influential *Transculturación narrativa en América Latina*, critics have often sought to locate Rulfo's work in a return to traditional, rural, indigenous and oral narrative forms; in the context of what Rama calls 'el repliegue dentro del venero cultural tradicionalista'.[1] Rulfo's narrative fiction, according to Rama, stands as a prime example of the way in which Latin American narrators wrote by turning their backs on European literary modernity: 'al relato compartimentado, mediante yuxtaposición de pedazos sueltos de una narración (en John Dos Pasos, en Huxley) se le opuso el discurrir dispersivo de las "comadres pueblerinas" que entremezclan sus voces susurrantes' (44). In this sense, Rulfo's work is considered to 'procede[r] de una recuperación de las estructuras de la narración oral y popular'; its fragmentary structure stems not from the influence of modern cultural forms, but from the 'reconocimiento de un universo dispersivo, de asociacionismo libre, de incesante invención que correlaciona ideas y cosas, de particular ambigüedad y oscilación' (44, 53). As Adam Sharman points out in his brilliant study of the relationship between modern Latin American fiction and tradition, this means that Rama effectively opposes the irrationalist, oral aspects of Rulfo's fiction with the Western modernist tendency to 'contest the dominant Western rationalist tradition'.[2] Formal fragmentation, in this view, is connected not with literary modernization and innovation, but rather with the retreat into a collective oral tradition.

In the same critical vein, Walter Mignolo argues that Rulfo's work is characterized not just by the fictionalization of orality, but more specifically by 'la ficcionalización de una oralidad que identifica la juxtaposición de tradiciones culturales nativas y colonizadas.'[3] The fragmentary form of Rulfo's work is attributed to the recuperation of oral Amerindian languages, to 'la lógica no-causal y aleatoria de culturas primariamente orales' (430). Again, the fragmentation of logical causality and temporal linearity are connected to orality, in stark opposition to what he calls 'alphabetic writing', which in turn is connected to temporal, linear and chronological organization (431).

While Mignolo focuses on residual form, Evodio Escalante focuses on residual content in his insistence that the time of Rulfo's fiction is 'el tiempo contrario al universo de la lectura':

> La remisión a un universo campesino, refractario al progreso [...], la pervivencia
> de un orden sincrético que sólo permanece para desmoronarse [...], bastan para
> indicar cuán incómodo, cuán resbaladizo, puede ser el trabajo de la lectura. Ese
> mundo no existe más. Mejor dicho: existe, resiste, pervive en lugares lejanos;
> acaso hay restos suyos en las periferias de las grandes ciudades, pero es difícil,
> animales urbanos como somos, que hayamos vivido su experiencia y que
> tengamos los parámetros adecuados para entenderlo.[4]

According to this reading, the archaic, or rather residual, traditions, beliefs, and orders that permeate Rulfo's world make it unapproachable, alien to any modern reader. In the light of this proposition, he questions the extent to which the urban reader might be prepared to accept its archaicism.

From an even more damning perspective, Bartra argues that Rulfo's melancholic evocation of the ghosts of Mexico's rural past is symptomatic of a dangerous romantic fetishization of 'Mexicanness' that characterizes post-revolutionary Mexico, and disguises a 'powerful nationalist will bound to the unification and institutionalization of the modern capitalist state'.[5] According to him, *Pedro Páramo* presents a subverted paradise, which constitutes 'the contemporary [inverted] image of an earlier, older place in which happiness reigned. But it is a past and faded happiness which reposes at a deep, mythical level, buried by the avalanche of the Mexican Revolution, through which we can only feel melancholy. It is a place in which present and past are confused in order to exclude the future' (18). Rulfo, from this perspective, takes part in the construction of a double myth: the modern myth of a mythical Mexican past. His fiction unwittingly provides fodder for the very nationalistic discourse against which he writes, by contributing to the myth of the prelapsarian paradise of traditional, rural Mexico upon which that discourse is erected.

My reading will be situated not in opposition to, but rather in dialogue with, these arguments. In other words, the aim is not to contradict this mode of thinking, which is to a certain extent justified by Rulfo's work, but to propose another dimension that will stand in a dialectical relationship with it, in order to reveal Rulfo's engagement with emergent forms and his contribution to the modernization of storytelling. In doing so, I shall offer some affirmative responses to Sharman's pertinent question, posed in relation to Rama's argument: 'If the transculturators were involved in a retreat back or re-immersion [...] into traditional culture, is this not because they have been out of traditional culture and have returned to it on the back of the experience of modernity?'[6] As we shall see, Rulfo's literary output is a transcultural mixture of themes, experiences and forms. The *mestizajes* in his writing reveal, in Martín-Barbero's terms, 'the interweaving of modernity and the residues of various cultural periods, the mixture of social structures and sentiments'.[7] As William Rowe observes in his brilliant critical guide to *El Llano en llamas*, though there are of course marks of orality in the stories, these are only ever partial:

> Their compositional techniques are those of modern, post-Joycean fiction,
> assembling a world by freely juxtaposing fragments of consciousness rather than
> aiming to produce naturalistic pictures of life. They combine modern literary
> techniques with an input from oral culture.[8]

Whereas as far as Escalante is concerned, Rulfo's territory is that of the archaic, the residual at best, my argument is that his work is punctured by emergent cultural forms. The terms 'archaic', 'residual' and 'emergent', here, are used in the sense offered by Raymond Williams: whereas archaic forms are relegated to museum displays, belonging as they do merely to the past, residual ones are fragments of past forms that are still actively present within cultural processes, and emergent ones constitute new modes and formations that have yet to be fully developed and established.[9] Notably, both the residual and the emergent are fragmentary cultural forms: the former because they are partial remainders of a former system that has collapsed or disintegrated, the latter because they have yet to take on full form or acquire meaning within dominant social structures. It is therefore hardly surprising that the transcultural properties of Rulfo's work are connected to its fragmentary quality, to the fact that, as Rowe affirms, 'Rulfo was one of the first writers in Latin America to thoroughly break up traditional narrative structures' (9). This reflects Rulfo's own views on his writing, expressed in an interview with Fernando Benítez in 1970:

> Yo quería leer algo diferente, algo que no estaba escrito y no lo encontraba. Desde luego no es porque no exista una inmensa literatura, sino porque para mí, sólo existía esa obra inexistente y pensé que tal vez la única forma de leerla era que yo mismo la escribiera.[10]

Rulfo sees his work as a necessary response to a gap and as a break from existent literature. Yet this is not to say that it is completely divorced from cultural forms that precede it; or that, as Manuel Durán suggests, twentieth-century Mexican literature should be divided into two great phases, 'Antes de Juan Rulfo y Después de Juan Rulfo'.[11] My contention is that Rulfo's innovation consists in his construction of a site in which residual forms are re-fashioned through emergent forms; in which inherited narrative forms are broken up and reconfigured in an active process of transculturation; in which tradition is renewed in the ruins of residual narrative forms.

On one level, this fragmentation or ruination is symptomatic of certain processes of socio-political fragmentation that characterize Rulfo's contemporary Mexico, a social situation that begs comparison with that discerned in the European context by Walter Benjamin. In 'The Storyteller' (1937), Benjamin attributes the death of the traditional storyteller to the decay of wisdom, which constitutes 'a concomitant symptom of the secular productive forces of history, a concomitant that has quite gradually removed narrative from the realm of living speech.'[12] The death of the storyteller is a symptom of a triple break from tradition, religion and authority, and the consequent decay of meaning and relations.[13] By bringing Rulfo's literary works and Benjamin's philosophical writings under a shared umbrella, we shall see how the death of the storyteller is not only implied and manifested in Rulfo's stories, but also staged and dramatized.

Yet, as I shall argue, the short story is not just a passive symptom of socio-historical circumstance, a negative product of social fragmentation. It also employs techniques of fragmentation to open up new aesthetic possibilities. As Philip Swanson explains, urbanization and modernization had a dual impact on writing in Latin America in the mid-twentieth century:

on the one hand, a rapidly changing technological environment promoted an awareness of new possibilities, a consciousness of the simultaneity of differing phenomena, and a desire to experiment, which resulted in the beginnings of new narrative forms; at the same time, that same shifting technological society caused an erosion of traditional values, generating instability, uncertainty and, ultimately, a sense of social and even metaphysical disorientation.[14]

Reversing the order of these two inter-related elements, this chapter will demonstrate how processes of erosion and fragmentation provide Rulfo with the materials from which to erect new narrative forms, which cannot be separated from the possibilities afforded by emerging technologies.

For Rulfo as for Cortázar, the modern writer's severance from the oral storytelling tradition is a positive, calculated aesthetic choice:

> la intención [en *Pedro Páramo*] fue [...] quitarle las explicaciones. Era un libro un poco didáctico, casi pedagógico: daba clases de moral y no sé cuántas cosas y todo eso tuve que eliminarlo porque no soy muy moralista y además... sí, fui dejando algunos hilos colgando para que el lector me... pues, cooperara con el autor en la lectura. Entonces, es un libro de cooperación.[15]

Rulfo's purpose is to break from systems of morality, rationality and didacticism in order to leave space for what Cortázar terms the 'lector cómplice'.[16] The consequent fragmentation of narrative results less in a loss to be mourned, than a gain to be celebrated: the democratization of the reading process through the elimination of a traditional storyteller whose traces, in Benjamin's terms, 'cling to the story the way the handprints of the potter cling to the clay vessel' (92). In an interview with Fernando Benítez, this process of authorial elimination is linked explicitly by Rulfo to the discipline of writing short stories: '*Pedro Páramo* es un ejercicio de eliminación. [...] La práctica del cuento me disciplinó, me hizo ver la necesidad de que el autor desapareciera y dejara a sus personajes hablar libremente'.[17] In other words, narrative fragmentation is not an inherited aspect of existent, residual oral forms, as Rama and Mignolo suggest; rather it is something artificial, inextricable from the labour of writing.

Moreover, I shall demonstrate that the 'técnica' of the short story, its art and craft, is inextricable from a different kind of 'técnica': the technology of photography. As is well known, Rulfo was a photographer himself, whose work has been celebrated in two collections: *Juan Rulfo: Homenaje nacional* (1980) and *Inframundo: el México de Juan Rulfo* (1983). These include some of the six thousand photographs whose negatives he kept and ordered in shoe boxes under his bed.[18] Taken in the 1940s and 50s, during Rulfo's period of literary productivity, these photographs bear a strong relationship with his writing.

This connection has already been pointed out in a small number of studies. In the opening section of her essay, entitled 'El ojo de la cámara', Yvette Jiménez de Báez claims that there is a close relation between the composition of *Pedro Páramo* and his photographic work. This is argued with specific reference to the collection *Juan Rulfo: Homenaje nacional*:

> Hay analogía entre esa secuencia de imágenes visuales [photos 28 to 39, whose centre is 33] y el centro del sentido en *Pedro Páramo*, que funciona en el plano

simbólico como Centro de las transformaciones (los 7 fragmentos, del 30 al 36, cuyo centro numérico es el 33).[19]

De Báez draws a connection between the 'Centre' of the *Homenaje* (capitalized by de Báez in spite of Rulfo's explicitly de-centring aesthetics) and the centre of *Pedro Páramo*. Yet the validity of drawing such an analogy is highly questionable, not least because the *Homenaje* was not ordered by Rulfo himself. As I shall demonstrate, it is precisely the dislocation of the Rulfian fragment from any fixed context that constitutes its power; it is its resistance to any sequential order, whether spatial (linear) or temporal (chronological), that gives it force.

Other critics have come closer to my reading of the connection between Rulfo's photography and his fragmentary fiction. Howard Fraser explores this connection in his article '*Inframundo:* Juan Rulfo's Photographic Companion to *El Llano en llamas*'.[20] His focus, though, is on content rather than form. He relates the subjects of Rulfo's photographs to the themes, characters and settings of the short stories, noting that they share scenes from his native region, the southern part of the central Mexican state of Jalisco: arid, desolate landscapes; ruined, collapsed buildings; indigenous people, often suspicious of camera and photographer alike. By looking more closely, and in more depth, at the *form* of Rulfo's short stories, I aim to gain a better insight into the relations between Rulfo's literary and photographic aesthetics. My theory is that his photographs are not simply the accompanying piece of his short story collection, a mere visual illustration or supplementation of its themes. Rather, they constitute a crucial ontological (absent-)presence in his writing, which is underpinned by the paradoxes inherent in the art of photography: the limited frame that opens onto a boundless beyond; the fleeting moment that is endowed with permanence; the past events that are revived through physical present-ness.

Fernando Benítez, in one of the essays accompanying the main edition of Rulfo's photographs, *Inframundo*, hints at this broader ontological connection:

> Sus fotos [...] retienen el misterio de *Pedro Páramo* o de *El Llano en llamas*; mujeres enlutadas, campesinos, indios, ruinas, cielos borrascosos, campos resecos. Una poesía de la desolación y una humanidad concreta, expresa un mundo que está más allá del paisaje y de sus gentes, construido en blanco y negro, con gran economía y nobleza.[21]

A link is established between photography and narrative not only in terms of common themes and subjects, but also in relation to a particular aesthetics of economy. Moreover, Benítez hints at one of the paradoxes enclosed in Rulfo's fragments: their intangibility and mystery stand in a dialectical relationship to their concreteness and directness. It is this concreteness that leads Eduardo Rivero to pinpoint the following formal connection: 'Rulfo, mediante sus fotografías y sus libros, parece estar diciendo: ¡Miren...! ¡Vean! Este mundo está aquí presente; nos lacera con el peso angustiante y funesto de su realidad tangible. ¡Asómense en él!'[22] His photographic and literary works alike, according to this account, have a presence, which is at once a phenomenological present-ness, a 'being now', and a physical existence, a 'being there'. The imperative to 'mirar', 'ver' and 'asomarse' suggests a link between the visual quality of Rulfo's writings and their physical presence, their power to cut into the reader's reality, and to invite him or her to participate in what they yield. Moreover, Rivero's use of the verb 'lacerar' points to the biting, wounding capacity of Rulfo's writing — one that will be aligned with what Cortázar, Benjamin and Barthes, respectively, have called the 'knock-out', the 'shock' and the *punctum*.

This chapter will offer a re-view of Rulfo's short story collection *El Llano en llamas* (1953) through its limits, its points of rupture — fault lines that, as we shall see, are manifested metafictionally within his highly self-conscious, introspective texts. I shall begin by exploring the ways in which Rulfo's short stories situate themselves at the limits of storytelling through their depiction of the death of the traditional storyteller and the corresponding decay of communicable meaning. I will then turn to explore the ways in which formal limits, cuts and breaks are posited not only as the symptom of residuality, loss and decay; but also as a point of departure, of lyrical and narrative openings onto new forms and paths. Finally, I shall examine the tales' rupture from narrative, that is, the point at which Rulfo's short story threatens to overspill its literary medium into the medium of photography.

The Death of the Storyteller and the Decay of Authority, Religion and Tradition

I shall begin by exploring the remnants, residues and shadows of the Benjaminian storyteller that persist in Rulfo's short stories, focusing on five key examples: 'Luvina', 'Es que somos muy pobres', 'Paso del Norte', 'Nos han dado la tierra' and 'El día del derrumbe'. I will return to these stories in more depth below, but the aim in this first section is to examine the links between the storyteller's dissolution and a broader process of fragmentation: that of communication, experience and community. In doing so, I hope to shed light on the ways in which the fragmentary form of the short story relates to the particular historical, social, political context of Rulfo's Mexico, namely the advent of a modern, urban, capitalist state, and the consequent rupture of traditional communities and relations.

In her analysis of *Pedro Páramo*, Jean Franco attributes the rupture of community that characterizes Rulfo's writing to the replacement of a tribal social order, based on human relations, by a new capitalist order dictated by monetary relations:

> *Pedro Páramo* puede ser consignada como una novela que no reproduce una visión coherente del mundo, sino la fragmentación y ruina de un orden social y moral, la supervivencia de códigos previos dentro de un nuevo orden social, y los conflictos y confusiones que surgen de la mezcla de lo nuevo y lo viejo. La intensa soledad de los personajes, señalada a menudo por los críticos, las escenas intensas pero aisladas que integran la novela son funcionales, vinculadas a la fragmentación de un orden, la ruptura de la tribu y su reemplazo por un código individualista.[23]

For Franco, the fragmentariness of relations and narrative in Rulfo's world is symptomatic of the disruption and displacement of the feudal system that formerly governed Mexico's rural communities without its full replacement by a bourgeois state. In this broadly Marxist reading, Franco sees money as an alienating force of mediation that replaces human relations with master–slave relations. By way of example, she posits the episode in which Susana San Juan is forced by her father to go down a mine to find gold coins. The rope that connects Susana to her father is read as a symbol of the precarious thread that ties humans together when filial ties are replaced by monetary ones. 'Sin relaciones plenamente humanas', Franco concludes, 'la comunidad muere' (774). The resonance with Benjamin's 'The Storyteller' displays a strong connection between Rulfo's Mexico and Benjamin's Europe, which have in common the rise of capitalism and consequent social fragmentation.

Though the focus of Franco's analysis is on *Pedro Páramo*, it will become evident that the stories of *El Llano en llamas*, too, are set against the backdrop of a triple fragmentation: the decay of traditional kinship and community relations; the loss of any authority that might mediate and communicate; the partial collapse of religious systems. As Gustavo Garza notes in *La urbanización de México en el siglo XX*,

> el acelerado económico entre 1940 y 1980 dinamizó el desarrollo urbano, transformando la organización de las actividades económicamente y la población en el territorio nacional. De inicio, entre 1940 y 1950 se observa una [tasa de urbanización] de 3.3, la más alta en todo el siglo XX, al crecer el [grado de urbanización] de 20.0 a 28.0%. Es necesario agregar que el aumento de la población urbana de 3.3 millones de habitantes, representó 53.5% de los 6.1 millones en que creció la total, y por primera vez en la historia del país la dinámica demográfica es mayoritariamente urbana.[24]

This vast demographic upheaval is the socio-cultural backdrop against which Rulfo's fiction is set: the emptying out of old communities, the loss of previous social ties, and the consequent alienation of the individual.

The decay of a rural community constitutes the historical backdrop against which 'Luvina' is staged. This story is narrated by a schoolteacher, who has returned from Luvina having failed in his didactic project, the vain attempt to transmit the messages of the modern state to the villagers. This might be read, as Rowe points out, as a critique of post-Revolutionary *desarrollismo* (26), adopted by the Comisión Económica para América Latina y el Caribe (Cepal) for the formation of its 1949 *Informe Económico de América Latina*. This theory of development is based on the premise of the intrinsic continuity of economic development, and on the mimetic replication of European models of modernization (whether economic, social, institutional, or ideological). In other words, the ideology of *desarrollismo* regards underdevelopment as the situation that precedes full economic development in a continuous line of progress.

More specifically, Rulfo's story might be read as a pointed reference to the policy of rural education adopted by the government of Lázaro Cárdenas (President, 1934–40). During this period, as Sergio López Mena explains, 'se dio gran impulso a la escuela rural. Miles de maestros acudieron por primera vez a lugares remotos con la idea cardenista de llevar la educación al campo para mejorar el país'.[25] The narrator of Rulfo's 'Luvina' is one of these school teachers, whose participation in the project of rural education is arguably the 'experiment' to which he refers in the following passage:

> En esa época tenía yo mis fuerzas. Estaba cargado de ideas... Usted sabe que
> a todos nosotros nos infunden ideas. Y uno va con esa plasta encima para
> plasmarla en todas partes. Pero en Luvina no cuajó eso. Hice el experimento
> y se deshizo...[26]

The teacher is left defeated by the peasants, whose entrenchment in traditional
values leads them to react with indifference to the grand ideas of the modern state.
The villagers' rejection of the government, on the basis that 'no tenía madre' (a
reference to the filial ties of their feudal order), is finally vindicated by the narrator.
The admission that 'tienen razón' (119) constitutes a resignation to the gulf between
Mexico's traditional social structures and the state system that came to occupy
their place. Feudal power, passed down paternal and maternal lines, is replaced by
the fragmented power of the state, represented here by the lone, withered teacher:
'Allá dejé la vida... Fui a ese lugar con mis ilusiones cabales y volví viejo y acabado'
(115). The bathetic juxtaposition of ideals and reality renders ridiculous Cárdenas's
educational project. Finally, all that remains for the teacher to transmit is his own
downfall, which reflects that of Luvina:

> un lugar moribundo donde se han muerto hasta los perros y ya no hay quien le
> ladre al silencio; pues en cuanto uno se acostumbra al vendaval que allí sopla,
> no se oye sino el silencio que hay en todas las soledades. Y eso acaba con uno.
> Míreme a mí. Conmigo acabó. (120)

Instead of counsel for his interlocutor (his successor, the next 'generation' of state
teachers), all the *maestro* has to offer is the proclamation of solitude and helplessness.
By pluralizing 'solitudes', Rulfo points to the connection between the isolation of
individuals as solitary beings and the sickness of tradition. The rural community
in the throes of death, whose silence is interrupted only by the roaring wind,
symbolizes the vacuity of the didactic project.

In 'Es que somos muy pobres', the triple break from tradition, authority and
religion, is enacted not at the level of the community, but rather at that of the family
unit, whose breakdown is caused by the daughters' prostitution:

> Mi mamá no sabe por qué Dios le ha castigado tanto al darle unas hijas de ese
> modo, cuando en su familia, desde su abuela para acá, nunca ha habido gente
> mala. Todos fueron criados en el temor de Dios y eran muy obedientes y no le
> cometían irreverencias a nadie. Todos fueron por el estilo. Quién sabe de dónde
> les vendría a ese par de hijas suyas aquel mal ejemplo. Ella no se acuerda. (55)

The girls' severance from a family tradition of god-fearing obedience and goodness
leads to incomprehension, isolation and alienation. Rowe points out the significance
of the mother's failure to explain her daughters' ill in terms of inheritance: 'the
failure of the parents' explanations is the inadequacy of authority and tradition,
i.e. of culture, to supply a language which can contain what is occurring' (71–72).
That is to say, the mother's amnesia is a manifestation of the tears in the fabric of
tradition, the web of past experience, that lead to an inability to make sense of
present experience. Moreover, the girls' rebellion from their Christian upbringing
is such that religious beliefs, displayed in the narrator's constant references to sin,
evil and punishment, are incapable of providing explanation or comfort. Their

prostitution — the ultimate manifestation of the more general Marxist paradigm of the prostitution of the labourer — indicates the replacement of a rural social order, based on human relations, by a new capitalist order dictated by monetary relations.

'Paso del Norte', a story about a son's desperate attempt to cross the US border due to the lack of employment in rural Mexico, also stages the 'death' of authority, of the father whose verse-reciting career is a permutation of the rural storyteller. The didactic nature of his verses is apparent in the words addressed to the son, 'apréndete mi sabiduría. Yo estoy viejo...' (127). This yoking of age and authority chimes with the figure of the Benjaminian storyteller, who derives his wisdom from experience and imparts his knowledge to the younger generations. Yet Rulfo's verse reciter is a subversion of the storyteller in many ways. Instead of passing on his wisdom to the son, he deprives him of it: 'nomás [me soltó] como caballo entre las milpas'; 'ni siquiera me enseñó usted a hacer versos' (128). His practical advice is reduced to isolated, fragmentary statements: 'Apréndete esto hijo: en el nidal nuevo, hay que dejar un güevo' (128); 'aprende algo. Andar por los caminos enseña mucho. Restriégate con tu propio estropajo, eso es lo que has de hacer' (129). These two moralizing verses are significant, since both point to human isolation and solitude: the first implies that parents are abandoned by children as they fly the nest; the second suggests that one must learn for oneself, the image of scrubbing oneself evoking the pathos of the helpless, solitary human condition. The father's only counsel, paradoxically, is a profound lack of counsel. His lesson is that men are united only by their solitude. This gains significance in the father's lament:

> Desde que tu madre murió me sentí solo; cuando murió tu hermana, más solo; cuando tú te fuiste vi que estaba ya solo pa siempre. Ora vienes y me quieres remover el sentimiento; pero no sabes que es más dificultoso resucitar un muerto que dar la vida de nuevo. (129)

The figure of the storyteller has been reduced to a solitary figure with no counsel. His metaphorical death is a vindication of Benjamin's prophecy: abandoned first by his wife and daughter (who die), then by his son (who leaves), the decay of paternal authority is a symptom of an emergent society in which every human is cut off from the other and from himself — a society that owes much to the powerful influence of the United States, which lurks behind the entirety of the story.

'Paso del Norte' therefore belies the attempt to locate Rulfo's work in a purely traditional, peasant culture. The son's departure is a manifestation of the more generalized trend of rural to urban migration, which results in the collapse of a traditional rural community.[27] As the supplementary narrator puts it, 'la gente de los pueblos se iba a las ciudades. En las ciudades la gente se perdía; se disolvía entre la gente' (129). The tale is underpinned by a dialectical movement between traditional, rural life in the *pueblos* and modern, urban life in Mexican and North American cities: the rearing of pigs and chickens, fruit-picking, and rural raconteurs, on the one hand, is set against urban, technological developments of gramophones, the firework industry and railway building. Whereas the traditional pig-rearing activities are failing, forcing the son to leave the village to find work in the city, 'el Carmelo volvió [de la ciudad] rico, trajo hasta un gramófono y cobra la música a cinco centavos' (126). Yet as is characteristic of Rulfo's fiction, the breakdown of any clear opposition between these two cultures gives way to transculturative processes. It is by bringing his gramophone back to his rural community that Carmelo earns a living. Similarly, the father 'gan[a] algo divirtiendo a la gente' (128), suggesting that storytelling functions as a money-making enterprise for the father as much as selling fireworks: 'mientras haiga funciones, le lloverá dinero' (126). The human relations with which traditional storytelling is inextricably connected are replaced by relations based on money, which links the rupture between father and son in this story to that between Bartolomé and Susana in *Pedro Páramo*. The socio-historical backdrop of this story, like that of *Pedro Páramo* as analysed by Franco, is the intrusion of capitalist relations into a rural community, causing the alienation of the individual, and the fragmentation of human relations.

Yet this process of social disintegration is not always presented by Rulfo as a passive symptom of capitalism, modernization, and progress. In other stories, it is portrayed as the result of a deliberate project: the exclusion of an entire community from the dominant cultural process, the post-Revolutionary nationalist project. As Monsiváis says in relation to *Pedro Páramo*, Mexico is a country in which 'marginalidad y amnesia han sido tácticas indispensables en la estrategia de la modernización y el crecimiento capitalista'.[28] Incommunication and alienation in Rulfo's world are not simply a symptom of historical circumstances (as Benjamin explains them in 'The Storyteller'), but also an active method of control and containment.

This can be seen clearly in 'Nos han dado la tierra', where the decay of communication is constantly reiterated:

> No decimos lo que pensamos. Hace ya tiempo que se nos acabaron las ganas de hablar. Se nos acabaron con el calor. Uno platicaría muy a gusto en otra parte, pero aquí cuesta trabajo. Uno platica aquí y las palabras se calientan en la boca con el calor de afuera, y se le resecan a uno en la lengua hasta que acaban con el resuello.
> Aquí así son las cosas. Por eso a nadie le da por platicar. (38)

The characters' resignation appears to stem from their belief in natural determinism, the notion that the human state is a direct result of his physical environment: the narrator asserts that their speech is literally dried out by the desert. Yet it later emerges that their silence is also the effect of socio-political circumstances, of the delegate's refusal to register their complaint that their allotted land is arid and infertile: 'no nos dejaron decir nuestras cosas. El delegado no venía a conversar con nosotros' (39); 'él no nos quiso oír' (40). Incommunication derives from the authority's indifference and from the consequent resentment, if not resignation. What is seen as a symptom of the natural surroundings is revealed to be a method of control and oppression in the revolutionary state, a means of keeping the peasants quiet. In the same vein, Rowe's analysis of 'Nos han dado' points out that the text creates ambiguity between fatalism as existential state and fatalism as method of control. For Rowe, the suggested message is that 'the peasants' anger is deprived of an outlet by the authorities who hide behind their bureaucratic mask; if their anger cannot be turned against its real cause, then a substitute must be found' (29). The peasants' attitude constitutes a defence mechanism, a means of survival in a post-Revolutionary state in which government bureaucracy functions as a means of social exclusion.

The use of bureaucratic masks for state control is also registered in Rulfo's 'El día del derrumbe'. Here, the state official, promising to provide support for a rural community in the aftermath of a devastating landslide, addresses the villagers thus:

> Conciudadanos — dijo —. Rememorando mi trayectoria, vivificando el único proceder de mis promesas. Ante esta tierra que visité como anónimo compañero de un candidato a la Presidencia, cooperador omnímodo de un hombre representativo, cuya honradez no ha estado nunca desligada del contexto de sus manifestaciones políticas y que sí, en cambio, es firme glosa de principios democráticos en el supremo vínculo de unión con el pueblo, aunando a la austeridad de que ha dado muestras la síntesis evidente de idealismo revolucionario nunca hasta ahora pleno de realizaciones y de certidumbre. (146)

His speech constitutes an accumulation of rhetorical structures that add up to nothing but a shimmering surface of signifiers. Grammatical structures lead nowhere; obscure, formal, bureaucratic terms fall into meaninglessness; contradictions are left unresolved. The speech is also ridden with irony: whilst he talks about togetherness, community and unity, he severs himself from the villagers through his inflated, and self-inflating, rhetoric. Rather than providing a communicative bridge, the delegate erects a barrier that serves to exclude, marginalize and subjugate. Wearing his bureaucratic mask, he creates an alienating persona that controls the community through sheer incommunicability.

In a sense, the delegate's vacuous words and excessive gestures turn him into a caricature of the traditional storyteller. As he is about to give his speech, the governor's movements are described thus: 'se fue enderezando, despacio, muy despacio, hasta que lo vimos echar la silla hacia atrás con el pie; poner sus manos en la mesa; agachar la cabeza como si fuera a agarrar vuelo' (146). The inflation of his bird-like gestures serves to satirize state rhetoric, which is exaggerated to the point of deflation: 'este lugar [...] antaño feliz, hogaño enlutecido, me duele. Sí, conciudadanos, me laceran las heridas de los vivos [...] me duele vuestra desgracia [...] ¡me duele!, con el dolor que produce ver derruido el árbol en su primera inflorescencia' (146–47). His grotesque attempt to feign empathetic suffering through the hyperbolic repetition of 'dolor' is self-defeating, divesting his words of any solemnity or significance. By caricaturing the figure of the storyteller, Rulfo theatricalizes the severance of community ties that results from the deliberate evacuation of communicative content.

A Poetics of (Un)Containment: From Text-as-Content to Text-as-Container

Rulfo's short story, however, is not just a passive product of the death of the storyteller, and the correlative dissolution of communicative content and meaning. It is also a purposeful severance from such an authority, a means of foregrounding form by changing the focus from message to medium. As we shall now go on to see, Rulfo's short story form is erected as a ghostly void that must be fleshed out, both by the characters or settings (that gain a life force of their own) and by the reader (who cooperates in their revival). Content, in this sense, is dependent not on the past, but rather on the future. This reading will be underpinned by Raymond Williams's theory of the emergent: 'what matters, finally, in understanding emergent culture, as distinct from both the dominant and the residual, is that it is never only a matter of immediate practice; indeed it depends crucially on finding new forms or adaptations of form'.[29] Because emergent cultures are in a gradual process of articulation and formation, form precedes meaning. Since Rulfo's literary work, as he himself claims, is an attempt to fill a gap, to find a language that has yet to be fully developed, his texts must be forged not as narratives that transmit pre-existing meaning, but rather as sites, containers or vessels that might *hold* new meaning(s). The attempt to find a form of expression for that which still evades understanding is linked to the following notion articulated by Williams:

> if the social is always past, in the sense that it is always formed, we have [...] to find other terms for the undeniable experience of the present: not only the temporal present, the realization of this and this instant, but the specificity of present being, the inalienably physical, within which we may indeed discern and acknowledge institutions, formations, positions, but not always as fixed products, defining products. And then if the social is the fixed and explicit — the known relationships, institutions, formations, positions — all that is present and moving, all that escapes or seems to escape from the fixed and the explicit and the known, is grasped and defined as the personal: this, here, now, alive, active, 'subjective'. (129)

The short story form is forged by Rulfo as a literary container for the inalienably physical, the undeniably present, the ungraspably mobile; for what Cortázar in 'Algunos aspectos del cuento' conjures through the evocative images of 'un temblor de agua dentro de un cristal, una fugacidad en una permanencia'.[30] In what follows, I shall examine the ways in which the narrative-as-container becomes the dialectical underside of the narrative-as-ruin — which are both in turn the decadent remains of the storyteller, of the narrative-as-content. In each example, I shall begin by indicating the ways in which the narrative container is figured metatextually by characters and settings, bodies and buildings, figures whose gaps, cracks and openings leave room for invasion, intrusion and infection, or, seen more positively, escape, reconstruction and imagination. I will then offer an analysis of the different literary techniques that are employed to produce these texts-as-containers. These techniques are inextricable from the spatio-temporal constraint of the short story, which is highlighted by Rulfo in his essay 'El desafío de la creación' (1986):

> Para mí el cuento es un género realmente más importante que la novela, porque hay que sintetizar, hay que frenarse; en eso el cuentista se parece un poco al poeta, al buen poeta. El poeta tiene que ir frenando al caballo y no desbocarse; si se desboca y escribe por escribir, le salen palabras una tras otra y, entonces, simplemente fracasa. Lo esencial es precisamente contenerse, no desbocarse, no vaciarse; el cuento tiene esa particularidad; yo precisamente prefiero el cuento, sobre todo, a la novela, porque la novela se presta mucho a esas divagaciones.[31]

For Rulfo, the short story is closer to poetry than to the novel; in fact its aesthetics of containment constitutes a reaction against the novelistic tradition of 'divagaciones', and a modern renovation of literary genre rather than a return to oral, traditional forms. In this respect, Rulfo aligns himself with the theories of Cortázar and Monterroso (see Introduction), which in turn are linked to that of Jorge Luis Borges. In 'El arte narrativo y la magia' (1932), Borges analyses the narratives of William Morris and Edgar Allan Poe, and implicitly forges an *ars poetica* for his own art of brevity, through a dictum by a master of poetry: ' "Nombrar un objeto", dicen que dijo Mallarmé, "es suprimir las tres cuartas partes del goce del poema, que reside en la felicidad de ir adivinando; el sueño es sugerirlo".'[32] In this way, Hemingway's tip of the iceberg technique is brought side by side with Mallarmé's (and Baudelaire's) notion of suggestion.

This is arguably the technique that Rulfo, in relation to the 1960s novel, illustrates through the following, suggestive image: 'está abierta la puerta y no nos dejan entrar'.[33] The barred space that remains concealed, suggested and imagined is precisely that which the short story creates through its poetic *técnica* of spatial restriction and temporal suspension. Taking these notions as a point of departure, I shall argue that the power of Rulfo's short story form derives from its eminently modern interplay between narrative suspension and poetic suggestion; that its uncontainable force is paradoxically potentiated by its strict containment.

In 'Es que somos', the severance from traditional structures is embodied by the character Tacha, who has lost her cow — her dowry — in a flood. The consequent 'falta de su vaca' (55) has, in the narrator's view, deprived her of her substance: 'se quedó sin nada' (54). She is left with nothing in the sense that she has lost her sole means of entering into the social institution of marriage. Her social ruination is underlined by the lyrical connection with a flooded building:

> [el río] estaba metiéndose a toda prisa en la casa de esa mujer que le dicen *la Tambora*. El chapaleo del agua se oía al entrar por el corral y al salir en grandes chorros por la puerta. *La Tambora* iba y venía caminando por lo que era ya un pedazo de río, echando a la calle sus gallinas para que se fueran a esconder a algún lugar donde no les llegara la corriente. (53)

Like the house, in which the normal content (the hens) are thrown out, and replaced by the intruding river, Tacha has been emptied out, left void, a mere vessel. The intrusion of the flowing river into *la Tambora*'s house, through two openings — that of the courtyard, and that of the door — becomes a negative metaphor for sexual penetration and rape, ominously foreshadowing Tacha's possible fall into prostitution. But it also foreshadows the possibility of release and liberation. Later, the overflowing river banks become a synecdoche for her overflowing emotions: 'de su boca sale un ruido semejante al que se arrastra por las orillas del río, que la hace temblar y sacudirse todita, y, mientras, la creciente sigue subiendo' (56). Uncontained and uncontrolled, her trembling body is depicted here not as a feeble, vulnerable structure (like *la Tambora*'s house) but rather as a site of power. Her mouth, an inlet for invasion, is also an outlet for a different language, a throbbing cry that, like the alien noise of the current, eludes human language. The overwhelming force of the flooding river is highlighted elsewhere:

> Allí nos estuvimos horas y horas sin cansarnos viendo la cosa aquella. Después
> nos subimos por la barranca, porque queríamos oír bien lo que decía la gente,
> pues abajo, junto al río, hay un gran ruidazal y sólo se ven las bocas de
> muchos que se abren y se cierran y como que quieren decir algo; pero no se
> oye nada. (53)

The narrator's impression is that the villagers' mouths have been invaded by the
sound of the river. Language, it seems, has been replaced by an irrational sound,
an unfathomable otherness, and an inalienably physical force, which does not
mean anything but simply *is* — a force which becomes synonymous with Tacha's
emotions, her suffering and her grief, her desire and her freedom.

As underlined by the dual imagery that connects her body both to the invaded
house and the invading river, Tacha is an uncontained container, a paradoxical,
hybrid figure that might be read as an incarnation of the short story form. On
the one hand, it is a residual form, a remnant of a past order, that demands to be
completed and filled; a container that can be invaded by the thoughts or emotions
of any reader. On the other hand, it is an emergent form, which has yet to
acquire fixed contours and always evades the grasp of any particular reading; an
uncontainable fount of thought and emotion. In brief, it is not merely a symptom
of the rupture of past relations, or relations with the past, as Benjamin suggests, but
also foregrounds the formation of new relations, based on the experience of the
present, and the presence of experience.

Some crucial questions, however, remain to be answered: how does Rulfo's
story communicate to the reader? How does it preserve the otherness of present
experience without assimilating it into narrative? How is the effect of present-
ness achieved when authorial presence is erased? The clue lies in the narrator's
description of the river as 'la cosa aquella'. As Rowe points out,

> The child's inability to rationalize, a feature in greater or lesser degree of all
> the characters, comes out in the way he uses language. The river has taken his
> aunt's tamarind tree away 'porque ahora ya no se ve ningún tamarindo'. He
> does not understand what is happening — and thus begin to come to terms
> with it — as a sequence of cause and effect: there is simply the raw fact of the
> tree's not being there. (71)

Similarly, by describing the river simply as 'la cosa aquella', the narrator presents
the flood as an unexplained occurrence, unassimilated and inassimilable into pre-
existing rational structures. Rulfo's text preserves the materiality — the thing-ness
— of the present experience, but also its strangeness, as the flood becomes an event
shrouded in mystery. As Eagleton points out, it is the short story's isolation of a single
moment that produces this effect of defamiliarization: 'if the novel is primarily a
cognitive form concerned to map the causal processes underlying events, the short
story, by contrast, can yield us some bizarre occurrence of epiphany or terror
whose impact would merely be blunted by lengthy elaboration.'[34] The exclusion of
explanation and rationalization allows otherness to remain as otherness, preventing
the folding of the strange back into the normal.

Moreover, the filtering of the story through the narrator's present experience has
an effect not only of estrangement, but also of narrative openness. Because the story

is recounted *in medias res*, starting at the point when the flood has already carried away Tacha's cow and perhaps her calf, the outcome of the flood is still uncertain:

> La única esperanza que nos queda es que el becerro esté todavía vivo. [...] Ojalá no se le haya ocurrido pasar el río detrás de su madre. Porque si así fue, mi hermana Tacha está tantito así de retirado de hacerse piruja. Y mamá no quiere. (54–55)

In this paragraph dominated by the subjunctive and the conditional, every sentence exudes provisionality, a temporality that contains two uncontained forces: a shred of hope (the 'only' hope that the calf might still be alive) and a glimpse of desire (albeit the mother's negative desire that she should *not* become a whore). As Bergson asserts,

> Time is what prevents everything from being given all at once. It retards, or rather, it is retardation. It must, therefore, be elaboration. Would it not then be a vehicle of creation and choice? Would not the existence of time prove that there is indetermination in things? Would time not be indetermination itself?[35]

The narrative's entrenchment in a restricted time frame is a paradoxically liberating one, as temporal enclosure results in indeterminacy. Like Tacha's mouth, the subjunctive mood constitutes an opening that renders the text inexhaustible. It is the same delay that allows Tacha to exceed the frame imposed by the narrator's gaze: 'crece y crece y ya tiene unos comienzos de senos que prometen ser como los de sus hermanas: puntiagudas y altos y medio alborotados para llamar la atención' (55–56). Her uncontrollable, unpredictable growth exceeds any complete knowledge. The temporality of the passage — its hyperbolic use of the present tense, emphasized by the childish repetition in 'crece y crece' — creates an effect of phenomenological present-ness. We might in this context draw attention to Williams's assertion, in his examination of emergent forms, that 'perhaps the dead can be reduced to fixed forms, though their surviving records are against it. But the living will not be reduced, at least in the first person; living third persons may be different' (129). The triumph of presence and present-ness in the text certainly prevents Tacha from being reduced to a fixed form. Yet it is precisely as the third person that Tacha resists reduction, as the restricted perspective of the first person narration endows her with both inalienable presence and unstoppable futurity.

In Rulfo's literary world, though, it is not just the living, but also the dead, that exceed reduction to fixed forms, as demonstrated by the corpse in 'Talpa':

> Quizá hasta empecemos a tenernos miedo uno al otro. Esa cosa de no decirnos nada desde que salimos de Talpa tal vez quiera decir eso. Tal vez los dos tenemos muy cerca el cuerpo de Tanilo, tendido en el petate enrollado; lleno por dentro y por fuera de un hervidero de moscas azules que zumbaban como si fuera un gran ronquido que saliera de la boca de él; de aquella *boca que no pudo cerrarse* a pesar de los esfuerzos de Natalia y míos, y que parecía querer respirar todavía sin encontrar resuello. De aquel Tanilo a quien ya nada le dolía, pero que *estaba como adolorido*, con las manos y los pies engarruñados y *los ojos muy abiertos* como mirando su propia muerte. Y por aquí y por allá todas *sus llagas goteando un agua amarilla*, llena de aquel *olor que* se derramaba por todos lados y *se sentía en la boca*, como si se estuviera saboreando una miel espesa y amarga que se derretía en la sangre de uno a cada *bocanada de aire*. (81, my emphases)

Tanilo's corpse defies death, maintaining a life-force that it expresses through its different openings, whether the mouth and eyes that refuse to close, or the wounds that continue to ooze puss. Tanilo's open mouth — the mouth through which he communicated, albeit with 'una voz apenitas', in his final days (75) — seems to carry on speaking through the buzzing flies, a kind of posthumous groan that exceeds ordinary language. Just as Tacha's body communicates through overflowing tears and quivering limbs that seem to gain almost autonomous power, Tanilo's corpse speaks through its otherness, through buzzing flies and oozing wounds. A different type of experience is foregrounded here: that of physicality, corporeality and death devoid of metaphysics.

This gains significance in the context of the complete breakdown of communication between the adulterous couple since Tanilo's death, which — though it might be explained externally by their rupture from traditional morality or from the shock of his death — is presented internally as a strange, alien experience: 'esa cosa de no decirnos nada'. Yet the thing-ness of the experience of fragmentation is precisely that which gives way to new relations between the characters, the corpse and the reader. It is through the fragmented, sensory effects of smell, taste and sound that Rulfo creates lyrical connections. The corpse is presented, or rather made present, to the reader less through story — through a rationalizing, causal narrative — than through lyrical effects, which connect the smell of the open wounds to a taste in the mouth of the characters, and perhaps the readers. The poetic technique, here, is akin to Baudelairean *correspondances*, whose principal device is synaesthesia. As Ihab Hassan puts it in his article on Baudelaire, 'a synaesthetic image reflects a certain totality uninhibited by logical classifications. It puts the reader in contact with a forceful sensory presence, a primitive wholeness or synthesis of impression.'[36] Rulfo's synaesthetic narrative, by producing unexpected connections between the senses, offers a different type of relation that might be seen as a solution to the state of incommunicability and fragmentation discerned by Benjamin: it communicates not in spite of a rupture from wisdom, knowledge, logic and rationality, but thanks to that; it achieves synthesis through fragmentation.

Tanilo's and Tacha's bodies, as vessels of unknown, unassimilated and unformed realities, might be regarded not only as the ruins of the storyteller, but also as metatextual figurations of the short story form. Rulfo, in 'El desafío de la creación', describes the modern writer as 'una especie de médium de cosas que uno mismo desconoce'.[37] Similarly, Cortázar proclaims that 'la gran mayoría de mis cuentos fueron escritos — cómo decirlo — al margen de mi voluntad, por encima o por debajo de mi consciencia razonante, como si yo no fuera más que un médium por el cual pasaba y se manifestaba una fuerza ajena' (517). As is becoming clear, it is not just Rulfo as author who constitutes a medium, but also his texts, which constitute vessels for realities that exceed narrative and linguistic configuration; mediations between the crumbling past and the uncertain future, between decay and growth, between death and life. To that extent, Rulfo's account of the challenge of literary creation might be supplemented: the challenge is not just for the author to become a facilitator, rather than an arbiter, of meaning; the greater challenge, to which Rulfo rises to an exceptional degree, is to craft a text that itself functions as a channel through which characters might be revived through the breath of new readers and readings.

In 'Talpa', it is not only the lyrical techniques of suggestion and *correspondances*, but also narrative constructions of ambiguity, which create openness and invoke readerly cooperation. Like most of Rulfo's narratives, 'Talpa' is seemingly self-enclosed and end-oriented: at the start, the narrator asserts that 'ahora todo ha pasado' (75); the narrative is framed by the verse-like sentence 'lo llevamos a Talpa ['allí' the second time] para que se muriera' (73, 80). Yet it soon emerges that the narrative is riddled with openings and indeterminacies: 'ahora Natalia llora por él, *tal vez* para que él vea, desde donde está, todo el gran remordimiento que lleva encima de su alma' (75); '*tal vez* de eso [llevar a Tanilo sobre los hombros] estábamos [...] con el cuerpo flojo y lleno de flojera para caminar' (78); '*tal vez* al ver las danzas [Tanilo] se acordó de cuando iba todos los años a Tolimán, en el novenario del Señor, y bailaba la noche entera hasta que sus huesos se aflojaban' (79, my emphasis). These are but a few illustrations of the way in which the narrator's limited perspective produces an effect of narrative openness: since he is unable to comprehend the thoughts, feelings and memories of other characters, he is reduced to conjecture. Every 'tal vez' leads the reader to question the causes or purposes of certain emotional and physical manifestations, whether Natalia's tears, the couple's weakness or Tanilo's dance; every 'quizás' produces a crack in the narrative through which another reality can be glimpsed, but only ever partially.

Indeterminacy comes to a head in the final section, which functions as a supplement to the story of Tanilo's fatal pilgrimage, destabilizing any finality through present-ness and futurity:

> Ahora [...] yo comienzo a sentir como si no hubiéramos llegado a ninguna parte, que estamos aquí de paso, para descansar, y que luego seguiremos caminando. No sé para dónde; pero tendremos que seguir, porque aquí estamos muy cerca del remordimiento y del recuerdo de Tanilo. (80)

Highlighted by the emphatic 'ahora', the blinkered vision of the narrator, restricted to the present, creates an opening in the narrative. The seemingly predetermined story is ultimately revealed to be indeterminate and incomplete. At the end of the single path of the pilgrimage that leads Tanilo to his predetermined death lies a Borgesian garden of forking paths, which opens the fate of the remaining two characters onto an uncertain future.

It is not just (living or dead) bodies, though, that embody the structural dialectic of containment and uncontainability in and of Rulfo's narratives, but also the settings. In the passage that opens 'El día del derrumbe', the trope of the ruin becomes a metaphor for the dialogic narrative from which it emerges:

> — Esto pasó en septiembre. No en el septiembre de este año sino en el del año pasado. ¿O fue el antepasado, Melitón?
> — No, fue el pasado.
> — Sí, si yo me acordaba bien. Fue en septiembre del año pasado, por el día veintiuno. Óyeme, Melitón, ¿no fue el veintiuno de septiembre el mero día del temblor?
> — Fue un poco antes. Tengo entendido que fue por el dieciocho.

> — Tienes razón. Yo por esos días andaba en Tuxcacuesco. [...] La gente salía de los escombros toda aterrorizada corriendo derecho a la iglesia dando de gritos. Pero espérense. Oye, Melitón, se me hace como que en Tuxcacuesco no existe ninguna iglesia. ¿Tú no te acuerdas?
> — No la hay. Allí no quedan más que unas paredes cuarteadas que dicen fue la iglesia hace algo así como doscientos años; pero nadie se acuerda de ella, ni de cómo era; aquello más bien parece un corral abandonado plagado de higuerillas.
> — Dices bien. Entonces no fue en Tuxcacuesco donde me agarró el temblor, ha de haber sido en El Pochote. (142)

Whereas the title leads the reader to expect the description of an earthquake on a particular date, he or she is instead presented with a series of disorientating questions: was the earthquake this September or last September, was it 21st September or a few days before, was it in Tuxcacuesco or in El Pochote? Any fixed reference points are eroded, leading to the substitution of substance and content with dialogue and invention. At the centre of the story lies a gap in knowledge which is filled by dialogic narrative. The story-ness of history here is laid bare in the way the past is subjected to personal feelings, active creations and subjective views. In turn, the narrative-filled historical void is figured by the image of the ruined church, a shell-like structure that has lost any fixed function or meaning, and has become a site of discontinuity, polyvalence and fluidity: it is reimagined as an abandoned farmyard, plagued not by a congregation, but by fig trees. As can be seen in the dialogic narrative, time and oblivion have led to metamorphosis and renewal; the ruins of history and memory have been filled by illusions and imaginings. The church functions as a spatial figuration of the temporality of the story, whose centre, like the epicentre of an earthquake, opens up deep cracks in the surrounding narrative ground.

Significantly, at the centre of the village lies another slippery structure, the symbolic statue of Benito Juárez (President of Mexico from 1858–72), which is also subject to oblivion, dislocation and metamorphosis:

> [El gobernador] habló de Juárez, que nosotros teníamos levantado en la plaza y hasta entonces supimos que era la estatua de Juárez, pues nunca nadie nos había podido decir quién era el individuo que estaba encaramado en el monumento aquel. Siempre creíamos que podía ser Hidalgo o Morelos o Venustiano Carranza, porque en cada aniversario de cualquiera de ellos, allí les hacíamos su función. (144)

History is decidedly demonumentalized, as Juárez's statue loses its fixity and solidity, dissolving into a fragile and malleable structure. Severed from its specific referent, it is transformed into a series of figures from different periods in Mexican history: the Wars of Independence (Miguel Hidalgo and José María Morelos) and the Revolution (Carranza). The emptying out of historical reference leads to infinite possible substitution and supplementation, as suggested by the repetition of the conjunction 'o'. Detached from any historical knowledge that would provide temporal continuity, the village community is left with a hole in the weft of tradition that it fills with plural inventions, multiple stories. Like the church, the statue might be regarded as a metaphor for the short story itself, which offers a site in which multiple narratives and temporalities, severed from a single voice of authority (a storyteller), are free to interlace and converge.

The trope of the text-as-ruin recurs in the central setting of 'Luvina', the hollow, decrepit church:

> Era un jacalón *vacío, sin puertas*, nada más con unos *socavones abiertos* y un *techo resquebrajado* por donde se colocaba el aire como por un cedazo. [...] Aquella noche nos acomodamos para dormir en un rincón de la iglesia, detrás del altar desmantelado. Hasta allí llegaba el viento, aunque un poco menos fuerte. Lo estuvimos oyendo pasar por encima de nosotros, con sus largos aullidos; lo estuvimos oyendo entrar y salir por los *huecos socavones de las puertas*; golpeando con sus manos de aire las cruces del viacrucis: unas cruces grandes y duras hechas con palo de mezquite que colgaban de las paredes a todo lo largo de la iglesia, amarradas con alambres que rechinaban a cada sacudida del viento como si fuera un rechinar de dientes. (116, my emphasis)

Like Tacha's body and *la Tambora*'s house, Tanilo's corpse and Tuxcacuesco's remains, the hollow shell of Luvina's ruined church, with its holes and openings, is an uncontained container; a space for invasion, this time by the howling wind. The physical, spiritual void at the core of the church — represented by the dismantled altar, the spatial and symbolic centre of the Christian ceremony — is a metaphor for the psychological emptiness of the teacher, narrator and storyteller (examined above). Yet the ruin, again, is a site to be filled. As the 'symbolic centre of the story', Rowe argues, the church is the space in which 'the various threads of symbolism are brought together' (62). Rowe's contention is that the dishevelled Christian building is occupied textually by indigenous Mexican symbolism. The wind as Christian symbol of the Holy Spirit is displaced by the Indian mythology of Quetzalcoatl as god of wind: anthropomorphized, it howls in a human voice and shakes the crosses with its hands. As Rama puts it, transculturation 'se trata de una fuerza que actúe con desenvoltura tanto sobre su herencia particular, según las situaciones propias de su desarrollo, como sobre las aportaciones provenientes de fuera.'[38] 'Desenvoltura' is an apt characterization of the vital force of the wind, of its indifference to moral and religious codes. The plural, pluralizing power of the wind — with its insinuating entrances and exits, threatening howls and violent knocks — is therefore a prime example of what Rama sees as the brazen force of transculturation.

Moreover, the church itself is reminiscent of a skull, with its eye sockets ('socavones abiertos'), grinding teeth (the crosses that 'rechin[an]') and death crown ('corona de muerto'). As Rowe points out, it symbolizes the cult of the dead, the Mexican mythology that has survived the Christianization of Mexico by occupying Christian spaces, whether physical or symbolic:

> Native beliefs and rituals related to death tend to survive precisely by adopting as an outer shell or protection the Christian symbols and practices which were supposed to replace them. This is the case with *el día de los muertos*, whose outer form is All Saints' Day, but whose dominant image in Mexico is the skull. (63)

The church is not merely a negative figure of decay, death and ruination, but also a figure of renewal — relevantly, the same renewal celebrated by Mexicans on the Day of the Dead. More broadly still, then, the church stands for the power of the fragmentary narrative itself, whose shell-like quality renders it open to infiltration or contamination by different readers, discourses and systems; whose transculturative power lies in its ability to mediate between different cultural practices and meanings.

Yet these processes, crucially, are dependent on an active reader who might tie different narrative, symbolic and cultural threads together; who, like the symbolic wind of 'Luvina', is able to insinuate himself through the narrative fissures. This cooperative reader is figured metatextually by the internal viewers who are forced to look through the partially open, cracked door:

> Allí tras las rendijas de esa puerta veo brillar los ojos que nos miran... Han estado asomándose para acá... Míralas. Veo las bolas brillantes de sus ojos... (116–17)
>
> Me detuve en la puerta y las vi. Vi a todas las mujeres de Luvina con su cántaro al hombro, con el rebozo colgado de su cabeza y sus figuras negras sobre el negro fondo de la noche. (118)

The meta-frame (the doorframe within the narrative frame) restricts vision, barring characters and readers alike from the secret world of the ghostly women of Luvina, and 'presenting' them through a sensual play of light and shadow: the internal viewers glimpse them through the tiny reflections in their glimmering eyes, as black spectres only minimally differentiated from the black background. Rather than seeing these spectral remainders face on, clearly, completely, we glimpse them as if in a mirror, in the darkness. As fleeting reflections, moving shadows and partially veiled figures, the ghosts of Luvina, like the corpse in 'Talpa', refuse to be reduced, in Williams's terms, to fixed forms. The totality — 'all the women of Luvina' — viewed through the restrictive doorframe functions as a *mise en abyme* of Rulfo's synecdochic artistic technique, which cuts narratives to the bare minimum in order to suggest, rather than to reveal, the totality; in order to produce a partial picture that only a cooperative reader can complete through imaginative participation.

Significantly, the frame in 'Luvina' is an overtly visual one, as emphasized by the continuous repetition of the verb 'ver' throughout the passages cited above. More specifically, its spatio-temporal limits and openings share the paradoxical quality of the photograph: the partial, restricted visions have an effect of expansion; the intermittent, flickering lights are endowed with futurity. Benjamin captures this paradox in his 'Short History of Photography' (1931), describing the photographic instant as 'the indiscernible place in the condition of that long past minute where the future is nesting, even today, so eloquently that we looking back can discover it.'[39] The photograph is characterized not only by the fleeting, vanishing moment — a ruin — but also by the suspension of completion, by the excess that always evades the prying gaze. Its tense is the future anterior; and the isolated instant bears an inextricable relationship with an untold, absent narrative. Many years later, Barthes's *Camera Lucida* (1980) would provide a seminal account of the dialectic of closure and openness, boundedness and boundlessness inherent in the photograph. As he affirms, the photograph's ontology is the past, or what he terms the 'ça a été' ('that-has-been'); the realm of certainty; the guarantor that something has happened.[40] Yet it also has the synecdochic ability to point to 'a kind of subtle beyond' (59), not only spatially, beyond the frame, but also temporally, beyond the instant. This beyond is described by Barthes as a 'blind field' (57), the spatio-temporal field that entails futurity, promise and possibility.

The technique of partial concealment that underpins Rulfo's (un)contained stories bears a strong connection with the art of photography as it is theorized by Benjamin and Barthes, but also as it is practised by Rulfo himself. Indeed, Rulfo takes the broad synecdochic logic of the photograph one step further in photographs that, through the subjects of collapsed buildings, decrepit branches or parched flowers, focus self-reflexively on the photograph's inherent fragmentation, partiality and fleetingness. This concern with the figure of the ruin is such that many of Rulfo's photographs sustain what one might call a second degree partiality: his photographs not only constitute ruins, but also present ruins; the opening *of* the photograph is supplemented by openings *within* his photographs; within the photographic frames, the viewer sees further frames. Emphasis is thus on the medium of photography rather than the content of the photographs.

One technique is that of imaginative aperture through physical, spatial restriction. A characteristic Rulfian photograph, no. 1 of the *Inframundo* collection portrays the empty shell of a ruined building that reminds one of the churches in 'Luvina' and 'El día del derrumbe' (see Fig. 2). The focus in this frame is on the empty doorframe, which constitutes an opening within the photograph. Through lighting effects, Rulfo emphasizes empty form rather than substantial content: the light that emanates from the white smoke conceals rather than reveals, barring any (visual) penetration into the ruin and deferring content; the contrasting darkness of the building in shadow preserves the ruin's obscurity. Likewise, no. 5 displays a meta-opening through the door of a ruined building, taken this time from inside rather than outside. Here, the presentation of small cracks in dilapidated doors draws attention to the limits of vision. In both cases, the Romantic ruin, symbol of past-ness, mortality and decay, is endowed with potentiality, stubbornly remaining what Borges in 'La muralla y los libros' calls the 'inminencia de una revelación que no se produce'.[41] A similar effect of obscurity is achieved in no. 49, this time a full-on view of a staircase, lit up in the midst of darkness. Since the revealing lighting of the staircase contrasts with the dark basement from which the photograph is taken, the latter remains an obscure underworld. Furthermore, the viewer cannot see where the staircase leads, though part of a laundry-laden clothes line is captured.

Another self-reflexive technique is that of overt temporal fragmentation in photographs that, like the stories from *El Llano en llamas* explored above, detach events not only from their outcomes, but also from their causes. A shot of an ornate church façade punctured with holes, no. 4 leaves the viewer to ponder on possible explanations: the holes could be the result of bullets holes, rendering the church the scene of violence or even a massacre; but they might also be the effect of weathering, and a consequent depiction of nature's triumph over civilization, time's triumph over man. By withholding any explanation, Rulfo's photograph necessitates the cooperation of the viewer in the same way that his stories require that of the reader. Similarly, in one photograph of three crosses (no. 35; see Fig. 3)

FIG. 2. Juan Rulfo, *Casa en ruinas en Tlaxcala* (1955).
© Sta. Clara Aparicio de Rulfo

Fig. 3. Juan Rulfo, *Huamantla*.
© Sta. Clara Aparicio de Rulfo

and another of a sign on a ruined building that says 'Earthquake of 16 April 1928' (no. 63), temporal segmentation not only functions as a *memento mori*, but also suggests a suspended story. The suggestive references to three deaths in the first case, and to an earthquake in the second, constitute partial witnesses to untold stories.

Rulfo's photographic work can in this context be viewed in relation to broader trends in Mexican photographic practice at the time when the large majority of his photographs were taken (the late 1940s and early 1950s). As Érica Segre explains, 'in the mid-1940s and 1950s photography had found its principal outlet in magazine illustration and reportage. Photographs "told a story"'.[42] Rulfo's work can be aligned with that of photojournalists like Héctor García and Nacho López: his work, though not intended as photojournalism in any strict sense, contributed towards his work for the *Instituto Nacional Indigenista*; towards a project that entailed documenting, and 'telling the story' of indigenous, rural Mexico. Yet in the case of Rulfo's photography, the story in question is never a told one, but always a latent one. As in *El Llano en llamas*, the object presented is valuable less because of its present content than because of its ghostly, suggestive form, be it an uninhabited collapsed building, unworn hanging clothing, or an unplayed musical instrument. The series of photographs of the band depict unattended instruments and empty stands, which promise music by withholding it (no. 78, see Figure 4). Drying laundry becomes a recurrent theme in photographs no. 50–53, where the ghostly clothes point to the absent-presence of their owners. Rulfo's photographic subjects therefore lay bare the fragmentary nature of his art: they do not represent reality, but present a frame through which another reality might be imagined; they present not palpable substance, but impalpable form; they open a door onto a future narrative, but do not let us in.

Howard Fraser refers to this presence of narrativity in his photographs: 'not only a life force but a narrative force seems to operate in his photographs as well.'[43] Yet it seems unfair to contrast his photography to his stories on this basis, as Fraser does in his assertion that, while the 'photographs outline the theme of hope', the stories 'frequently end on a note of despair' (60). As we have seen, his short stories contain the same dialectic of death and life, fatalism and freedom, despair and hope; just like his photographs, they consist of Cortazarian apertures onto some beyond that exceeds the instant that they inhabit. The most fatalistic of Rulfo's tales are punctured by indeterminacy; even when his characters seem irremediably trapped, there is always a possibility of escape; even when they die, they seem to keep on breathing.

As is becoming clear, Rulfo's photographic narratives and narrative photographs break down the opposition between story and snapshot, and by the same token, between photography and film. As fleeting moments pregnant with the expectation of succession, photographs capture suspended motion. It is this paradox which leads the novelist and screenwriter José Revueltas, in an influential article entitled 'Lugar del cine en el arte' (1947), to problematize the distinction between 'la fotografía fija y [la] fotografía en movimiento'.[44] By way of illustration, he cites the photographer Manuel Álvarez Bravo (1902–2002), Rulfo's contemporary, whose photographs are viewed by Revueltas as arrested moving images rather than stills. 'Not coin-

FIG. 4. Juan Rulfo, *Instrumentos musicales*, Photograph no. 78
© Sta. Clara Aparicio de Rulfo

cidentally,' Érica Segre observes, 'Álvarez Bravo during the 1940s had begun to collaborate in a number of films (it is presumed principally as a stills photographer), and was a close friend and associate of the outstanding *camarógrafo* Gabriel Figueroa and various directors' (126–27). Similarly, Juan Rulfo, who also enjoyed Figueroa's friendship,[45] was increasingly tempted by the art of cinematography, completing three film scripts gathered in *El gallo de oro y otros textos para cine*, writing another draft that was published posthumously in his *Cuadernos*,[46] and collaborating with the director Rubén Gámez on the script of *Fórmula secreta* (1964). Segre expands on this connection between image and narrative in the context of what she terms the literary *captionalization* of film and photography in 1950s Mexico, with the effect that 'the contingent moment becomes subject to narrative recuperation and an integrative imperative' — a narrativization which she connects with the fact that 'in the immediacy of a staged or captured moment the future subsists' (151).

In the following section, I wish to explore the ways in which the dialectic of image and narrative is played out in Rulfo's short stories. As we shall see, the relationship between short story and photograph transcends Cortázar's metaphorical analogy. It is not enough to say that the short story is like a photograph. Through the theoretical lenses of Benjamin, Cortázar and Barthes, I shall demonstrate that the rupture of narrative continuity in Rulfo's fiction is related to a broader *sensorium*, to shifting modes of perception, presentation and reception that result from emerging forms of experience, production and consumption — forms that are entangled with the technology and phenomenology of photography.

Beyond Metaphor: Fragmented Visions and the *Técnica* of Photography

Walter Benjamin's 'On Some Motifs in Baudelaire' (1939), which as we have seen functions as a theoretical counterpart to his essay 'The Storyteller', describes the experience of modernity and the correlative rupture from tradition in terms of a qualitative shift in the structure of experience, from *Erfahrung* to *Erlebnis*. Rapid developments in social, economic and technological realities have 'subjected the human sensorium to a complex kind of training', placing the shock experience at the heart of day-to-day life.[47] The photograph is one of Benjamin's principal examples of this phenomenon: the technology of photography allows the finger to freeze the instant at the push of a button and to produce a 'posthumous shock' (see Introduction). As García Canclini affirms in relation to new technologies in the 1980s, photographs 'debilitan el sentido histórico y las concepciones macroestructurales en beneficio de relaciones intensas y esporádicas con objetos aislados'.[48] These 'intense relations' or 'shock experiences' bear an important relationship with the 'knock-out' that for Cortázar defines the short story:

> en ese combate que se entabla entre un texto apasionante y su lector, la novela gana siempre por puntos, mientras que el cuento debe ganar por knockout [...] La novela acumula progresivamente sus efectos en el lector, mientras que un buen cuento es incisivo, mordiente, sin cuartel desde las primeras frases. (514)

From this perspective, brevity, intensity and *violence* are essential and constitutive, since the short story concentrates its strength in the vanishing instant. The effect of the short story is dependent on an intense, momentary relation that is akin to a knock-out in boxing, or in Benjaminian terms a passing moment (*Erlebnis*) cut out from cumulative *Erfahrung*.

With this in view, it is perhaps not surprising that Cortázar's essay on the short story chimes, to a large extent, with Barthes's work on the photograph, *Camera Lucida*. Both elaborate theories that connect the reader's or viewer's response to the particular temporality of the artworks in question. For Barthes, the *punctum* as a form of reception functions in a dialectical relationship with the *studium*. Whereas the latter is a gradual, cerebral labour of 'studying' that is embedded in shared cultural codes and accumulated experience, the former is a sudden, emotional sting produced by a photograph, that is to say, an intrinsically singular, disembedded experience. The violence of the *punctum* corresponds to that of the 'knock-out': it is 'this element which rises from the scene, shoots out of it like an arrow, and pierces me'; it is 'this wound, this prick, this mark made by a pointed instrument'.[49] As indicated by the accumulation of terms, that confuse speed and fleetingness ('prick', 'shoots', 'arrow') with prolonged duration and permanence ('wound', 'mark'), the *punctum* encloses a temporal dialectic. The stab produced by the photograph constitutes a sudden awareness that what the photograph presents is in fact irretrievably lost.[50] The same duality is captured by Sontag in her equally personal account of a set of photographs of Nazi concentration camps:

> Nothing I have seen — in photographs or in real life — ever cut me as sharply, deeply, instantaneously. Indeed, it seems plausible to me to divide my life into two parts, before I saw the photographs (I was twelve) and after, though it was several years before I understood fully what they were about. [...] When I looked at those photographs, something broke. Some limit had been reached, and not only that of horror; I felt irrevocably grieved, wounded, but a part of my feelings started to tighten; something went dead; something is still crying.[51]

Like the Winter Photograph for Barthes, these photographs have a dual effect on Sontag: the impact is at once brief and never-ending; something in her breaks, something is attached to her forever; it will remain inexpressible, yet she will always be bound by the attempt to express it.

A crucial difference must be highlighted between Barthes's and Sontag's personal accounts of photographic reception and Cortázar's theory of short story writing — a theory of production. Whereas the *punctum* is a contingent effect of the photograph (of any part of any photograph on the viewer), the 'knock-out' is formalized and, to a certain extent, predetermined by what Cortázar terms the 'great' short story (512); it derives from literary technique, from calculated craft. But a crucial connection remains: though the photograph is a *memento mori*, a residual remnant of the past, it also bears an important relation with the present moment, the instant of the experience, the *punctum*; the experience within the photograph, but also the experience of viewing the photograph. My argument is that the connection between the Rulfian short story and the reader, like that between the photograph and its viewer, is an inherently temporal one. Concerned with the fleeting moment, the remaining shard, the short story is enacted in the ever-changing present into which it cuts, a fleeting experience that is closely connected with the emerging conditions of consumption outlined by critics like Sillars and Sarlo: the experience of reading on a train journey or on a tram platform.

Ángel Rama's analysis of the first image of 'No oyes ladrar los perros' is an interesting starting point. For him, the 'sombra larga y negra de los hombres', the 'sola sombra tambaleante' that opens the story (137), is a monstrous image of a mythological animal with two voices, two mouths and two heads. Though Rama regards this as a poetic image, it is an eminently visual one, based on effects of light and shadows. Indeed, the moon is as much the subject of the story as the characters or plot:

> Allí estaba la luna. Enfrente de ellos. Una luna grande y colorada que les llenaba de luz los ojos y que estiraba y oscurecía más su sombra sobre la tierra.
> — No veo ya por dónde voy — decía él.
> Pero nadie le contestaba.
> El otro iba allá arriba, todo iluminado por la luna, con su cara descolorida, sin sangre, reflejando una luz opaca. (138)

The foregrounding of moonlight privileges presentation over representation, effect over meaning. By placing the reader behind the walking pair, the narrative perspective displays only the moon — which dazzles and blinds the reader as it does the characters — and the shadow it creates. The narrative is infused with visual tricks of lighting, framing and angles, in particular the play of opaque reflections on the son's bloodless face which endow him with a spectral quality. Unsurprisingly, then, Rama's description of Rulfo's short story resonates with Barthes's characterization of photographic presentation:

> Si lo real es la impresión del ojo que no ha tenido tiempo, ni fuerzas, ni suficiente información, para reinstalar la sensación dentro de un estable sistema cognoscitivo, podríamos definir esa imagen inicial del cuento como *lo real en su estado puro*.[52]

The Photograph is never anything but an antiphon of 'Look,' 'See,' 'Here it is'; it points a finger at certain *vis-à-vis*, and cannot escape this pure deictic language.[53]

What both thinkers describe here is that which Benjamin sees as a feature of modern experience: the shock of a sudden, isolated experience, uncushioned by any rational defence system. The pure presentation of the poetic or photographic image produces a sensation that is disconnected from any accumulated experience, both because of its temporal present-ness and because of its material thing-ness. As Rama points out, the singularity of Rulfo's work lies in its aesthetics, which he characterizes as three-fold: 'la brevedad, la violencia y la precisión con que se aplican las matrices trópicas a la construcción de un cuento'.[54] By framing his short stories through a fragmenting photographic lens that violently ruptures any unified relation to a stable cognitive system, Rulfo undermines any totalizing narrative system.

It is perhaps in 'La cuesta de los comadres' that the underlying photographic principle of Rulfo's short stories is most evident. In this story the Torricos, the landowners of the eponymous 'cuesta', use the hill as a viewpoint:

> los Torricos venían a sentarse aquí también y se estaban acuclillados horas y horas hasta el oscurecer, mirando para allá sin cansarse [...] Únicamente se ponían a ver el camino: aquel ancho callejón arenoso que se podía seguir con la mirada desde el comienzo hasta que se perdía entre los ocotes del cerro de la Media Luna.
>
> Yo nunca conocí a nadie que tuviera un alcance de vista como el de Remigio Torrico. Era tuerto. Pero el ojo negro y medio cerrado que le quedaba parecía acercar tanto las cosas, que casi las traía junto a sus manos. (45)

The Torricos' blinkered vision reflects their single-minded interest in taking possession of other people's crops and animals. Incessantly, tirelessly and mechanically, the Torricos' eyes track the path like surveillance cameras. Remigio's single-minded focus on the path constitutes a metatextual representation of the short story's photographic principle: the paradoxical need to crop the content, to limit the frame in order to achieve Edgar Allan Poe's 'unity or totality *of effect*'.[55] In fact, Remigio's cycloptic vision shares some features with photographic technology: it enables him to see distant objects that exceed the normal field of vision and to produce close-up images; to flatten everything onto the same, two-dimensional plane. The black, half-closed eye suggests the limited aperture of the camera lens. Finally, the inhuman ability to see that which normally remains unseen is interestingly located in the name of the setting, the Half Moon, also the setting of *Pedro Páramo*; a name that points towards the barriers between seen and unseen, presence and absence, possibility and impossibility; barriers that are partially eroded by Remigio's inhuman vision.

Indeed violence and precision, identified by Rama as a structural principle in Rulfo's fiction, are linked to visual form. This is demonstrated by the following description of the scene in which the narrator kills Remigio:

> al quitarse él de enfrente, la luz de la luna hizo brillar la aguja de arria, que yo había clavado en el costal. Y *no sé por qué*, pero de pronto comencé a tener una fe muy grande en aquella aguja. Por eso, al pasar Remigio Torrico por mi lado, desensarté la aguja y sin esperar otra cosa se la hundí a él cerquita del ombligo. (50, my emphasis)

Spontaneously compelled by a minute play of light on his needle, the narrator kills Remigio. By removing layers of explanation and rationality ('no sé por qué'), Rulfo leaves narrator and reader alike to grapple with the sudden, raw experience itself. Rationalizing narrative gives way to raw experience, causality to mere effect. The entire focus, of both the narrator-protagonist and the reader, is suddenly on the momentary gleam of moonlight on the tiny needle, which gives the ordinary object an almost supernatural power. Spatially, the narrative produces a close-up which focuses on the minute detail, as suggested by the diminutives 'cerquita' and later 'más arribita'. Temporally, the photographic flash arrests time at the fleeting moment at which the narrator sinks the needle into Remigio's stomach. Narrative condensation, abruptness and precision combine to produce the Cortazarian 'knock-out', or what Gordimer terms the 'flash of fireflies'. The needle prick could be regarded as a *mise en abyme* of the text itself, which functions by cutting down narrative accumulation in order to produce instant images that jump out at the

reader; which revives the fleeting past experience through a violent encounter, a
momentary relation: the present moment of reading or viewing.

Similarly, in 'El Llano en llamas', the violent climax is rendered through the
photographic snapshot, in the scene in which a bullet pierces a hole through a
soldier's chest:

> Sólo cuando *vio* su sangre dándole vueltas por la cintura dejó de moverse. Se
> asustó y trató de taparse con sus dedos el agujero que se le había hecho en las
> costillas, por donde le salía en *un solo chorro* la cosa aquella colorada que lo hacía
> ponerse más descolorado. (98, my emphasis)

The hole in his chest punctures the story with what Benjamin terms *Erlebnis*; an
effect achieved formally by the severance of the sight of the blood from the cause
of the injury. The single gush of blood produces a poignant effect on the reader not
through clarity but rather through obscurity: the subject of violence, thanks to the
grammatical construction 'se le había hecho', refuses to be named; the blood, because
the peasant does not understand what is happening to him, preserves its thing-ness
as 'la cosa aquella'. The soldier's experience seems to point simultaneously towards
two intersecting sensibilities: a traditional, irrational worldview, divorced from
scientific, medical reasoning on the one hand, and a modern, fragmented *Erlebnis*
on the other. Traditional experience, again, is traversed by a modern sensorium as
theorized by Benjamin and Barthes. For the latter, the photograph's poignant effect
is coterminous with its unnameable quality: 'what I can name cannot really prick
me'.[56] Like the Barthesian photograph, the camera lens of the narrative frame points
at the event, presents it, without naming or rationalizing it; this withdrawal of
explanation, seen by Eagleton as a defining characteristic of the short story, creates
the *punctum*.

The fragmentary vision is made yet more overt in the snapshot of the single rain
drop that falls on the barren plain in 'Nos han dado la tierra':

> Cae una gota de agua, grande, gorda, haciendo un agujero en la tierra y dejando
> una plasta como la de un salivazo. *Cae sola*. Nosotros esperamos a que sigan
> cayendo más. (38, my emphasis)

A photographic perspective is evident here, as the rain drop, large and plump, is
captured in a blow-up that produces the effect in the reader that the raindrop has
on the characters. The hole carved into the parched earth in this passage — like the
hole in the ground from which lizards later appear — momentarily opens a window
of hope and futurity in the otherwise stagnant, despairing narrative. Notably, the
anaphoric repetition in the passage — 'Cae una gota [...] Cae sola' — signals the
solitariness of the raindrop: it is not only spatially isolated, but also temporally
severed from the normal flux of experience, from the chronological passage of time.
As an isolated instant, it resounds with Benjamin's theory of the *Erlebnis* that characterizes the modern structure of experience. In Benjamin's account, as Wolin puts it,

> events take on a desultory and isolated, overwhelmingly *private* character;
> where 'experiences' are at best meaningful for the individual, but have forfeited
> the attribute of *universality* from which the element of wisdom, the moral of the
> story, traditionally derived.[57]

The experience of modernity, for Benjamin, has destabilized tradition, and with it the possibility of a continuous, universal experience, of *Erfahrung* understood as shared experience that is passed down from one generation to the next. As *Erfahrung* declines, it gives way to *Erlebnis*, to single, lived experiences that resist assimilation. The writer's struggle to communicate particular reactions to isolated, momentary experiences or stimuli becomes a struggle with language itself: the struggle to punch holes in a common, homogenizing language, in order to glimpse isolated, private, heterogeneous experiences.

The link between the fragmentation of vision and the isolation of the individual from the crowd is portrayed vividly in 'Talpa'. As in 'La cuesta', one of the climaxes of the story is provided by a photographic close-up:

> Tanilo comenzó a rezar y dejó que le cayera *una lágrima grande*, salida de muy adentro, apagándole la vela que Natalia le había puesto entre sus manos. Pero no se dio cuenta de eso; la luminaria de tantas velas prendidas que allí había *le cortó esa cosa con la que uno se sabe dar cuenta de lo que pasa junto a uno*. Siguió rezando con su vela apagada. (79, my emphasis)

Here, the enlargement of the tiny tear drop, suggested by the emphatic adjective 'grande', produces a striking image, a *punctum* that is supplemented by the pathetic image of Tanilo praying with an extinguished candle, without hope. The dazzling effect of the light on the character, which cuts Tanilo from his normal consciousness, is a metatextual figuration of the reader's severance from any collective experience. By connecting the reader with the text not through a shared narrative but through an inherently isolated, physical *punctum*, Rulfo's text reproduces in the reader Tanilo's experience of being dazzled by the bright light: the effect of violent severance; severance from rationality, from the knowledge of 'lo que pasa'; that is, rupture from story. Plot is replaced or displaced by visual effect. Yet a paradox underlies this effect, which depends on simultaneous illumination and blindness.

This dialectical interplay of visibility and invisibility is a structural one in 'El Llano en llamas', as demonstrated in the following views of the burning plain:

> Los miramos pasar [...] Daba gusto mirar aquella larga fila de hombres [...] se veía muy bonito ver caminar el fuego en los potreros; ver hecho una pura brasa casi todo el Llano en la quemazón aquella, con el humo ondulando por arriba. (95)

> Desde aquí veíamos arder día y noche las cuadrillas y los ranchos [...] Era bonito ver aquello. Salir de pronto de la maraña de los tepemezquites [...], y verlos atravesar el Llano vacío, sin enemigo al frente, como si se zambulleran en el agua honda y sin fondo que era aquella gran herradura del Llano encerrada entre montañas. (97)

By linking the violence of the fire with the aesthetic appeal of the light, Rulfo lays bare the raw, photographic perception of his narrator, stripped of any explanation or moral judgment.[58] Yet this visual display is paradoxically characterized by visual restriction and invisibility. Though the narrator claims in the first description to see the entirety of the plain, this is gradually undermined. The narrator's camera-eye vision creates an effect of fragmentation: the smoke emitted by the flames, and the mountains that enclose the otherwise boundless plain, produce spatial restriction; the suddenness of the vision ('de pronto'), and the fleetingness of the undulating smoke and spreading fire, produce temporal limits. Moreover, the narrative itself exceeds the realm of the visual, through its subjunctive mood: the 'como si' supplements the photographic image with the poetic image of the bottomless lake, invoking the reader's imagination to fill in the emptiness, to give form to the formlessness of the empty plain. The recourse to trope is a necessity: since the momentary images and visions around which the text gravitates exceed language, narrative, story, they can only acquire form and permanence through simile, simulation.

This reliance on trope is manifested later on in the story, in the climactic scene in which the train is sabotaged, a scene that shares the dual temporality of the photograph. On the one hand, the derailing of the train is the unrepeatable, particular moment *par excellence*; a singular moment whose fleetingness is emphasized by the adverbial phrase 'a toda prisa' (101). On the other hand, it creates a sudden stillness, as the soldiers are 'acalambrados de miedo' (101). The unrepeatable instant is constantly repeated in the narrator's memory: 'todavía veo las luces de las llamaradas que se alzaban allí donde apilaron a los muertos' (100). It is crucially the momentary, visual impact of the flash of the flames that haunts the narrator, marking him permanently. His lasting memory, produced by an intense image, reminds us of the irrevocable wound produced by the Holocaust photographs on Sontag: it is experienced as both a numbness (depicted in his paralysis) and a lasting rawness (displayed in the vividness of his memory); a singular experience from which he is forever severed, and an ever-repeated moment that will haunt him forever. As Barthes says of the photographic instant,

> it is the absolute Particular, the sovereign Contingency, matte and somehow stupid, the *This* (this photograph, and not Photography), in short, what Lacan calls the *tuché*, the Occasion, the Encounter, the Real, in its indefatigable expression.[59]

It is this singular, unassimilable moment that is reproduced *ad infinitum* by the technology of mechanical reproduction, through what Benjamin terms the 'posthumous shock' of the photograph. Similarly, the traumatic encounter of the derailing incident is a shock experience that exceeds comprehension. Hence it can only be imitated, simulated by the writer (who is immersed in language, which Lacan locates in the realm of the Symbolic) through *technique*, in this case through the trope of the 'como si' that recurs here: 'Después todo se quedó en silencio *como si* todos, hasta nosotros, nos hubiéramos muerto' (101, my emphasis). The certainty of the past tense, the 'ça a été' that Barthes attributes to the photographic image as an index of a historical moment, is dialectically intertwined with the ambivalence of the Rulfian subjunctive, the 'como si (hubiera sido)' that constitutes the formalization of the *tuché*. The encounter with the real, the shock or trauma, cannot be made visible to the reader in itself, but rather in its momentary effect of deathly silence and paralysis. This 'como si' recurs in the description of the hanging corpses:

> como los colgaban alto, allá se estaban campaneándose al soplo del aire muchos días, a veces meses, a veces ya nada más las puras tirlangas como si alguien las hubiera puesto a secar allí. Y uno sentía que la cosa ahora sí iba de veras al ver aquello. (102)

Again, there is a link between the visual image of the hanging trousers and the truth, or at least a truth effect. It is the *sight* of the corpse ('al ver aquello') that creates in the narrator an impression of present-ness ('ahora'), thing-ness ('la cosa') and truth ('de veras'). The demonstrative pronoun used by the narrator creates an effect of photographic presentation; as Eduardo Rivero puts it, the text calls out, '¡Miren...! ¡Vean! Este mundo está aquí presente'. This encounter with the real (the 'ça a été'), again, is simulated by the 'como si', the poetic image of the drying clothes that serves to reproduce in the reader the effect of the sight in the character.

In 'La herencia', too, literary technique is intrinsically connected to photographic technology. Initially, the death of the mother and wife is recounted through a series of snapshots: Matilde 'engordó. Tuvo un hijo. Luego murió. La mató un caballo desbocado' (152). The text turns into a series of fragmentary, dislocated moments, producing what Cortázar terms a narrative of 'knock-out'. The shock experience is portrayed metatextually in the paralysis of the characters: Matilde's face bears the mark of her dying moment, 'la boca torcida por la angustia' (153); her husband, Euremio Cedillo, is frozen stiff as a board, 'parado como horcón' (154). Yet the paralyzing event is far from a moment of illumination:

> sólo me acuerdo que era un animal rosillo. Pasó junto a nosotros como una nube gris, y más que caballo fue el aire del caballo que nos tocó ver [...] todavía siento pasar junto a mí ese aire, que apagó la llamarada de su vida, como si ahora estuviera soplando; como si siguiera soplando contra uno. (153)

At this point, the narrative style progresses from journalistic clarity to mystifying obscurity. The scene is characterized by blurriness: through the narrator's eyes we do not see the horse that caused Matilde's death, but rather the cloud that resulted from it, a cloud that shrouds it in mystery. A photographic image is conjured through the interplay of light and shadow, the 'llamarada' and the 'nube gris'. Yet as in 'El Llano', a poetic image is called upon to fill in the gaps in the visual image, the black hole produced by the traumatic experience in the narrator's memory. Like the wind that fills the clothes in 'El Llano', the 'como si' fills in the gaps, the holes in the initial visual image. Trope invokes the imagination to make visible that which the camera-lens eye cannot capture: the 'aire del caballo', that is, invisibility itself. And just as it is a fragmentary remnant that will haunt the narrator as a 'sombra o si acaso una brizna de recuerdo' (153), it is the fragmentation of Rulfo's narrative of concealment that contains the power to haunt the reader. In a sense, Cortázar's narrative images are less akin to fully formed photographic ones than to undeveloped photographic negatives; inverted images whose light must be translated into shadow and shadow into light; images that are not consumable and disposable, but rather resistant to these processes.

We might in this context provide a tentative answer to Cortázar's question regarding the lasting power of great short stories: '¿*Por qué* perduran en la memoria?' (519–20, see Introduction). Paradoxically, it is the element of the narrative that exceeds narrative that makes the story endure. The effect of shock, knock-out, or *punctum* produces a tear in the narrative, a hole which — like the hole in the soldier's chest in 'El Llano' and the furrow in the plain in 'Nos han dado' — constitutes a window onto another reality. Contrary to Pattee's claim that the short story makes no deep impress in the reader since it is based in the temporary sensation (see Introduction), my argument is that the force of Rulfo's art lies precisely in its tantalizing brevity, in its *punctum*.

My argument also differs from that of Joseph Sommers, who reads Rulfo's fiction through Richard Chase's interpretation of myth:

> El mito cumple la función catártica de dramatizar los choques y las armonías de la vida en un ambiente social y natural. Pero el mito puede ser entendido como el fenómeno estético que reconcilia o hace tolerables [...] profundos disturbios neuróticos.[60]

I would suggest, on the contrary, that Rulfo's aesthetics of brevity disembeds shocks from any continuous narrative (mythical or otherwise), refusing any such reconciliation or alleviation. By detaching violent, traumatic experiences from causality, explanation and morality, Rulfo's work not only foregrounds the direct, unadulterated, irrational instant of shock, but also the shock of the instant itself. What is at stake is not so much the mythification of violence, but rather its demythification, its connection not with the timeless but rather with the temporal, not with the lost past but rather with the inescapable present, which the short story writer produces artificially through the textual *punctum*. A Rulfian short story has the power to *perdurar*, to survive, because its narrative has a function not of catharsis, but rather of haunting.

A more influential reading in relation to which my own study might be situated is that of Carlos Fuentes in 'Juan Rulfo: El tiempo del mito'. Fuentes regards *Pedro Páramo* as a 'novela mítica', and goes so far as to suggest that the focal plot development, Juan Preciado's death, is caused by 'el mito de la muerte', a myth into which his death is then re-inscribed.[61] For Fuentes, Rulfo's work is steeped in an intemporal narrative of myth, in a linguistic construction. My argument is that the shocks in *El Llano en llamas* are produced not by mythical constructions, by pre-existing linguistic, narrative fabrics, but rather by tears in those fabrics produced by literary-cum-photographic *técnica*. Whereas for Fuentes as for Bartra, the pathos of Rulfo's writing lies in great mythical constructions, my contention is that it lies rather in the tiny pinprick, the minute intrusion that punctures any totalizing mythical construction. The mythical wound of Mexico's originary conflict that Bartra locates at the centre of Rulfo's work is displaced by singular, deeply personal shocks. Whereas mythical narrative is characterized by the abstract, the essential, the archetypal and the collective, Rulfo's photographic stories are characterized by the concrete, the contingent, the singular and the solitary. The collective aspect of myth, one of its principal facets, is described by Fuentes through a Jungian psychoanalytical model as 'lo que es creído siempre, en todas partes y por todos' (931). However, timelessness, permanence and universality — which González Echevarría sees as defining features of the *cuento* (see Introduction) — are undercut by Rulfo's modern, demythifying, singularizing aesthetics.

The Rulfian instant, severed from totalizing narrative structures, bears a strong relationship to Henri Cartier-Bresson's 'decisive moment' (the title of the preface to the 1952 US edition of his *Images à la Sauvette*). As Cortázar puts it, Cartier-Bresson defines the photographic moment as a 'recorte [que] actú[a] como una explosión que abre de par en par una realidad mucho más amplia' (516), an opening onto something new that has yet to come, to grow, to form. Cortázar's view of Henri Cartier-Bresson's aesthetics contrasts that which Fuentes offers in his preface to the photographer's *Mexican Notebooks*. In this account, which opens with the melancholic assertion that 'wounds sear the whole landscape of Mexico', Fuentes integrates Cartier-Bresson's fleeting moments fully into the myth of Mexico as 'one enormous wound'.[62] Fuentes's reading of Cartier-Bresson's photographs chimes with Bartra's reading of Rulfo's writing as a melancholic memorial of the wound of the conquest, as a contribution to the construction of a homogenized myth of Mexico. In the following assertion, Fuentes subsumes the instantaneous into the eternal, the particular into the universal, the temporal into the timeless: 'Henri Cartier-Bresson photographed Mexican eternity from the Mexican moment, which is the only time that accords universality with the camera'.[63] In this sense, Fuentes's view of Cartier-Bresson's photographs coincides with his reading of Rulfo's work, as inextricably connected with eternal sameness, mythical return and archetype, a view that my own reading has sought to question through a focus on the particularity of the Rulfian instant. As Cortázar suggests, the narrative-cum-photographic 'cut' constitutes not a wound inscribed in totalizing mythical structures, but rather a window that opens onto stories that have yet to be unravelled.

Temporary Conclusions: Rulfo's Short Story as Emergent Form

In this chapter, we have seen how *El Llano en llamas* self-consciously stages the rupture from the traditional storyteller, who transmits meaning through inherited, rational, didactic narrative; and the correlative birth of the medium of the short story, which communicates through narrative rupture, 'knock-out' and *punctum*. The limit of storytelling, posited by Benjamin as a death to be mourned, is fashioned by Rulfo as a birth to be celebrated. My argument might be rearticulated as discerning two principal movements in Rulfo's stories, which correspond with different, intersecting relationships with tradition: the evacuation, or emptying out, of narrative content; and the fragmentation of narrative into scattered shards. These movements turn the stories into writerly texts that demand to be 'filled', on the one hand, and reconstructed, on the other.[64]

First, textual corpses and ruins become containers of present-ness, vessels that paradoxically enclose the uncontainable: the present moment. In a sense, this logic parallels that of Kafka's writing, as read by Benjamin in his essay entitled 'Max Brod's Book on Franz Kafka'.[65] For Benjamin, as Rebecca Comay succinctly puts it,

> the eclipse of meaning by the material force of its presentation [in Kafka's writing] defines the sickness of tradition (the complete evacuation of any deter- minative content to be handed down) and, paradoxically, the latter's supreme vindication (a transmission that occurs in the absence of anything to transmit and which indeed transmits essentially its very absence).[66]

Rulfo's mausoleum-like short stories constitute not a return to traditional form, but a vindication of the survival of tradition through modern — participative, democratic — form. Like Luvina's church, Tuxcacuesco's remains or Juárez's statue,

Rulfo's texts uphold tradition *as* ruin, as a shell-like form, or formal shell, that can be filled by anything and anyone. As I have argued, this empty shell might be regarded as the remains of the traditional storyteller: the uncontained container that can be filled by any reader, but that simultaneously exceeds any given reading, is the liberating product of the decay of wisdom.

Second, the photographic fragments, severed from a causal narrative continuum, are reactivated by the cooperative reader. This reactivation, linked to Benjamin's posthumous shock, Barthes's *punctum* and Cortázar's 'knock-out', can be seen not only within the texts themselves, as explored above, but also in their after-lives. One such case is that of the story '¡Diles que no me maten!', whose title is a recurrent motif in its narrative of violence. As Rowe explains, these words

> were painted on a wall in the Universidad Nacional Autónoma de México, the main university in Mexico City, in 1977, at a time when the university, occupied by the students, was being strafed by police helicopters. This [...] shows how Rulfo's writing has the power to imprint itself on the public memory and to speak in a public space. There can be few writers whose words have the power to become a message on the wall. (54)

Because of the present-ness of the narrative and its isolation from any linear historical context, it can be recontextualized and transculturated in new contexts. The instant around which it is structured, by grafting itself onto any reader's present, ruptures Bartra's 'cage of melancholy' by creating openings onto an undecidable future. Rulfo's narrative therefore shares the quality of the photograph as described by Sontag and Cortázar, respectively: 'a photograph is only a fragment, and with the passage of time its moorings come unstuck';[67] 'no congela el tiempo, como suele decirse, lo libera de su versión primaria'.[68] Because of its fragmentariness, the Rulfian short story, like the photograph, is free from any determined time, place and form: the pastness of the story gains presentness; the rural tale becomes an urban tool; the peasant's words turn into the students' *graffiti*. The short story therefore not only *results* from, but also has a particular capacity to *produce*, transculturative processes: ruptured from its author, it unleashes new forms of collectivity, participation and solidarity.

Whereas critics have often situated the fragmentariness of Rulfo's writing in relation to a folding back into tradition, my argument is that, far from a mimetic replication of oral narrative styles, his fiction constitutes the calculated product of artistic labour. The 'yuxtaposicion de pedazos sueltos de una narración' discerned by Rama must be seen as the result not of the calque of oral forms but rather as a hybrid creative process, configured not only in the ruins of traditional narrative, but also through emergent literary-cum-photographic forms. In this vein, I might propose a response to John Szarkowski's insistence that,

> notwithstanding frequent claims to the contrary, photography has never been very successful at telling stories. This is not surprising if one considers that isolating single fragments out of the continuity of time — what photographs do — is very close to the opposite of what narrative does.[69]

As we have seen, Rulfo's short story technique undermines this opposition, appealing to the reader through instant experiences, experiences of the instant, that constitute shards of narratives that have been forgotten and lost, or have yet to be forged or fleshed out. It is by tearing single moments out of continuous, chronological time that Rulfo's narrative establishes an active, immediate, *instant* relation with the reader, producing ever-changing visions and re-visions. Whereas Escalante insists that the time of Rulfo's fiction is 'el tiempo contrario al universo de la lectura' (cited above), I must insist, on the contrary, that the time of Rulfo's fiction is precisely the present time: the moment of reading or viewing.

Rulfo's short story, in this sense, calls for an expansion of Williams's terms, since it is not only an emergent form but also a form of emergence: the temporality of the irretrievable past is always dialectically intertwined with the unpredictable future; the logic of the decaying remainder with the suspended supplement; the tone of irredeemable despair with unending hope. In other words, not only does the short story, as emergent aesthetico-cultural form, or adaptation of existing forms, constitute a cultural opening; but more importantly, each fragment of *El Llano en llamas* produces different narrative, lyrical, photographic apertures that promise new meanings, forms and relations. Its poetics of (un-)containment render the short story a vessel of infinite potential in which narrative content gives way to unassimilated experience, whether isolated events, physical sensations or subjective present-ness. Figured in the texts' internal residues (whether narrative or photographic), Rulfo's short story foregrounds form *as* ruin which will continue to move in and through the present; in and through which the present will continue to move.

Notes to Chapter 1

1. Ángel Rama, *Transculturación narrativa en América latina* (Mexico City: Siglo XXI, 2004), p. 44.
2. Adam Sharman, *Tradition and Modernity in Spanish American Literature: From Darío to Carpentier* (New York: Palgrave Macmillan, 2006), p. 153.
3. Walter Mignolo, 'Escribir la oralidad: la obra de Juan Rulfo en el contexto de las literaturas del "Tercer Mundo"', in Juan Rulfo, *Toda la obra*, ed. by Claude Fell, pp. 429–45 (p. 430).
4. Evodio Escalante, 'Texto histórico y texto social en la obra de Rulfo', in Juan Rulfo, *Toda la obra*, ed. by Claude Fell, pp. 561–81 (p. 561).
5. Roger Bartra, *The Cage of Melancholy: Identity and Metamorphosis in the Mexican Character* (New Brunswick, NJ: Rutgers University Press, 1992), p. 3.
6. Sharman, *Tradition and Modernity*, p. 152.
7. Martín-Barbero, *Communication*, p. 2.
8. William Rowe, *Rulfo: El Llano en llamas* (London: Grant and Cutler, 1987), p. 9. Hereafter, all references to this edition will be made within the body of the text.
9. Raymond Williams, *Marxism and Literature* (Oxford: Oxford University Press, 1977), pp. 122–23.
10. Fernando Benítez, 'Conversaciones con Juan Rulfo', in Juan Rulfo, *Inframundo, El México de Juan Rulfo* ([Hanover, NH]: Ediciones del Norte, 1983), pp. 3–9 (p. 7).
11. Manuel Durán, 'La obra de Juan Rulfo vista a través de Mircea Eliade', *Inti*, 13–14 (1981), pp. 25–33 (p. 25).
12. Walter Benjamin, 'The Storyteller: Reflections on the Work of Nikolai Leskov', *Illuminations*, p. 87.
13. In his brilliant analysis of *Pedro Páramo*, Sharman argues that the triumvirate of religion, authority, and tradition in Rulfo's world reveals the 'legacy of the "Roman trinity" that underpinned Western society for centuries, and which, duly exported, becomes the Mexican Roman trinity' (Sharman, p. 139). Like the society analysed by Benjamin in 'The Storyteller', the Roman trinity is underpinned by the belief in the need for continuity, of an order that links one generation to the next.

14. Philip Swanson, 'Introduction: Background to the Boom', in *Landmarks in Modern Latin American Fiction*, ed. by Philip Swanson (London; New York: Routledge, 1990), pp. 1–26 (pp. 13–14).
15. Cited by Sharman, *Tradition and Modernity*, p. 155.
16. Cortázar, *Rayuela* (Madrid: Cátedra, 2006), chapter 79, p. 518.
17. Fernando Benítez, in *Inframundo*, pp. 3–9 (p. 6).
18. Marisa Giménez Cacho, 'Juan Rulfo, fotógrafo', *Luna Cornea*, 6 (1995), pp. 50–58 (p. 51). Available online at <http://issuu.com/c_imagen/docs/lunacornea_6/53> [accessed 6 April 2014].
19. Yvette Jiménez de Báez, 'Historia y sentido en la obra de Juan Rulfo', in Juan Rulfo, *Toda la obra*, ed. by Claude Fell, pp. 583–608 (p. 583).
20. Howard Fraser, '*Inframundo*: Juan Rulfo's Photographic Companion to *El Llano en llamas*', *Chasqui*, 17.2 (November 1988), pp. 56–74.
21. Fernando Benítez, 'Conversaciones con Juan Rulfo', in Rulfo, *Inframundo*, pp. 3–9 (p. 4).
22. Eduardo Rivero, 'Juan Rulfo, escritura de la luz y fotografía del verbo', in Carlos Fuentes and others, *México: Juan Rulfo fotógrafo* (Barcelona: Lunwerg Editores, 2001), pp. 27–32 (p. 30).
23. Jean Franco, 'El viaje al país de los muertos', in Rulfo, *Toda la obra*, ed. by Claude Fell, pp. 763–74 (p. 772).
24. Gustavo Garza, *La urbanización de México en el siglo XX* (Mexico City: El Colegio de México, 2003), p. 43.
25. Juan Rulfo, *Toda la obra*, ed. by Claude Fell, p. 113.
26. Juan Rulfo, *El Llano en llamas* (Madrid: Cátedra, 1985), p. 115. Hereafter, all references to this edition will be made within the body of the text.
27. More specifically, this story deals with illegal immigration to North American cities. The title is a reference to the real Paso del Norte border bridge on the Rio Grande between Mexico and Texas, through which immigrants, today, as in Rulfo's time, seek to cross the border.
28. Carlos Monsiváis, 'Sí, tampoco los muertos retoñan, desgraciadamente', in Rulfo, *Toda la obra*, ed. by Claude Fell, pp. 833–42 (p. 834).
29. Williams, *Marxism and Literature*, p. 127.
30. Cortázar, 'Algunos aspectos', p. 512.
31. Rulfo, 'El desafío de la creación' (1986), in *Toda la obra*, ed. by Claude Fell, pp. 383–85 (p. 385).
32. Jorge Luis Borges, 'El arte narrativo y la magia' (1932), in *Discusión*, pp. 102–15 (p. 109).
33. Rulfo, 'Situación actual de la novela contemporánea' (1965), *Toda la obra*, ed. by Claude Fell, pp. 371–79 (p. 378).
34. Terry Eagleton, *Heathcliff and the Great Hunger* (London: Verso, 1995), p. 150.
35. Henri Bergson, *The Creative Mind: An Introduction to Metaphysics*, trans. by Mabelle L. Andison (New York: Wisdom Library, 1946), p. 93.
36. Ihab H. Hassan, 'Baudelaire's 'Correspondances': The Dialectic of a Poetic Affinity', *The French Review*, 27 (1954), 437–45 (p. 439).
37. Rulfo, 'Desafío', pp. 383–85 (p. 384).
38. Rama, *Transculturación*, p. 34.
39. Benjamin, *One-Way Street, and Other Writings*, trans. by Edmund Jephcott and Kingsley Shorter (London: NLB/Verso, 1979), p. 202.
40. Roland Barthes, *Camera Lucida: Reflections on Photography*, trans. by Richard Howard (London: Vintage, 1993), p. 85.
41. Jorge Luis Borges, 'La muralla y los libros' (1951), in *Otras inquisiciones* (Madrid: Alianza, 1997), pp. 9–13 (p. 13).
42. Erica Segre, *Intersected Identities* (New York; Oxford: Berghahn Books, 2007), p. 131.
43. Fraser, '*Inframundo*', p. 61.
44. José Revueltas, 'Lugar del cine en el arte', *Anthropos*, 1 (1947), 2–10 (p. 2).
45. Cacho, 'Juan Rulfo, fotógrafo'.
46. Juan Rulfo, *Los cuadernos de Juan Rulfo* (Mexico City: Era, 1994).
47. Benjamin, 'On Some Motifs in Baudelaire', in *Illuminations*, p. 176.
48. Néstor García Canclini, *Culturas híbridas*, p. 286.
49. Barthes, *Camera Lucida*, p. 26.
50. Barthes, *Camera Lucida*, p. 85.
51. Susan Sontag, *On Photography* (London: Penguin, 1979), p. 20.

52. Ángel Rama, 'Una primera lectura de "No oyes ladrar los perros"', in Rulfo, *Toda la obra*, ed. by Claude Fell, pp. 790–99 (p. 793).

53. Barthes, *Camera Lucida*, p. 5.

54. Rama, 'Una primera lectura', p. 894.

55. Edgar Allan Poe, 'Review of *Twice-Told Tales*', pp. 59–72 (p. 66).

56. Barthes, *Camera Lucida*, p. 51.

57. Richard Wolin, *Walter Benjamin: An Aesthetic of Redemption* (Berkeley and Los Angeles; London: University of California Press, 1994), p. 219.

58. Although in this context it is the photographic principle that underlies the text more than the filmic, we could also relate these descriptions to the cinematic medium. Indeed, battles of the Mexican revolution were aestheticized and made into films. Francisco Villa, for example, staged his battles, delayed them for the purposes of lighting effects. See Steven Boldy, *The Narrative of Carlos Fuentes: Family, Text, Nation*, Durham Modern Languages Series (Durham: Durham University Press, 2001), p. 189.

59. Barthes, *Camera Lucida*, p. 4.

60. Joseph Sommers, 'A través de la ventana de la sepultura', in Rulfo, *Toda la obra*, ed. by Claude Fell, pp. 728–40 (p. 738).

61. Carlos Fuentes, 'Juan Rulfo: el tiempo del mito', in Rulfo, *Toda la obra*, ed. by Claude Fell, pp. 825–33 (p. 827).

62. Henri Cartier-Bresson, *Henri Cartier-Bresson: Mexican Notebooks, 1934–1964* (London; New York: Thames and Hudson, 1995), p. 5.

63. Cartier-Bresson, *Henri Cartier-Bresson*, p. 11.

64. The term 'writerly' is used to designate a text in which the reader is no longer the consumer, but rather the producer. It is borrowed from Barthes, *S/Z*, trans. by Richard Miller (Oxford; New York: Wiley-Blackwell, 1990), p. 5.

65. Benjamin, 'Max Brod's Book on Kafka and Some of My Own Reflections', in *Illuminations*, pp. 141–48.

66. Rebecca Comay, 'Benjamin and the Ambiguities of Romanticism, in *The Cambridge Companion to Walter Benjamin* (Cambridge: Cambridge University Press, 2004), pp. 134–51 (p. 143).

67. Sontag, *On Photography*, p. 71.

68. Cortázar, *Alto el Perú* (Mexico City: Siglo XXI, 1994), cited by Marcy Schwartz and Mary Beth Tierney-Tello, in *Photography and Writing in Latin America: Double Exposures* (Albuquerque: University of New Mexico Press, 2006), p. 132.

69. *Looking at Photographs: 100 Pictures from the Collection of the Museum of Modern Art*, ed. by John Szarkowski (New York: Museum of Modern Art, 2009), p. 154.

CHAPTER 2

Julio Cortázar, the World-Opener

Introduction: Between Closure and Aperture

Julio Cortázar, in his 1982 article 'El escritor y su quehacer en América latina', reflects that the task of the Latin American writer is to

> inventar nuevas formas de contacto, abrir otro espectro de comunicaciones en todos los niveles, y es ahí donde los estereotipos profesionales (digamos vocacionales si se quiere, pero agregando que escribir no es sólo vocación, sino traslación, comunicación), es precisamente ahí donde nuestros estereotipos demandan una autocrítica profunda que no todos hemos sido capaces de hacer hasta ahora.[1]

The writer's role, for Cortázar, is necessarily interwoven with a self-conscious reflection on form, and more particularly with the search for new means of expression and communication; with the rupture of established communicational boundaries; and therefore with the severance from his own vocation as a writer, from the mould of literature, from his 'writerliness'. In what follows, I shall examine the ways in which Cortázar's short stories transgress existing narrative and literary structures in order to forge new forms of contact. In order to do so, I shall use the concept of intermediality, which might be considered, as Lars Elleström suggests, 'a result of constructed media borders being trespassed'.[2] It involves the pushing of boundaries between one mode of communication and other modalities, whether material, sensorial, spatio-temporal or semiotic (17). By incorporating into the literary text the formal principles of other media, from photography and cinema to journalism and telephony, Cortázar breaks down the exclusive walls of the institution of literature. The consequent intermediality of his texts might be contextualized by Cortázar's notion, put forward in his 'Teoría del túnel' (1947), that

> este avance en túnel, que se vuelve contra lo verbal desde el verbo mismo pero ya en un plano extraverbal, denuncia a la literatura como condicionante de la realidad, y avanza hacia la instauración de una actividad en la que lo estético se ve reemplazado por lo poético, la formulación mediatizadora por la formulación adherente, la representación por la presentación.[3]

Cortázar's desire is to move away from a literature that takes part in the conditioning of reality, notably, realism. Indeed, as Swanson argues, the defining — though no doubt problematic — feature of the 'nueva novela' is the 'desire somehow to re-evaluate or reject the values, belief systems and formal or stylistic patterns that lie at the roots of traditional realism.'[4] The principal criticism launched against Regionalist authors like Ciro Alegría, Rómulo Gallegos and Ricardo Güiraldes was that, while they claimed to offer an objective representation of the outside world, they in fact coaxed their readers to accept their own ideological, socio-political perspective, and replicated a pre-existing, bourgeois status quo. For Cortázar, the rupture from this model seems to involve a movement from literature to poetry, from representation to presentation, from reproduction to production, from mediation to adherence.

Immediacy, or what Cortázar terms 'adherence', is thus placed in opposition to mediation. A parallel might be detected between this opposition and that constructed by the literary critic Charles May in his attempt to contrast the short story with the genre of the novel: whereas long fiction deals with 'experience, conceptually created and considered', the short story focuses on '*an* experience, directly and emotionally created and encountered'.[5] Yet my contention is that, in his quest for immediacy, Cortázar paradoxically supplements the literary medium of the short story with extra-literary media. The supposed directness of the short story form, as we shall see, is achieved through multiple interwoven layers of artifice.

In what follows, I shall seek to destabilize the polarity of directness and indirectness that Cortázar and theorists have constructed. Doubtless, Cortázar's short stories are driven by the desire to create participation through immediacy. As Morelli insists in *Rayuela*, present-ness is necessary to the creation of a complicit reader: 'el lector podría llegar a ser copartícipe y copadeciente de la experiencia por la que pasa el novelista, *en el mismo momento y en la misma forma*: sólo vale la materia en gestación, la inmediatez vivencial' (Cortázar's emphasis).[6] Yet I shall argue that this experiential immediacy is achieved paradoxically through the proliferation of different media within the narrative. In this sense, Cortázar's stories capitalize on what David Trotter calls, in relation to the presence- and absence-effects of modernist literature and cinema, 'the conflict between immediacy and hypermediacy constitutive of mediation itself'.[7]

In the same vein, I shall dismantle the opposition that Cortázar and his critics have established between his short stories and the rest of his literary production. As Cortázar suggests in 'Algunos aspectos', 'la novela se desarrolla en el papel, y por lo tanto en el tiempo de la lectura, sin otro límite que el agotamiento de la materia novelada; por su parte, el cuento parte de la noción de límite, y en primer término de límite físico.'[8] He does, nonetheless, partially undermine this opposition in 'Volviendo a Eugenia Grandet', affirming that the short stories 'son en su mayoría de la misma estofa que [sus] novelas, aperturas sobre el extrañamiento'; that, in his *cuentos* and novels, 'la actitud central sigue siendo la misma'.[9]

According to Gustavo Pellón, Cortázar 'expanded his writing practice from the crafting of classically perfect short stories (which he never abandoned) to the examination of open forms: *Hopscotch* and the collage books, *La vuelta al día* and *Último round*.'[10] His literary progression is therefore seen as a process of expansion from perfect, circular, closed short stories to open, multimedial, collaborative forms.

Saúl Yurkievich expands on this notion in *Mundos y modos*, in which he insists on a clean distinction between the 'closed textuality' of the short story and the 'open textuality' of the rest of his artistic production, his novels and collage works.[11] For him, the short story 'presupone una nítida atribución genérica. No se abre, no se mezcla, no se ramifica, no se dilata. Cortázar acata la cerradura autárquica del cuento, la practica ortodoxamente' (14). My contention is that the short story's closure and enclosure are in fact paradoxically a means of producing open texts; that its sharp, defined generic limits are the site through which it is infiltrated by other media; that its constitutive spatio-temporal rupture is in fact a point of contact with other modes of production and communication. Far from representing 'la literatura literaria, celosa de su dominio' as Yurkievich suggests (15), Cortázar's short stories invade, and are invaded by, extra-literary forms; by popular or mass media that undercut the literary dominion.

I shall argue against Yurkievich's rather black-and-white assertion that 'no es la producción propiamente cuentística la que nos permite conocer a Cortázar, ese abremundos' (15). As we shall see, the short story breaks down its linguistic limits to open doors, cracks and fissures in existent literary structures. What Yurkievich says of the collage works is already noticeable in his earliest short story collections: 'la obra [...] se deja invadir por las otras inscripciones, por la bullanga colectiva, por el fragor del extratexto, por el ruido de fondo' (20). Whereas this suggests that background noise and extratextual clamour are excluded by the short story, I shall argue that their fragmentary form is in fact a site for invasion and contamination not only by other texts, but also by other media, other modes, and other worlds.

Marcy Schwartz, in her excellent study of Latin American urban writing, also implies a straightforward distinction through the division of Cortázar's work into two chapters: the short stories and the photo-narratives, *Prosa del observatorio* (1972) and *Alto el Perú* (1984). In her examination of the latter, she argues that 'la fotografía en colaboración con la palabra ofrece sistemas alternativos que requieren nuevas estrategias para leer la realidad'.[12] As emergent, interstitial forms, his collage works propose alternative channels through which to 'read', view or re-view, reality. Schwartz continues thus: 'la coincidencia o co-participación de los medios verbal y visual anuncia este umbral urbano donde el lenguaje cede el paso a la imagen porque no puede contra la vasta expansión iluminada' (159). I shall demonstrate that the intermingling of verbal and visual media upon which Schwartz insists in her reading of the collage works might also be detected within the content, form and structure of his short stories. My argument is that Cortázar's fiction does not simply follow two trajectories, as Yurkievich affirms and as Schwartz implies through the structure of her chapters. Operating on the point of narrative breakdown, his short stories lie at the limits of the verbal, the narrative, and the literary.

One reading against which I shall situate my argument is that of Saúl Sosnowski. His thesis, entitled *Julio Cortázar: Una búsqueda mítica*, is encapsulated in his introductory comment that 'hemos considerado la determinación de la búsqueda mítica problema central en la obra de Cortázar, ya que tiene como fin el *retorno* a la *unicidad* integrada por el hombre y el universo' (his emphasis).[13] My approach to the short story form problematizes the notion of a unidirectional backward movement: as we shall see, any return to pre-lapsarian, pre-linguistic unity in Cortázar's work is invariably conjugated with the renewal of literary form, the transformation of reality, and the opening up of new worlds. This is seen most clearly in *Rayuela*, the ultimate example for Sosnowski of a 'mythical search', which also constitutes itself as an eminently experimental, modern form. Inseparable from the notion of the return for Sosnowski is that of unity. Yet this must be squared with Cortázar's aesthetics of the fragmentary and the fleeting, which admittedly, and no doubt problematically, bears a dialectical relation with the desire for wholeness and timelessness. Finally, I shall question the possibility of 'una aproximación a una visión totalizadora de la narrativa de Cortázar' towards which Sosnowski sets out (2). My study, which takes spatio-temporal fragmentation to be a fundamental structure and process in Cortázar's work, will be limited by the frames in the work itself, which as I shall argue also entail ever-evolving ways of seeing.

Dominic Moran's reading of Cortázar's work is an important approach with which mine will intersect. Working on the foundations of Steven Boldy's work, Moran argues that the majority of Cortázar's writing is fuelled by a struggle between the hegemonic structures and strictures of Western metaphysics and that which remains extrinsic to them. In order to support this view, he brings in the notion of 'framing', the unambiguous division — created by different discourses and schema — between self and other, essence and accident, good and evil, and so on. It follows that the short story is of particular interest to Moran. As it is theorized by Cortázar in his 1962 lecture 'Algunos aspectos del cuento', it seems to suffer the pitfalls of framing: it is defined by its limits, and opposed to the novel. Yet both in Cortázar's theory and practice, Moran analyses the ways in which the short stories self-consciously problematize and complicate the notion of the frame, blurring inside and outside and laying bare its paradoxes, the slipperiness of any boundaries.

Moran lays some fascinating theoretical foundations for a study of the paradoxes of enframing, invoking Derrida's notion of the parergon. 'The parergon', for Derrida, 'inscribes something extra, *exterior* to the specific field [...], but whose transcendent exteriority touches, plays with, brushes, rubs, or presses against the limit and intervenes internally only insofar as the inside is missing'.[14] For Moran, the logic of parergonality applies to Cortázar's attempted differentiation between short story and novel, and to the corresponding distinction between photography and film.[15] The notion of the 'parergon', also termed the 'supplementary hors-d'oeuvre',[16] intersects with the dual structure of the supplement that underlies Derrida's thought. On the one hand, 'the supplement adds itself, it is a surplus, a plenitude enriching another plenitude, the fullest measure of presence'. On the other hand, 'the supplement supplements. It adds only to replace [...] If it fills, it is as if one fills a void [...] Compensatory and vicarious, the supplement is an adjunct, a subaltern instance which *takes-(the)-place*'.[17] This Derridean approach is useful for a study of the short story, whose art is founded upon the haunting or invasion of a delimited sphere. The undecidable barrier between interior and exterior, between the work ('ergon') and that which lies outside the work ('parergon'), is essential to a genre which at once seeks to discard that which is ornamental and non-essential and to open the door to that which lies outside its boundaries.

In what follows, we shall see how the irreducible structure of interference, which for Derrida is at work within any discourse, schema, or structure, is capitalized upon by the short story writer: it is potentiated, used inventively, made to work as a technique as well as a mere fact. By problematizing the false polarity between his short stories and the rest of his artistic corpus, I shall unveil the creative processes of (de)construction and reconstruction that underlie his short fiction. Following Cortázar's own model of the tunnel — the notion of destroying in order to build — I shall argue that the supplementary relationship between the short story and different genres, forms and media creates new ways of producing, seeing, and experiencing. By breaking literary limits, generic frames and medial borders, Cortázar's stories forge multiple tunnels and passages, windows and lenses that open up different views of the world and demand alternative strategies to approach it.

In this sense, my approach plays with the different types of interference that drive the plots of the stories. As Steven Boldy points out, the stories can be classified into two broad types: *lo otro* is either 'consciously and intentionally visited by a character dissatisfied with his primary reality', or it is an unconscious, unintended and unwelcome event, 'far more passive on the side of civilization [the 'inside'...] involving metaphorical possession by incubi and succubi, the return of ghosts', and so on.[18] My reading renders ambiguous the distinction between active and passive, conscious and unconscious: on a formal level, the processes of interference result simultaneously from conscious, calculated techniques and unconscious affinities or accidental relations.

I am not the first to have considered this angle of Cortázar's short fiction. Most notably, the many critics who have dedicated articles and book sections to 'Las babas del diablo' (*Las armas secretas*, 1959) have paid due attention to these kinds of concerns.[19] This is doubtless because of the highly self-reflexive nature of this story, which is overtly about the problems of representation, the intermedial relations between narrative/image and photograph/film, and the complicity of the reader/viewer. Carmen de Mora Valcárcel notes that the concept of open form, of *how to tell a story*, is at the self-conscious heart of this story (55–56). Sosnowski touches on the photographic logic of the story in his analysis of visual limits and frames: 'la razón explica la realidad empírica mediante principios que limitan la visión total a marcos determinados' (66). Graciela de Sola comments on 'la libre utilización de técnicas cinematográficas' in 'Las babas' (71). Keith Cohen expands on this notion in an article on the filmic nature of Cortázar's writing that focuses almost exclusively on 'Las babas'. Valeria de los Ríos, in an article dedicated to this story, looks at photography and cinema in relation to the question of translation. Among others, Terry Peavler examines the film version of the story, *Blow-Up*, in his 'Reconsideration of Antonioni's Infidelity to Cortázar'. Dan Russek delves further into the different media that permeate Cortázar's writing, showing the evolution of Cortázar's engagement with photography, journalism and travel writing from 'Las babas del diablo' and 'Apocalipsis en Solentiname' to *La vuelta al día en ochenta mundos* and *Último round*.

In what follows, I shall look beyond 'Las babas del diablo' to demonstrate that the logic of intermediality, whether explicitly or implicitly, self-consciously or unconsciously, permeates Cortázar's art of the short story. By the same token, I shall dismantle the essential opposition constructed by Eva Valcárcel between 'relato popular' and 'cuento literario'.[20] Using the theories of Jesús Martín-Barbero, Néstor García Canclini and Beatriz Sarlo as points of departure, I shall argue that his literary narratives are permeated by emergent, contemporary forms of the 'popular'.

I shall begin by focusing principally on three stories from his 1966 collection *Todos los fuegos el fuego*, starting with 'La isla a mediodía', moving on to the one that bears the collection's name, and ending with the final story of the collection, 'El otro cielo'. These stories share certain features: they are couched in Cortázar's concept of *figuras*, of two divergent realities that are brought together through constellations of correspondences;[21] they involve spatio-temporal rupture, and the consequent invasion of the past into the present, of *el lado de allá* into *el lado de acá*;[22] they incorporate mechanical modes or media, and corresponding stimuli and shocks, into their narrative substance and structure. In order to bolster — and, literally, illustrate — my argument that the logic of extra-literary media underlies the literary form of stories, I shall suggest some of the important relations they bear with the advertisements from the magazines and journals in which Cortázar's works were first published. These tend to gravitate around products related to visual media, mass communication and international transport: cameras, films, televisions, telephones, teleprinters, transatlantic flights, and so forth. The resulting resonances will help to delve into the formal intermedial unconscious that underlies Cortázar's short stories. Finally I shall argue that, since these texts push the genre of the short story to its very boundaries, they often bear striking resemblances to Cortázar's later collaborative and mixed-media projects, particularly *Buenos Aires Buenos Aires* (1968) and *Fantomas contra vampiros multinacionales* (1975).

I shall then turn to his later collection, *Queremos tanto a Glenda* (1982), in which the logic of intermediality is much more explicit and self-conscious, inscribed as it is within the plot, as well as the form, of the short stories. In this section, I continue to dismantle the opposition between 'relato popular' and 'cuento literario', demonstrating the ways in which these stories engage self-critically with popular forms of expression and action. I shall examine two instances in which Cortázar self-reflexively flirts with the limits between literature and a wide variety of artistic and non-artistic media, whether press clippings, testimony, sculpture or graffiti: 'Recortes de prensa' and 'Graffiti'. My contention is that the writer's role as inventor of 'new forms of contact', in Cortázar's own words, is intensified in these later works, which use formal experimentation to produce encounters between otherwise separate experiences, places, and realities.

The Promise of Intermediality: Photography, Cinema, Journalism and Telephony in *Todos los fuegos el fuego*

A glance through some of the journals in which Cortázar published his work gives a good idea of the changes that awakened the Argentine urban imagination at the time when his short stories were written and first read. As Sarlo insists in relation to Argentine cultural journals from 1920s Buenos Aires (like *Martín Fierro*, *Caras y Caretas* and *El Hogar*), 'la publicidad expresa cambios que afectaron las prácticas culturales en el sentido más amplio, incluidas las de las elites [...] Los avisos dan una idea de la penetración en el imaginario colectivo de estos dispositivos modernizadores' (22). Under the same conviction, I shall open this section with a sample of advertisements from three journals from the 1940s to the 1960s: the literary review *Los Anales de Buenos Aires* in which Cortázar published his first short stories, 'Bestiario' and 'Casa tomada', in 1946; *Confirmado*, a current affairs magazine that published a fragment of Cortázar's 'Autopista del sur' in 1967; and *Visión*, marketed as 'la revista de noticias de mayor circulación', that published some of Cortázar's *Modelo para armar* in 1969. Most notably, the advertisements promise speedier modes of transport and communication, lighter machines and more accurate storage media.

It must be noted that Cortázar emigrated to France in 1951, where he would spend the rest of his life. Of these three journals, therefore, only *Los Anales* published his work while he was still living in Buenos Aires. One should not overlook his consequent detachment from — or, from another perspective, indirect attachment to — the cultural context in which his work was being consumed. Indeed, this is in itself significant, placing the onus on the reader rather than the writer. Cortázar, it must not be forgotten, was the sponsor of the writerly text, of the *lector cómplice*, and of the necessary severance of the text from its author:

> Un verso admirable de Pablo Neruda: *Mis criaturas nacen de un largo rechazo*, me parece la mejor definición de un proceso en el que escribir es de alguna manera exorcizar, rechazar criaturas invasoras proyectándolas a una condición que paradójicamente les da existencia universal a la vez que las sitúa en el otro extremo del puente, donde ya no está el narrador que ha soltado la burbuja de su pipa de yeso.[23]

Cortázar's well-known theory of writing as exorcism carries the message, rendered in psychotherapeutic terms, that the severance of the short story from its author is crucial to its effect. The writer gets rid of demons, cleanses himself, by transferring his obsessions to the reader. Significant to the current argument is the paradox of globality and locality set up in this passage — or the glocal, as it has become known more recently.[24] The dislocation of the text at once endows it with universality and isolates it 'on the other side of bridge'. In practical, geographical terms, Buenos Aires is this other side; and the story is the bubble that has travelled across the ocean separating France from Argentina; a bubble that ends up in an Argentine journal, under the devouring gaze of a *porteño* reader, and next to an advert for a national or international company. It is at this juncture that the bubble floats, circulates and bursts, infiltrated by the contemporary, popular cultural imaginary of the Argentine readership. These adverts, then, might constitute the starting point of a cultural history (which has yet to be written) of the reception of Cortázar's work in Argentina, as well as a hint of the modes of production that underlie or invade his writing.

Adverts for visual and communication media prevail in these magazines. *Pentax*, the lightest of all single-lens reflex cameras, transports its users from the intimate and marvellous world of microphotography to the extraordinary, inspiring feats of telephotography (see below, Fig. 7). Elsewhere, *Kodak* photography promises a quick and economical method to print on almost all types of materials, accurately reproducing attractive designs and enabling you, for example, to 'poner una sola flor en mil vestidos de mujer'. *Cinematografía interamericana*, based in Buenos Aires and boasting $1 million in venture capital, sells itself as a distributor of films from Mexico, Argentina and Chile, but also France and North America.[25] *Televa*, the new personal television set, is light and portable, weighing only six and a half kilos.[26] 'El aire está lleno de imágenes' is the advertising slogan for the new television channel, *Canal 13 de Corrientes*, as depicted by the image of signals filling the sky.[27] The *Unión Telefónica* advertisement constitutes both a promise of communication across geographical barriers, and a set of instructions on how properly to use one's phone — the message being that you have to wait for the dialling tone before making a call (Fig. 9). A *Siemens* teleprinter or teletypewriter tempts the consumer with the possibility of transforming his or her messages into electric impulses, allowing them to cross borders and oceans within a fraction of a second.[28] The slogan of the *Compañía argentina de electricidad* (CADE), 'the magic wand of your well-being', is followed by triumphant exclamations such as: 'Hace girar una perilla, y la radio le trae música, novelas, informaciones!'[29]

The magazines are also filled with advertisements for media in the broader sense proposed by Marshall McLuhan, 'the extensions of man': electricity, lighting, and transport. *CADE* guarantees the illumination of Buenos Aires, with a scintillating image and description of Florida Avenue at night, flooded with lighting that turns the street into the dazzling 'Milky Way of the City' (Fig. 5). *Philips* also vaunts its newest lighting technologies, with a slogan claiming that 'la ciencia arroja luz sobre la luz'.[30] *Esso* petrol, the 'vía láctea por donde fluye la vida interior de cada motor', circulates in the motors of the vehicles that are incessantly running through streets, avenues and roads.[31] *Trans World Airlines* advertises its new jet thus: 'StarStream, el más moderno de los jets, desarrolla una mayor velocidad: cuatro motores jet DynaFan con más de 70,000 libras de empuje'.[32] *Boeing*, similarly, urges the reader to 'escog[er] entre 150 ciudades y 75 países y lleg[ar] en cuestión de horas en aeronaves Boeing a reacción'.[33] *Air France* (Fig. 8), *Pan American*, *Alitalia* and *Varig* are other competitors.

In what follows, I shall examine the fantasies about telekinesis, transport and intensified communication that fuel Cortázar's short stories. His texts, as we shall see, cannot be separated from their contexts: from the radical transformation of society brought about by shifting modes of production, circulation and consumption in the mid-twentieth century; from the explosion of communication and transport media in the 1960s; and from the magazines in which they were published. With regard to 1960s Argentina and Brazil, García Canclini notes that

> se constituía un nuevo sistema de circulación y valoración que, a la vez que proclamaba más autonomía para la experimentación artística, la mostraba como parte del proceso general de modernización industrial, tecnológica y del entorno cotidiano, conducido por los empresarios que manejaban esos institutos y fundaciones.[34]

Cortázar's work, as we shall see, displays this paradox: artistic freedom is counter-balanced by art's ties to rising technologies, and therefore to national and

FIG. 5. CADE Advertisement. *Los Anales de Buenos Aires*, May 1947, No. 17.
Hemeroteca de la Biblioteca Nacional de la República Argentina

ESTO LO ESCRIBIÓ JULIO CORTÁZAR

EXCLUSIVO

INVITADO POR "EL GRAFICO", JULIO CORTAZAR PRESENCIO EL COMBATE DEL SABADO. EL DOMINGO POR LA MAÑANA ACEPTO ESCRIBIR ESTAS LINEAS. LA PRODUCCION ESTUVO A CARGO DE NUESTRO COLEGA ALBERTO PERRONE, QUE APARECE A SU LADO EN LA FOTO. DESPUES DE 22 AÑOS, TAL COMO CORTAZAR SE LO CONFESO A PERRONE, EL GRAN ESCRITOR ARGENTINO VOLVIA AL LUNA PARK Y A SU ENCUENTRO CON UNA NOCHE DE SABADO TOTALMENTE PORTEÑA.

ABRIL 10 DE 1973

UN TRIUNFO CON ALGUNAS NUBES

Como es lógico, el público fue a ver ganar a Castellini. Como también es lógico, Castellini ganó. La única cosa ausente en tanta lógica fue lo que justifica y da su auténtica belleza al deporte: la alegría. A la victoria del argentino le faltó todo, salvo la fuerza del punch, y ni siquiera éste pudo definir una situación que por lo menos dos veces se volvió crítica para Doc Holliday. Fue una victoria chata, sin nada que permitiera festejarla como se esperaba. Frente a Castellini hubo un hombre que en buena ley deportiva merecía los aplausos que tan sin ganas cosechó el vencedor. Pero Doc Holliday fue además otra cosa: el símbolo amenazante del futuro. Si Castellini no aprende todo lo que le falta aprender, de nada le valdrán las interminables instrucciones que le gritaba Ringo Bonavena. En la actualidad no faltan los Doc Holliday a la espera de su hora y algunos, además de la alegre y clara técnica del yanqui, tienen punch. Cualquiera de ellos puede malograr la carrera de Castellini si éste no se decide a convertir la potencia física en ese mecanismo más complejo y eficaz que define a los grandes boxeadores, y que da a sus victorias el esplendor que tanto faltó anoche.

Julio

13

FIG. 6. Julio Cortázar, 'Un triunfo con algunas nubes', *El Gráfico*, 10 April 1973, p. 13. Hemeroteca de la Biblioteca Nacional de la República Argentina

transnational corporations, from *CADE* to *Trans World Airlines*. It therefore sustains a dual relationship with what García Canclini terms the 'industrial bourgeoisie' (86), which accompanied and propelled productive modernization and new consumer habits in the 1960s, using its resources and habits while questioning its foundations and principles.

Cortázar's active engagement in mass culture is displayed by his love of boxing. On 10 April 1973, the popular Argentine sports magazine *El Gráfico* featured an article by him on a boxing match between Miguel Angel Castellini and Doc Holliday (figure 6). As demonstrated by the bold, capitalized heading, 'Esto lo escribió Julio Cortázar', and the picture of Cortázar with the *Gráfico* journalist Alberto Perrone, the magazine capitalizes not only on his writing, but perhaps more importantly, on his image, his fame, and indeed his autograph. This is a manifestation of a broader trend identified by García Canclini and Martín-Barbero, in which the 'culto' is incorporated into mass culture. As the former affirms,

> 'las revistas de moda o decoración vendidas en puestos de periódicos y supermercados llevan las innovaciones literarias, plásticas y arquitectónicas a quienes nunca visitan las librerías ni los museos'.[35]

The movement is not uni-directional, though, since the mass media are also incorporated into 'high-brow' culture, as demonstrated by the advertisements in the literary and cultural magazines in which Cortázar published his work. In what follows, I shall ask how the popular urban imagination is reworked in Cortázar's short stories; how it is used to produce encounters between *el lado de acá* and *el lado de allá*, and to rearticulate disconnected parts into new configurations.

It seems appropriate to start off by looking at a story whose setting and plot is furnished by the aeroplane. On a basic level, 'La isla a mediodía' is a story about an air steward, Marini, who becomes obsessed with the Greek island Xiros over which his plane repeatedly flies. His evasion to the almost uninhabited island has been read by critics as the enactment of a fantasy, the realization of a mythical return. According to Sosnowski, 'El camarero Marini alcanzó a concretar su pasión porque una fuerza trans-humana lo extrapoló fuera de las coordenadas espacio-temporales que la razón puede determinar.'[36] The transhuman force that allows him to escape his own reality is from Sosnowski's perspective the result of primitive irrationalism. It involves the reversal of the Western historical process and the return to a magical, mythical, poetic vision of reality. Yet as I shall argue, Marini's realization might be read not as the escape into a mythical, unchanging time, but rather as the product of an eminently modern temporality: the precise instant (the titular midday) at which the plane flies over the island, which coincides with the moment that precedes his death.

From the very start of the story, the fleeting, constricted vision is granted a privileged position: the island is seen by the air steward through 'el óvalo azul de la ventanilla', for 'unos segundos' (109). The narrator encourages the reader to see this spatio-temporal frame as a photographic one by pointing out that Marini once takes a blurry photograph. Later, Marini thinks about buying a camera to film the island, but saves the money for a trip to the island, in the hope of transferring the fantasy into reality, of shifting from representation to presence. 'Forget filming', the narrative suggests, 'just go there'. Yet this rejection of representation is overturned as

the island is presented as a fake construct, the repetition of a fantasy-filled vision:

> Nada de eso tenía sentido, volar tres veces por semana a mediodía sobre Xiros era tan irreal como soñar tres veces por semana que volaba sobre Xiros. Todo estaba falseado en la visión inútil y recurrente; salvo, quizá, el deseo de repetirla, la consulta al reloj pulsera antes de mediodía, el breve, punzante contacto con la deslumbradora franja blanca al borde de un azul casi negro. (111)

This passage suggests various, inter-related connections between Marini's view of the island and the viewer of a photograph. An aerial view under the dazzling midday sun, the island's qualities are not inherent and unchanging, but rather the result of a temporally, spatially restricted perspective. The sight of dazzling white sand against an almost black sea evokes a black-and-white print, echoing the narrator's depiction of the breaking, foaming water as 'la orla de un blanco deslumbrante y como petrificado' (109) — a single, dazzling border, petrified as if in a photograph. Moreover, the narrator's desire to see the island again is inextricable from the 'brief, puncturing contact' produced by the fleeting vision. This undoubtedly resonates with another photographic logic, notably Barthes's theory of the *punctum*, the momentary, violent impact which endows the picture with an eminently physical reality: 'this element which rises from the scene, shoots out of it like an arrow, and pierces me'.[37] The real-ization of the instant, for Marini as for Barthes, is inextricable from the realization of the contingent, desiring, wounding gaze.

What the reader experiences throughout the story is a gradual photographic zoom, as broad swaths of dark blue and brilliant white are transformed into a crystallized, detailed picture. The first time Marini sees the island, distance leads to pure conjecture: 'la mancha plomiza cerca de la playa del norte podía ser una casa, quizá un grupo de casas primitivas' (110). Yet this distant world is gradually brought closer to the viewer, as hesitation and uncertainty give way to assertion and certainty; as the tiny, leaden stain becomes 'las casas plomizas' (113). In this context, we might be reminded of the Pentax advertisement, which promises to 'llevar[le] a usted desde ese mundo íntimo y maravilloso de la microfotografía hasta los extraordinarios trabajos — verdadera inspiración de la imaginación — de la telefotografía' (Fig. 7). The imagination, both advert and story suggest, is not unique to the aesthetic, but also a commoditized product of technological advances: Marini's vision (in both senses of the word) is inextricable from a telephotographic ability to capture distant objects, combined with a microphotographic ability to capture the tiniest details with an 'enfoque claro y positivo' (Fig. 7).

A related photographic technique that seems to drive the narrative forward is that of blow-up: every repetition of the image seems to bring the island closer, gradually supplementing the original view, revealing a different reality, and bringing life to what is at first seen as a desert island. In this sense, this story resonates with 'Las babas del diablo', in which the gradual blow-up of the photograph leads to a disturbing revelation. In both cases, repetition and reproduction lead to change and transformation. The transformational aspect of photographic reproduction contrasts with the repetitive task that defines Marini's daily routine: the 'infinitas bandejas de comida, cada una con la sonrisa a la que tenía derecho el pasajero' (112). The repeated smile, one might note, is immediately comparable to that advertised by

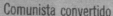

FIG. 7. *Asahi Pentax* Advertisement. *Visión*, 9 March 1962, p. 35.
Hemeroteca de la Biblioteca Nacional de la República Argentina

FIG. 8. *Air France* Advertisement. *Visión*, 23 February 1962.
Hemeroteca de la Biblioteca Nacional de la República Argentina

Air France (Fig. 8) in its guarantee of an enjoyable, friendly flight experience — an advertisement that, in turn, is reproduced and multiplied by the *Visión* magazine. As an artificial, constructed image, repeated *ad absurdum*, the fake smile is also comparable to the tortoise-island. What differentiates the infinite repetition of the dutiful smile (in the story and the advert) with the obsessive reproduction of the turtle-island, however, is the privileging of desire and imagination over duty and imitation. Like the Kodak advertisement, which vaunts the capacity to produce a thousand different dresses from an identical floral pattern, the repeated image of the island is ever-changing and ever-evolving, using the same base material in different configurations. It is the product of the active enactment of a dream, the construction of a whole world from a fragmentary vision. In the light of these correspondences between text, photograph and advertisement, it seems fitting to align Marini's act of communion on Xiros with Benjamin's theory of mechanical reproduction:

> la isla lo invadía y lo gozaba con una tal intimidad que no era capaz de pensar o de elegir. La piel le quemaba de sol y de viento cuando se desnudó para tirarse al mar desde una roca [...] lo aceptó todo en un solo acto de conciliación que era también un nombre para el futuro. (115)

> Even the most perfect reproduction of a work of art is lacking in one element: its presence in time and space, its unique existence at the place where it happens to be [...] Every day the urge grows stronger to get hold of an object at very close range by way of its likeness, its reproduction.[38]

The process of mechanical reproduction, as Benjamin points out, severs the artwork from its original spatio-temporal context and hands it over to the consumer. This might explain the short circuit between distance and proximity that is produced in 'La isla a mediodía'. What the reader witnesses in the above quotation is the foregrounding of the bodily, the sensation as the site of communication between two distinct realities. The dialectical interplay between physical distance and imaginative intimacy, irretrievable past and experiential presence might be regarded as the culmination of photographic reproduction, which enables the viewer to get hold of an otherwise unobtainable object, to capture an unrepeatable instant.

'La isla a mediodía' therefore contains at its core an instance of what Cortázar calls a 'nueva forma de contacto'. The plane window offers a different mode of contact, a brief, violent vision that is in turn connected to the medium of photography: it offers a 'camera lens' through which to view the world, one which frames and transforms the object viewed. Though Peter Standish is justified in suggesting that Marini's journey (imagined or real) constitutes an 'escape from modern technology into primitivism',[39] it must also be noted that it is only through the means of modern technology that he is able to carry out his escape. Key to his evasion and metamorphosis is the special sight that he is afforded through the plane window, which is described as a tactile experience: 'sentir el frío cristal como un límite del acuario donde lentamente se movía la tortuga dorada en el espeso azul' (114). Marini's physical sensation of the limit pre-empts Michel de Certeau's characterization, in the context of rail travel, of the windowpane:

paradoxically, it is the silence of these things put at a distance, behind the windowpane, which, from a great distance makes our memories speak or draws out of the shadows the dreams of our secrets [...] This cutting off is necessary for the birth, outside of these things but not without them, of unknown landscapes and the strange fables of our private stories.[40]

Cortázar's story foregrounds the distant image, which is inflated and blown up through the creative participation of both character and reader. The experience of severance and the severance of experience — represented by the windowpane and culminating in the story's disastrously destructive finale — lead to suggestion and imagination, movement and transformation, endless productions and reproductions.

I shall now move on to the story that bears the name of the collection, 'Todos los fuegos el fuego'. Readings of this tale have tended to follow a similar line of argument to that of Sosnowski in relation to 'La isla a mediodía', locating it in a unifying, mythical vision. Alberto Paredes suggests that 'la idea que origina este cuento es la de mostrar la pervivencia de ciertos problemas íntimos dentro de la cultura occidental, la prolongada relevancia de ciertas figuras del discurso amoroso: amor, celos, indiferencia, soledad, hastío, venganza'.[41] The tale, according to this interpretation, is rooted in the Western cultural narrative that revolves around the experience of love. For Manuel Benavides, 'el amor, la muerte y el fuego se unen en el relato de Cortázar siguiendo una tradición tan vieja como los mitos y la literatura, como la humanidad misma'.[42] These age-old themes, then, constitute a continuity with tradition, notably the narrative traditions of myth and literature. Fire is a unifying, eternal element that links the two love triangles through a 'verdad única' (488).

Similarly, Lagmanovich concludes his analysis of the structure of the story by suggesting that the fact that it is 'absolutamente unitario' comes from its 'ámbito temático'.[43] Identifying, like Benavides, 'el amor, la lucha, la muerte y el fuego' as the common thematic elements of the two stories, he affirms that 'su permanente resonancia en los episodios del primer nivel afirman de manera definitiva la forma del cuento' (385–86). In spite of the fragmentary structure or form of the tale, then, its content gives it an underlying unity. More broadly, Joan Hartman concludes her article on Cortázar's search for *figuras* thus: 'Cortázar, en su persistente lucha por una visión totalizadora y unificadora del hombre como parte de un sistema cósmico de supra-relaciones, es un nuevo Pitágoras en busca de la armonía en un mundo fragmentado.'[44]

I wish to distance myself partially from these readings insofar as their attempt to locate unity, continuity and myth at the heart of the tale causes them to underestimate the role played by processes of fragmentation and rupture in its formal structure. As I shall argue, the background noises that Yurkievich locates in Cortázar's 'open work' are crucial to this supposedly 'closed' story, which clears a space for interruptions, disruptions, and interferences. I shall focus on two extra-literary media which disrupt the narrative unity of 'Todos los fuegos' — whether implicitly, in the case of photographic or cinematic visual effects, or explicitly, in the case of telephonic interference.

The prominence of the visual in this story is apparent in the very opening line:

'así será algún día su estatua, piensa irónicamente el procónsul mientras alza el brazo, lo fija en el gesto del saludo, se deja petrificar por la ovación de un público'.[45] Less important than the plot is the way in which a certain gesture would be recorded for posterity — that is, the way in which his body would be petrified into its artistic representation, whether the statue imagined by the character, the Roman proconsul, or the photographic snapshot that this petrified figure might conjure for the modern reader. Similarly, the character of the gladiator is presented to the reader through an abrupt apparition: 'En un brusco silencio de expectativa que lo recorta con una precisión implacable, Marco avanza hacia el centro de la arena; su corta espada brilla al sol, allí donde el viejo velario deja pasar un rayo oblicuo' (138). The text thus produces the effect on the reader that Marco's entrance has on the crowd: just as silence generates a visual impression, outlining the gladiator's figure sharply against the arena, narrative progression is displaced by the momentary image of his sword glistening under a single light beam; by the same truth-revealing instant that is at the core of modern thinking about the photograph and its ontological purchase.

The visual, then, is linked with phenomenological present-ness and deictic presentation. Lagmanovich suggests this in his assertion that, 'como domina el uso del presente, puede decirse que la narración es presentada simultáneamente a la vista del lector'.[46] Yet whereas Lagmanovich focuses on the grammatical effect of tense and uses sight as a metaphor for presentation, I would propose that his statement might be reversed, and that the visual crucially goes beyond metaphor: as I have already argued in relation to Rulfo, it is the predominance of the visual in the narrative that creates the (illusory, mediated) effect of present-ness in the reader. Expanding on Lagmanovich's concept of the 'retícula bipolar', I shall argue that the process of visual disarticulation underlies the dual narrative structure, which is built on scattered images.

Formally, the two plots are connected through jerky, abrupt shifts; through the underlying technique of montage, the type of editing that came first from the Soviet experimental cinema of the 1920s. As Susan Hayward explains, 'a first principle of montage editing [...] is a rapid alternation between sets of shots whose signification occurs at the point of their collision.'[47] This can be seen, for instance, in the climactic scene of the gladiator Marco's death, which is linked to the implied scene of Jeanne's suicide through the spatio-temporal focus on the final movement of a single limb. In one narrative strand, Marco's final movement is repeated three times: 'Marco mueve lentamente un brazo [...] Irene ve moverse el brazo de Marco, un lento movimiento inútil' (149); later Irene is haunted by 'un brazo moviéndose lentamente como si acariciara la tierra' (150). In the Parisian plot, we are presented with a close-up on Jeanne's hand, then finger: 'su mano sigue inmóvil junto al gato y apenas si un dedo busca todavía el calor de su piel, la recorre brevemente antes de detenerse otra vez' (149). The close-up shot of the finger, and the freeze-framing of its brief, final movement, produces a collision between this narrative strand and the other. The 'retícula bipolar' must therefore be regarded not just as metaphor, but more crucially as a structural technique of montage that not only breaks reality up into fragments, but also allows new images and meanings to emerge from their juxtaposition — an emergence that depends on the participation of the 'lector cómplice' or the spectator.[48] Hence Hayward's description of Sergei Eisenstein's concept of montage chimes with Cortázar's description of the short story:

> For Eisenstein, montage has as its aim the creation of ideas, of a new reality, rather than the support of narrative, the old reality of experience.[49]

> Un cuento es significativo cuando quiebra sus propios límites con esa explosión de energía espiritual que ilumina bruscamente algo que va mucho más allá de la pequeña y a veces miserable anécdota que cuenta [...] que nos insta a salir de nosotros mismos y a entrar en un sistema de relaciones más complejo y hermosos.[50]

The conflict, shock and collision between narrative fragments or cinematic shots are crucial to the process of opening onto a new, different configuration of reality and relations. In his essay *Montage of Attractions* (1923), Eisenstein characterizes these clashes or 'attractions' in terms of an 'aggressive moment in [an artwork], i.e. [... an] element that can be verified and mathematically calculated to produce certain emotional shocks in a proper order within the totality'.[51] The same experience of shock, the result of sudden, unpredicted events or experiences, connects the two narratives in 'Todos los fuegos'. The sudden 'lluvia de chispas' that falls on the audience as the fire starts in the circus (141) links it with the minimal, fleeting 'chispas de sonido' (141) on the telephone line. The pang of pain, experienced by Marco's dying rival as 'ese último instante en que el dolor es como una llama de odio' (149), links his death with the flames that engulf Roland's room in the final scene.

In the Parisian plot, Sonia's blunt announcement about her relationship with Roland to the innocent Jeanne is unexpected, hence her shock, highlighted self-consciously by Roland: 'Sonia se ha precipitado, yo quería evitarte ese golpe' (147). Likewise, the arrival of the monumental adversary in the Roman plot is experienced by the crowd as a shock, as highlighted by the repetition of the word 'sorpresa' throughout the opening passages (137, 140, 141). Similarly, the sight of the giant has a powerful physical effect on Marco: 'todo su cuerpo se contrae' as he 've dibujarse la gigantesca silueta del reciario nubio, hasta entonces visible contra el fondo de piedra mohosa [...] su cuerpo sigue contraído como si tuviera miedo' (140). The internal shock caused by the stature of the rival is reproduced by the narrative perspective, which filters the reader's gaze through the terrified eyes of Marco, blowing the rival up to gigantic proportions and presenting him in raw, undiluted terms.

The use of shocks as a means of mediating between two ontological levels can be seen very clearly in 'La noche boca arriba', in which the *figura* of Aztec warfare and sacrificial ritual intertwines with that of a motorbike accident and its aftermath; in which the main character dies, at once, under the sharpened stone of an Aztec priest and under the scalpel of a surgeon. In this story, it is explicitly the trauma caused by the motorbike accident that produces the intrusion into one order by another, a shock effect to which the narrator refers repeatedly throughout the story: 'junto con el choque, perdió la visión. Fue como dormirse de golpe'; 'estaba bajo los efectos de un shock terrible'; 'el choque, el golpe brutal contra el pavimento'.[52] The shock — both the physical effect of the accident and the psychological experience of trauma — tears the narrative into two convergent narrative lines, slicing the reality of the present moment through with another reality. On the one hand, it is a fleeting experience, from which the motorcyclist awakens quickly: 'volvió bruscamente del desmayo' (170). On the other hand, 'tenía la sensación de que ese hueco, esa nada, había durado una eternidad. No, ni siquiera tiempo, más bien como si en ese hueco él hubiera pasado a través de algo o recorrido distancias inmensas' (175–76). This might be seen as a metafictional comment on the 'knock-out' that for Cortázar defines the short story. By puncturing a hole in spatio-temporal continuity, the shock produces an opening onto boundless time and space. The gap functions, in Cortázar's theoretical terms, as a 'recorte [que actúa] como una explosión que abre de par en par una realidad mucho más amplia'.[53]

Shocks punctuate both strands of the narrative. The initial shock of the accident is followed by a series of after-shocks: 'no brinque tanto, amigazo', his roommate cautions him (172); a nurse 'le clavó una gruesa aguja' (173); his eyebrow 'chirriaba a veces una punzada caliente y rápida' (173). These jolty, sporadic shocks correspond with the shocks of tribal warfare: 'una soga lo atrapó desde atrás' (175); 'el chirriar de los cerrojos lo sacudió como un látigo' (177); 'de golpe vio la piedra roja' (178–79). The series of shocks, like the drum beat of the Aztec warriors, create a pace and a rhythm which are structural to the story. Moreover, the tactile, visual and auditory shocks tear the dying man out of his reality and connect him to that of tribal Mesoamerica. This corresponds to the effect that, as Cortázar insists in 'Del cuento breve', a great short story should have on its reader; notably 'hacerle perder contacto con la desvaída realidad que lo rodea, arrasarlo a una sumersión más intensa y avasalladora'.[54] The fragmentation of experience into disconnected, unassimilated shocks that for Benjamin characterizes modernity therefore serves on a formal level to produce a series of reconnections.[55] Specifically, the montage technique produces a dialectical encounter, as the primitive returns within modern experiences; as modernity mirrors those forms that are supposed to be antithetical to it. As in 'La isla a mediodía' and 'Todos los fuegos', then, dislocated instants permit escape, aperture and metamorphosis.

It is therefore no coincidence that the visual image as a site of transformation and transfiguration is foregrounded in this story. The protagonist's state of shock produces an altered state of consciousness in which

> las cosas tenían un relieve como de gemelos de teatro, eran reales y dulces y a la vez ligeramente repugnantes; como estar viendo una película aburrida y pensar que sin embargo en la calle es peor; y quedarse.
> Vino una taza de maravilloso caldo de oro oliendo a puerro, a apio, a perejil. Un trocito de pan, más precioso que todo un banquete, se fue desmigajando poco a poco. (173)

The hospital room, viewed through the eyes of the protagonist, is defamiliarized, becomes unreal, a fictional construct. As if flattened by binocular or camera lenses, the objects around him take on strange qualities. The reference to filmic vision serves to highlight the intermeshing of reality and fantasy that is structurally crucial to the process of fragmentation and metamorphosis in this story. In the very next paragraph, the patient's distorting vision transforms the dull hospital soup into a marvellous golden stew and the tiny piece of bread into a delicious banquet. It is the falsifying lenses and frames that produce an effect of defamiliarization and transformation.[56] Quite the contrary of a totalizing, unifying vision, these are fragmented frames, as suggested by the separation of the soup into its constituent parts (leak, celery, and parsley) and the crumbling of the bread into tiny pieces. These fragments are increasingly visual:

> la botella de agua tenía algo de burbuja, de imagen translúcida contra la sombra azulada de los ventanales. Jadeó, buscando el alivio de los pulmones, el olvido de esas imágenes que seguían pegadas a sus párpados. Cada vez que cerraba los ojos las veía formarse instantáneamente. (178)

First, the bottle is seen through a distorting lens as a bubble. Immediately after, it becomes a translucent image, a fragile, barely visible simulacrum of a bottle. Pre-empting the ending of the tale, the reality of palpable things becomes a mere bubble that is about to burst, a construction that is about to crumble. The image of the bottle is displaced by a stronger set of images: those of the dream world that itself is built on the shards of the patient's fragmentary experience. Persistent and obdurate, these images 'stick' and become more palpable and three-dimensional than his immediate reality, which appears flat and false.

The effect of defamiliarization is also linked to another aspect of technology, notably the dangers and intense shocks associated with it — in the case of this story, the cranial injury caused by the high speed of the motorbike. This is the negative underside of the comfort and safety promised by the sponsors of technology, whether politicians, technocrats or advertisers. Ernst Bloch has characterized the technological accident as a sudden reminder that the very machine that is supposed to provide ease carries potential danger and violence: 'only the accident reminds us of it sometimes, with the crash of collision, the roar of explosion, the cries of maimed people — a production that knows no civilized schedule.'[57] These violent experiences have fuelled certain artistic movements. Hal Foster, in *Compulsive Beauty*, points out modernism's involvements in desire and trauma, in industrial shock, mechanical warfare and technological development. The surrealist movement to which Cortázar has often been linked,[58] and with which he strongly associated himself,[59] is a principal example. Foster tells the following story to introduce these notions:

> In 1916 André Breton was an assistant in a neuro-psychiatric clinic Saint-Dizier. There he tended a soldier who believed that the war was a fake, with the wounded made up cosmetically and the dead on loan from medical schools. The soldier intrigued the young Breton: here was a figure shocked into another reality that was also a critique of this reality.[60]

Hal Foster sees this encounter between Breton and the traumatized soldier as the unacknowledged origin story of surrealism: beauty, for the surrealists, is the con-vulsion, subversion and explosion of reality through shock (23). The story resonates with 'La noche boca arriba', in which Cortázar's motorcyclist, like Breton's soldier, is shocked into another reality that is simultaneously a critique of that reality. Indeed, by the end it is not just single objects like the bottle that take on marvellous qualities, but his whole reality: at the end, he realizes that the marvellous dream had not been that of the *guerra florida* between Aztecs and Motecs, but rather that of the 'ciudad asombrosa, con luces verdes y rojas que ardían sin llama ni humo, como un enorme insecto de metal que zumbaba bajo sus piernas' (179). He has therefore realized the Cortazarian dream, at least momentarily, of seeing the same world in a different way, and forcing the reader to do so by the same token.

The very modern technology that produces the world-opening accident is now seen from the other side. Just as I argued, in relation to Rulfo's work, that modern forms are put to the service of traditional ones, here technology is used against itself and viewed critically, from 'el otro lado', by the protagonist. On the one hand, flickering electrical lights and vibrating motors produce the excessive stimuli and shocks that serve to create world-opening cracks within the narrative and to drive the double plot forward. On the other hand, the invasion of modern reality by a former, archaic reality provides the lenses through which that very reality is critiqued. As García Canclini affirms in relation to the geometric painters and sculptors César Paternosto and Alejandro Puente in the 1960s, 'el retorno a los orígenes premodernos [es un] recurso para descentrar, diseminar, la mirada actual'.[61] Yet in the case of Cortázar, it is the combination of modern and pre-modern optics that produces a profoundly decentring effect.

I shall now return to 'Todos los fuegos el fuego' to examine another medium from which the technique of spatio-temporal fragmentation is inextricable: telephony. At various points in the Parisian plot, the telephone enables seemingly disconnected words to infiltrate the story. At one point, 'como un diminuto dibujo a lápiz, alguien que podría ser una mujer tímida pregunta entre dos chasquidos: "¿La estación del Norte?"' (144). A meagre, barely audible sentence interrupts the conversation, destabilizing the linearity of the plot and disorienting characters and readers alike. Like the telephone, which detaches the voice from its bodily source, the fragmented narrative severs the miniature narrative fragment, the train journey, from any known origin. The *estación del Norte* is unfixed and dislocated. The words take on a life of their own, turning into marks, traces, shapes that are closer to unreadable drawings than to signifying, end-oriented words.

The main telephonic interference that punctuates the story, though, is 'una voz distante que dicta números a alguien que no habla' (141). This distant voice irritates, amuses and fascinates the characters, supplementing the narrative with seemingly insignificant, unsignifying digressions: 'se lo oye como desde muy lejos. Trescientos cincuenta y cuatro, doscientos cuarenta y dos' (143). Such supplementarity renders problematic Saúl Yurkievich's notion that the *cuento* 'no tolera digresiones, pasajes parásitos, demoras de la acción'.[62] The telephonic interferences in this story are precisely such digressions. Described as an 'organizado mundo de hormigas' (146), the repeated numbers are tiny parasites that penetrate into the deepest recesses of the storylines through the insidious gallery of the phone line. The ants swarm beneath and between the two strands of this story, turning the dying gladiator into 'un enorme insecto brillante' (149). We might even say that Marco *is*, in fact, the parasitic ant that has invaded Jeanne's story — an invasion that constitutes the second type of contact delimited by Steven Boldy (as outlined above), since Jeanne and Roland receive it passively rather than searching for it, and with annoyance and hostility rather than with pleasure and elation.

Such interferences contribute to the destabilization of identity that is crucial to the formal aperture of the story. Jeanne finds it difficult to believe that her voice on the phone is her own, 'negándose a creer [...] que la voz que acaba de repetir: "Soy yo", es su voz, al borde del límite' (141). This limit, as well as the verge of ridicule that she is about to cross, is the limit of her-*self*. Telephonic communication produces a severance between the self and the voice, enabling her story to be infiltrated by that of others. Hence Jeanne has a sudden feeling that 'va a decirle a Roland eso que exactamente la incorporará a la galería de plañideras telefónicas' (141). Jeanne feels connected with a group of women that is unknown yet familiar, distant yet close, disparate yet unified. This interconnectedness is related to what McLuhan sees as a characteristic of the electric age, namely that our 'central nervous system is technologically extended to involve us in the whole of mankind and to incorporate the whole of mankind in us'.[63] By disconnecting words from their author, the short story, like the telephone, incorporates different strands of reality, thus enabling the Roman love triangle to blend with the modern one.

It also resonates with the advertisement from *Los Anales de Buenos Aires*, with its image of multiple hands and dials communicating through a great machine (Fig. 9). The central switchboard, with all its cogwheels and wires, is the extension of the individual nervous system, as depicted by the impulses firing into it from the dialling fingertips. This 1940s advertisement is therefore a brilliant illustration of the 'crepitación de comunicaciones mezcladas' on the phone line in 'Todos los fuegos el fuego' (138) — which in turn is a self-conscious reference to the narrative structure of the story, one which is intimately connected with the modern medium of telephony. Yet just as Jeanne's sense of connectivity to a 'galería de plañideras telefónicas' is a negative, ironic, self-conscious one, Cortázar's story forces the reader to adopt a critical position towards the incorporating, homogenizing effects of technology. As in 'La noche', the technology of telephony is turned against itself insofar as it allows the infiltration of a different order which serves to defamiliarize and critique the status quo: the telephone line through which the couple have their final conversation becomes the gallery in which the Roman gladiators battle to the death.

Formally constructed on principles adopted from visual and telephonic media, 'Todos los fuegos el fuego' foreshadows Cortázar's *Fantomas contra vampiros multi-nacionales*, a 1975 multimedial work that also combines two increasingly inter-connected narrative strands: the 1974 Russell Tribunal II in which the narrator Julio participates as part of the jury, as he did in real life; the burning of libraries across the globe in the *Fantomas* comic strip, which Julio starts reading on his journey back from the Tribunal, and in which he features as a character. In *Fantomas*, Cortázar stages the gradual merging of different modes of communication. The work hovers between prose narrative and comic strip, but also incorporates elements of telephonic communication, oral testimony, short story, journalism, cinema and photography. On the phone to the character Susan Sontag, the narrator Julio observes that 'en ese teléfono pasaban cosas raras, además de las palabras venían imágenes más bien borrosas pero reconocibles'.[64] The intrusion of fragmentary words and images from the Russell report intensifies until a climactic moment: 'del hueco sonoro venían voces, acentos, gritos, llamadas, afirmaciones, noticias; se sentía

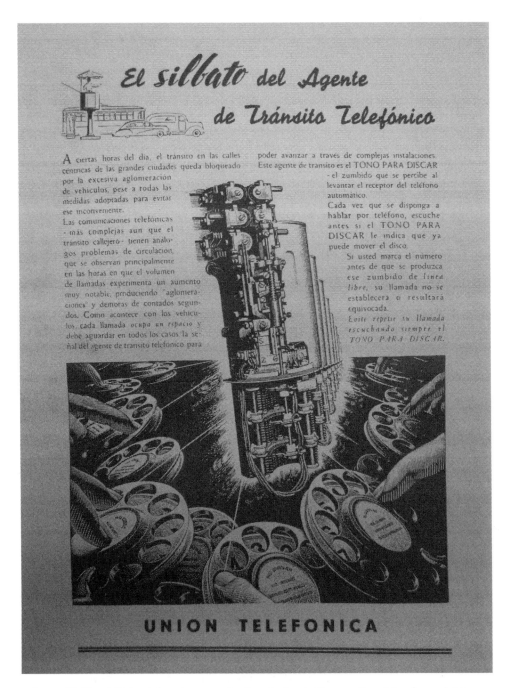

FIG. 9. *Unión telefónica* Advertisement. In *Los Anales de Buenos Aires*, March 1946, No. 3. Hemeroteca de la Biblioteca Nacional de la República Argentina

como si muchedumbres lejanísimas se juntaran en el oído del narrador para fundirse en una sola, incontenible multitud' (80). The telephone therefore becomes a site of connectivity, endowed here with huge revolutionary potential. This is arguably the same potential that Marshall McLuhan sees more generally in the electric media, which promise to connect people in such a way that certain marginal groups 'can no longer be contained, in the political sense of limited association. They are now involved in our lives, as we are in theirs, thanks to the electric media.'[65] *Fantomas* stages this notion of connectivity and reflexivity. Since the reality that the multitude is striving to express is uncontainable, no single medium is sufficient; hence the words on the phone are supplemented by images; and hence the choice of Sontag, an iconic theorist of photography, as a character. In its multiple connections and disconnections, in its interweaving of visual and verbal media, and in its merging of print fiction with telephonic communication, 'Todos los fuegos el fuego' prefigures this multimedial work.

I shall now turn to look at the final story from the collection *Todos los fuegos el fuego*, 'El otro cielo', which is also fragmented into two distinct times and spaces: Buenos Aires from the 1920s to the end of the Second World War; Paris in the 1870s, the time of the Franco-Prussian War. Critics have agreed on the active part played by the urban setting of the story. Marcy Schwartz sees the galleries as sites of productive encounters: 'Los pasajes [...] funcionan como puentes que conectan fragmentos de realidades posibles', connecting the protagonists to otherwise inaccessible or forbidden territories.[66] For Jorge Rodríguez Padrón, the never-ending journey of Cortázar's tales is driven by 'el espacio urbano, cuya contingencia y multiplicidad [...] no se limita a ser ámbito que contenga las anécdotas, de modo pasivo, sino que es trama, motor de la misma.'[67] Similarly, Paredes asserts that the urban space animates and *creates* the protagonist's intimate life, showing that 'el medio crea al hombre y hay ambientes que tienen su historia que contar'.[68] A link is therefore established by all three critics between the plot of 'El otro cielo' and its urban setting. I shall extend their arguments by highlighting that it is not just the urban setting per se that generates the plot, but also the multiple media that characterize and indeed create that urban space, from newspapers, magazines and advertisements to photography and cinema.

The *pasaje Güemes* is a site of mediation, which allows the narrator to wander seamlessly from one territory to another: from adolescent innocence to adulthood, or vice-versa; from Irma to Josiane; from Buenos Aires to Paris. Its multi-sensory quality is at first sight that which permits these transitions:

> el Pasaje Güemes era la caverna del tesoro en que deliciosamente se mezclaban la entrevisión del pecado y de las pastillas de menta, donde se voceaban las ediciones vespertinas con crímenes a toda página y ardían las luces de la sala del subsuelo donde pasaban inalcanzables películas realistas. (154)

The Güemes Gallery produces a synaesthetic mixture of sensory impressions, sights, sounds and tastes. Yet this experiential immediacy is inextricable from the different modes and media that stimulate the protagonist's senses. The burning lights are those of the cinematic projector and the sounds are the cries of newspaper sellers. Stimulation is inextricable from simulation, whether the illusions of realist cinema or the fabrications of sensationalist news. The direct, emotional experience, that for Charles May constitutes the short story, is therefore paradoxically channelled through multiple media.

As is made explicit, the language of the narrator is tied to that of the daily press. The prostitutes of the *Pasaje Güemes*, encountered in 'los presuntos paraísos en lo más alto', are 'mujeres de la vida y amorales, como les llamaban en los diarios, con bebidas preferentemente verdes en copas biseladas, con batas de seda y kimonos violeta' (154). As betrayed by the adjective 'presuntos', the adolescent protagonist lacks any direct, real encounter with these prostitutes, imagining them instead through the words and images of the yellow press. This suggestion is strengthened by the preceding passage, in which the narrator describes his memory of 'olores y sonidos, algo como una expectativa y una ansiedad, el kiosco donde se podían comprar revistas con mujeres desnudas y anuncios de falsas manicuras' (154). The impression of sensory immediacy is belied by the multiple frames through which those senses are mediated, notably the images of naked women and advertisements of fake manicures in magazines. This resonates with the *CADE* advertisement, in its combination of the artifice of advertising and that of electrical light, which together create the 'rutilante Vía Láctea de la ciudad' (Fig. 5) — an artificial galaxy that mirrors the 'falso cielo' of the *Pasaje Güemes* (154). Even the wording, the 'torrentes de luz que emergen de los suntuosos escaparates y de los letreros multicolores', foreshadows the evocative, sensual language of 'El otro cielo'.

Similarly, the narrative (dis)located in the Parisian *Galerie Vivienne* is not only characterized by, but also propelled by, the media. It is *through* the newspapers that the collective imagination is awoken and sustained: 'en un principio todo parecía ordenarse en torno al gran terror del barrio, alimentado por lo que un periodista imaginativo había dado en llamar la saga de Laurent el estrangulador' (159). The terror that propels this narrative strand is not a raw, unmediated emotion, but rather a product of the melodramatic aesthetic of the sensationalist press — an aesthetic that permeated the popular press in Latin America from the mid-nineteenth century.[69] 'Extensions of man' in the sense proposed by McLuhan, the endlessly reproduced newspapers create connections not only between Buenos Aires and Paris, but also between different symbolic fields and social spheres. In fact, the narrative of 'El otro cielo' is inseparable from the rise of mass culture in the mid-nineteenth century which, as Martín-Barbero notes, turns culture into a '*mediating factor*, that is, covering over differences and reconciling tastes [...], cover[ing] over the conflict between the classes by producing a uniting resolution at the level of imaginative symbols' (122). It is through this collective imagination that different levels of society intersect in 'El otro cielo': a businessman and a prostitute, the middle classes and the underclasses, the public domain and the criminal underworld.

Indeed, the press fuels the relationship between the prostitute Josiane and the narrator, as he accompanies her through the galleries to protect her from Laurent, the criminal protagonist in the crafty journalist's narrative saga.[70] The widespread name Laurent is soon revealed to be a mystification, seen by the local voyeur in her glass ball, appropriated and perpetuated by 'los gacetilleros [que] se cuidan de no contrariar los instintos del público' (160). At the end, *Laurent the strangler* is revealed to be 'un marsellés de pelo crespo, un miserable cobarde [que] se llamaba Paul' (177). This revelation causes the world of the Vivienne Gallery to collapse for the narrator.

The link between sensation and sensationalism, fear and mediation is suggested in the following description of Josiane's friend: 'En la mesa de al lado Kikí se estremece ostentosamente y suelta unos grititos que se multiplican en los espejos' (160). Multiplied not only in echoed sounds, but also in reflected images, the theatrical screams might be seen as a *mise en abyme* of the mechanically reproduced newspapers that fuel the urban collective imagination: newspapers that, as Martín-Barbero notes in the Chilean context, are characterized by 'prominent graphics illustrating the stor[ies]' and the 'melodramatization of a discourse gripped by violence and the macabre'.[71] We might thus return to Martín-Barbero's insistence on the distance between what the culture industry offer (the yellow press in the case of this story) and the manner of its appropriation. To illustrate his point, he quotes Monsiváis's analysis of urban popular culture in the Mexican context: 'groups without political power or social representation assimilate what is offered them, making melodrama sexy, constructing satire out of bad jokes [...] The underclasses "take" — because they have no choice — a vulgar and pedantic industry and turn it into self-indulgence and degradation but also into an enjoyable and combative identity'.[72] The prostitutes Kikí and Josiane, representatives of the underclasses, turn sensationalism into sex appeal, criminal sagas into romantic narratives, and use journalistic phrases to remould their images. The *other sky*, in a sense, is the product less of architectural design than of journalistic design: the combination and reconfiguration of gripping words and striking graphics.

The importance of the image is emphasized later in the same paragraph, when the narrator ponders on the following thought: 'a la primera imagen que se me ocurre de Josiane y que es siempre Josiane en la banqueta del café, una noche de nevada y Laurent, se agrega inevitablemente aquél que ella llamaba el sudamericano, bebiendo su ajenjo y dándonos la espalda' (161). His memory, therefore, is built on a chain of supplementary characters, or actors, that displace one another: Josiane, Laurent (Paul) and the South American (who later turns out to have a French name that the narrator forgets immediately). Significantly, it is the superposition of two images that brings the figures of Josiane and the South American together. The repeated references throughout the story to the South American, back turned and brooding, and Josiane, on the purple bench, fix the two figures in the same place and position. The immobilized, photographic images, ruptured from space and time, permit the narrator to access the past, imaginary world of the Parisian gallery from his present reality: Buenos Aires just before the elections of February 1946 that would put Juan Perón into power.

Flickering images are in fact fundamental to the *figura* in this story, to the correspondences between the two narrative realms: Buenos Aires, Irma, and the *Pasaje Güemes*; Paris, Josiane and the *Galerie Vivienne*. The motif of the garland that runs through the narrative becomes a *mise en abyme* of the weft of the multiple, converging plots: 'las cosas se tejían como las flores en una guirnalda' (172–73). It is surely significant, then, that this motif stems from a material object in the *pasaje Güemes*, as revealed in the description of 'las figuras de yeso que el pico de gas llenaba de temblores (las guirnaldas iban y venían entre los dedos de las Musas polvorientas)' (156). The garland-cum-narrative is a gas illumination, the product of intermittent lights and reflections. Similarly, Josiane's fear is described as 'el ávido terror parpadeando en sus ojos azules' (160). The terror that propels the narrative, reproduced in her blinking eyes, is therefore inextricable from flickering visions.

The role of fleeting images in the fragmentary narrative is most obvious in the final Parisian scene, in which the group of friends go to watch the public execution of 'el envenenador' (170). This must be regarded as an instance of a dual relationship set up by Cortázar in a number of his stories between the bourgeois orderliness of Buenos Aires (manifested by attributes such as marriage, family and middle-class values) and the barbaric otherness of the 'elsewhere' (displayed by violence, crime, or monstrosity): as Boldy points out, 'Buenos Aires is civilization in "Lejana", "El otro cielo", "Reunión", the other term being situated in Budapest, Paris and Cuba.'[73] As we shall see, the mediation between one realm and the other in 'El otro cielo' is achieved through instant images.

The journey in a horse-drawn carriage to the infernal Parisian spectacle is depicted thus: 'remontamos la rue de la Roquette vagamente iluminada por reverberos aislados, entre sombras movientes [...] rostros iluminados un instante por un yesquero' (171). Fleetingly illuminated by the flashes of reflectors and cigarette lighters, the narrative turns into a series of intermittent visions. The restriction of vision to isolated frames intensifies the characters' emotions, hence Josiane 'hundía las uñas en el brazo [of the narrator] y temblaba', 'volvía a clavar[le] las uñas', and '[le] mordió histéricamente [la boca]' (172). Experienced as a sequence of brief visual stimuli, the scene produces a series of momentary, violent reactions. By linking the violence of the pinch with that of the kiss, the narrator highlights the mingling of fear and desire, the dual emotion that propels the narrative and that is in turn linked to the photographic instant. Later on, the scene of the guillotining is similarly fragmented:

> En la sombra que los dos reverberos de la puerta agitaban sin ahuyentarla, la mancha blanca de una camisa surgió como flotando entre dos siluetas negras, apareciendo y desapareciendo cada vez que una tercera sombra voluminosa se inclinaba sobre ella. (174)

Like the garlands between the Muses' fingers, the 'envenenador' flickers in and out of visibility, under the agitated light of the two reflectors and behind the large shadow of a figure that leans over him. The harsh lighting reduces him to a white stain framed by two dark silhouettes. Temporal, spatial fragmentation creates the effect of a series of black-and-white photographs. Emphasized further on by the almost oxymoronic 'relámpagos de sombra entre gabanes y brazos' (174), the interplay of light and shadow, flashes and darkness, visibility and invisibility, structures the narrative. The ceremony has to be reconstructed by the spectators, by the narrator's group who leave, 'comentando lo que cada uno había creído ver y que no era lo mismo, no era nunca lo mismo' (174). The photographic snapshots that puncture the narrative therefore open holes that create passages into multiple realities or fantasies.

Arguably, the photographic principle that underlies 'El otro cielo' foreshadows the collection of photographs and textual fragments, *Buenos Aires Buenos Aires*, published jointly by Cortázar, Alicia d'Amico and Sara Facio in 1968. Story and collage work alike are permeated by the logic of 'posthumous shock' that for Benjamin is enabled by the reproductive technology of photography.[74] In 'El otro cielo', the narrator's return to the *Pasaje Güemes* long after losing his youthful innocence marks him with

> un brusco recuerdo delicioso: al entrar una vez más en el Pasaje Güemes me envolvió de golpe el aroma del café, su violencia ya casi olvidada en las galerías donde el café era flojo y recocido. Bebí dos tazas, sin azúcar, saboreando y oliendo a la vez, quemándome y feliz. (167)

The intense aroma and taste of the coffee produce a tear in the temporal continuum, allowing the older narrator to enter the otherwise forgotten realm of the porteño *Pasaje*. Similarly, in *Buenos Aires Buenos Aires*, Cortázar's texts highlight the photograph's quality as a site of passage. Looking melancholically at the photographs of the Buenos Aires that he last saw one November evening in 1954, he sees a reality that is both irretrievable and permanent: 'la luz, el sesgo de las caras de las muchachas, la silueta solitaria del hombre del café, y las azoteas con palomas y toallas al viento son una vez más la misma cosa'.[75] Here, Cortázar creates an atmosphere of nostalgia by highlighting the fragmentariness of the images: recording the fleeting moment, they restore the lost past. As Cortázar, the alienated viewer of Buenos Aires, peruses these photographs, a sudden effect of presentness is felt: 'de golpe algo como una felicidad de puro presente lo mezcla con viento de río y olor de calle, de recova y de café, con la viviente respiración de su ciudad recobrada desde tan lejos' (25). The photographs restore the multi-sensory experience of the city, the brush of the wind, the smell of the streets, arcades and coffee. Memorial absence turns into experiential presence; tiny fragments revive a lost world. Like the narrator of 'El otro cielo', whose fleeting happiness comes from the violence of the instant, the sip and smell of a strong coffee, Cortázar feels something like happiness as the distant, past world of Buenos Aires is revived temporarily through the medium of photography. Once again, pure, direct experience seems to require the intervention of a mediated form.

These readings of the *Todos los fuegos el fuego* collection might be used to shed light on the role of modern modes of production and mediation in Cortázar's short stories. Technological media, whether telephony or photography, journalistic sensationalism or cinematic montage, function as sites of passage. They create openings in the texts at the level of content, plot and narrative, permitting the characters insights and adventures into realms of experience from which they are otherwise severed and barred, be it temporally or geographically, culturally or socially. Moreover, they produce apertures at the level of form, tearing the reader out of known, familiar territories and providing him or her with tunnels, channels or vessels through which to access unchartered, unfamiliar modes of experience. In this way, Cortázar's short stories function as machines of production, narratives that internally create other forms and formations. Breaking down literary limits and generic frames, the short stories are an essential part of Cortázar's success as an 'abremundos', to use Yurkievich's term: by fragmenting narrative form, Cortázar forges multiple passages and mediations, windows and lenses that open, from the closed form of the short story, onto different views, realities and worlds. What remains to be seen is the way in which Cortázar's use of intermediality develops in his later short stories; the relationship between his continued experimentation with form and his increasingly political outlook; and the possible ethics of his *abremundos* aesthetics.

From Sculpture to Graffiti: The Politics of Mediation in *Queremos tanto a Glenda*

Having explored the configurations of the fragment in *Todos los fuegos el fuego*, I shall now turn to examine one of Cortázar's final short story collections, *Queremos tanto a Glenda*. This collection is perhaps the culmination of Cortázar's intermedial art of the short story, which pushes narrative to points at which it merges with other artistic media; which combines different cultural fragments in new syntheses. What Cortázar says of Keats's 'Ode on a Grecian Urn' might be said of *Queremos*, which stages 'el paso de lo pictórico a lo verbal [o vice versa], la inserción de valores musicales y plásticos en el poema [o en el cuento], la sorda y mantenida sospecha de que sólo exteriormente se aíslan y categorizan las artes del hombre'.[76] The movement that can be most clearly perceived from the 1968 collection to the 1982 collection is one of heightened self-reflexivity surrounding forms of mediation. Cortázar's later stories self-consciously flirt with the limits not only of language and representation, but also of a wide variety of artistic and non-artistic media, whether narrative, musical or visual, fragments of which constantly supplement and supplant one another. Focusing on the stories 'Recortes de prensa' and 'Graffiti', I shall demonstrate that the writer's role as 'abremundos' is heightened in these later works, which self-consciously stage metamorphoses between different modes, vessels and media.[77]

The second striking element of *Queremos tanto a Glenda* is its overtly political content, something that is seemingly lacking from *Todos los fuegos el fuego* — with the obvious exception of *Reunión*, Cortázar's take on Che Guevara's diaries, which constitutes one of Cortázar's few direct homages to the Cuban Revolution. Critics Aníbal González, Maurice Hemingway and Frank McQuade, and Amanda Holmes have analysed and explained the political subject matter of the stories 'Graffiti' and 'Recortes de prensa'.[78] Yet what remains to be ascertained is the link between political content and experimental, intermedial form. Why is 'Reunión', for example, underpinned by formal experimentation, incorporating into the narrative elements of music and pictorial art? Why, more generally, should Cortázar's most political writings be engaged in experiments with multiple forms and media, in the dismantling or fragmentation of narrative and its relation to reality? And finally, can these connections help address what Swanson, in relation to the 'nueva novela', sees as the biggest problem for critics, notably, 'how to reconcile the political dimension with the issue of the problematisation of reality and literature's relation to it'?[79]

In order to approach these questions, I first need to ascertain what Cortázar's political preoccupations *were* in the 1980s, which I shall do by turning initially to some of Cortázar's non-literary writings. One of his principal concerns, as Aníbal González points out,[80] is the dilemma of the Latin American writer as a result of the widespread illiteracy across the continent. In 'La literatura latinoamericana a la luz de la historia contemporánea' (1980), he talks about the 'responsabilidad cultural' of the Latin American writer, who faces 'problemas de orden moral o ético' that distinguish him or her from writers in more developed countries.[81] Cortázar affirms that the new generation of writers is increasingly conscious of this cultural responsibility, to which he attributes the dynamism and creative capacity of their works (273). One example of this, Cortázar affirms, is the extraordinary success of testimonial literature (275), which displays the desire to break down the exclusive walls of literature, to articulate writing with experience, aesthetic creativity with political action, invention with solidarity. As Roberto González Echevarría notes, the documentary novel of the Cuban Revolution manifests 'the struggle to transcend, to go beyond or to remain outside of the literary'.[82] Paradoxes and ironies notwithstanding, the intermediality of Cortázar's later short stories must be seen in relation to this sense of cultural responsibility, to this alignment with a new generation of Latin American writers who 'saben que sus libros forman parte de las vivencias totales de sus lectores' (276) — in political processes and fights for freedom.

The problems of incommunication related to high levels of illiteracy are compounded with the deliberate tactics of dictatorial regimes. In his 1980 speech for the Literary Prize of the *Casa de las Américas*, Cortázar praises the work of a cultural institution that displays a strong resistance to the persistence of dictatorial regimes in the Southern Cone — regimes that imprison, alienate and murder millions of Argentinians, Paraguayans, Chileans and Uruguayans. In these conditions, Cortázar insists, 'toda comunicación cultural con el exterior es cada vez más precaria y se cumple al precio de un riesgo que muchas veces puede ser mortal'.[83] It is in this context, and against the egotistical satisfaction of elite intellectuals, that he upholds the collective work and mass audiences of the *Casa de las Américas*, whose magazines Cortázar claims to have seen in the most varied of places, in the most unexpected of hands (298). Apparent in this speech is Cortázar's increasingly prominent desire to incorporate literature into a collective movement, into a global revolutionary process that denounces any injustice, any violation of human rights — hence his declaration of 'la razón del socialismo' (300), and his avowed return to the achievements of the Cuban Revolution (301). The speech thus marks a decided turn away from an intellectual elite, towards a popular, mass movement.

This alignment with 'lo popular' is most evident in Cortázar's support of the Sandinist Revolution against Somoza's dictatorial regime in Nicaragua in 1979, and the cultural campaigns that succeed this overthrow. In 'Discurso en el Recibo del Orden Rubén Darío' (1983), Cortázar lauds Nicaraguan government members who have 'empujado la palabra *cultura* a la calle como si fuera un carrito de helados o de frutas, se la han puesto al pueblo en la mano y en la boca con el gesto simple y cordial del que ofrece un banano'.[84] Extending his culinary metaphor, Cortázar affirms that culture is not seen by Nicaraguans as the salt and pepper that adds flavour to a dish, but rather that the dish and the culture are one and the same:

en última instancia la cultura está presente en cada uno de los avances, de las iniciativas y de las realizaciones populares, que no es ya el privilegio de los que escriben muy bien o cantan muy bien o pintan muy bien, sino que la noción parcial de la cultura ha explotado en miles de pedazos, que se recomponen en una síntesis cada vez más visible y que comporta igualmente miles de voluntades, de sentimiento, de opiniones y de actos. (481)

Cortázar thus upholds Nicaragua as a place where culture has been detached from 'lo culto', in the academic, intellectual sense of the term. Exploded into thousands of pieces that are recomposed anew, culture is symbiotically connected with revolution. It belongs to nobody and everybody. This, Cortázar insists, is apparent in the way crowds respond to artistic manifestations of all types, whether music, popular theatre, dance or visual arts (484); in 'el gran camaleón del arte y de las letras, de las artesanías y de las músicas' that represents Nicaragua's hybrid cultural scene (485); in the cultural supplements of revolutionary newspapers, radio and television shows (487). Multimediality, then, is linked to the uncontainable force of what Cortázar terms the 'gran ola de la movilización cultural masiva' (484–85). It is in order to produce this wave of freedom that Nicaraguan cultural politics is opening up 'en todas las direcciones posibles y por todos los medios a su alcance' (486). *Queremos tanto a Glenda* must be read as a manifestation of a profound desire to open culture up to the masses, to multiply forms of contact and modes of mediation.

It is not surprising, therefore, to find that his personal musings in 'Nicaragua desde adentro' (1982) are based on intermedial processes. The first section of this piece opens with an affirmation that, rather than a journalistic representation of Nicaragua's geopolitical situation, these notes must be seen 'a la manera de esas voces en off que completan el sentido de una imagen, o tal vez, mejor, como imágenes que permiten entender mejor el discurso racional'.[85] These analogies — the cinematic voix-off and the illustration of a text — suggest from the outset that this subject requires different types of media, that verbal and visual forms of representation supplement one another. The text culminates in a visit paid by Cortázar and a friend to Brenda Rocha, a member of the *Juventudes Sandinistas*, who lost an arm in a struggle to defend her people — a fight against ex-Somozist guards who assault and murder villagers, rob and loot rural communities and harass the Sandinist militia. Cortázar recognizes Brenda immediately because her smile recalls that of the photograph published daily in Nicaraguan newspapers at the time: 'su sonrisa, de la que todos hablan, se ha grabado en las memorias y en los corazones con tanta fuerza como si fuera una consigna de lucha, una bandera o una canción revolucionaria' (456); one of his friends says she smiles like Giotto's angels, but Cortázar sees it as closer to that of the statue of the smiling angel in Reims Cathedral.

Multiple media are thus invoked to depict the force of her smile: a photograph, a phrase, a symbol, a song, a painting, and finally a sculpture. As in *Todos los fuegos*, intermediality is the paradoxical manifestation of the desire to render direct, immediate experience, to represent 'ese rostro que vio la muerte y el horror de frente, y sin embargo no está marcado por el sufrimiento o la cólera' (457). The implication is that the articulation of multiple media permits the transformation of Brenda's personal experience into a collective experience. It is by conjugating different ways of seeing, expressing and representing that Cortázar reaches his affirmative conclusion: 'sí, la sonrisa de Brenda es también la sonrisa de Nicaragua, que se reconoce en ella y la hace suya' (457). As I shall argue in relation to *Queremos tanto a Glenda*, the multiplication of media is used by Cortázar as a means of producing a short circuit between the individual and the collective, between the singular act and the popular movement.

Cortázar's desire to articulate aesthetic freedom and ethical responsibility is part of a broader trend, which García Canclini situates in the varied artistic contexts of Surrealism, Bauhaus and Constructivism (42).[86] He notes the paradoxical logic of these movements, which were based on the belief that 'era posible profundizar la autonomía del arte y a la vez reinscribirlo en la vida, generalizar las experiencias cultas y convertirlas en hechos colectivos' (43). On the one hand, García Canclini suggests a possible connection between cultural mediations and political power: 'la búsqueda de mediaciones, de vías diagonales para gestionar los conflictos, da a las relaciones culturales un lugar prominente en el desenvolvimiento político' (326). Yet from his Leninist position, he also deeply doubts the possibility of this link, suggesting a divide between action and acting, between political praxis and simulated or symbolic action. Works of art, he suggests, cannot constitute effective interventions in the material structures of society, because their performative capacity to generate immediate and verifiable change is hardly ever enacted (327). Artistic experimentation, from this perspective, is irreconcilable with any democratizing insertion into the social fabric.

In what follows, I shall explore the ways in which Cortázar multiplies media in the attempt to incorporate — at least on a formal level — a broader cultural fabric into the literary work, and the literary text into a wider cultural experience. Holmes, in her *City Fictions*, comes closest to underlining this crucial connection between formal experimentation and political message:

> By locating possibilities for communication in unusual media and form, [the stories] detail aesthetic production that extends the limits of creativity to include the expression available to ordinary man, presenting new art forms as metaphoric representations of a disquieting urban space.[87]

I shall develop and expand this idea in order to emphasize the role of intermedial experiments in Cortázar's *Queremos tanto a Glenda*. As with 'El otro cielo', I shall argue that morphing media are not mere metaphors, but rather the 'vías diagonales' — to use García Canclini's term — by which Cortázar gropes towards new forms of contact, new ways of relating, communicating and being.

'Recortes de prensa', like the *figura* stories examined above, interweaves two narratives: the torture and murders of Laura Beatriz's family in the 1970s by members of the Argentine military *Junta*; and a sado-masochistic domestic crime in Paris or Marseille. Fragmentation lies at the core of this tale, which creates a strong connection between bodily violence and narrative disintegration. As Holmes affirms, this story 'disintegrat[es] the form of the coherent narration in a repeated movement between representations'.[88] Indeed, the art of the short story is combined with, and supplemented by, different media: principally sculpture and press clippings, but also music, poetry, photography and film. As will become evident, the intermedial metamorphoses that characterize the story are crucially connected with the need to find, and create, ever new forms of communicating and commemorating the experience of violence.

From the very start of the narrative, the interaction between different media is placed at the fore, through an opening scene in which the writer Noemí views her friend's sculptures before agreeing to write a text to accompany a collection of photographic reproductions of his work. First, we are afforded an insight into the visual, material art of the sculptures, which displace words and narrative:

> casi no hablábamos ahora, [las esculturas] tenían la palabra y [...] nac[ían] de alambres o de botellas pacientemente envueltas por el trabajo de los dedos y la espátula, creciendo desde latas vacías y objetos que sólo la confidencia del escultor me dejaba conocer por debajo de cuerpos y cabezas, de brazos y de manos.[89]

By drawing attention to the materials from which the sculptures are made, the narrator places the focus on form rather than theme. Concrete, palpable bodies emerge from ordinary objects like bottles and empty jars — containers that are filled with new meanings by the sculptor's manipulation. The political content entailed by the denunciation of violence thus springs forth from the material forms and textures of everyday life.

Significantly, a correspondence is set up from the start between the sculptures and the press clippings brought by Noemí, which consist of an open letter written by a victim of the Argentine military regime asking for justice. Noemí shows her friend this testimony even though, as she puts it, 'no es necesario que lo leas después de lo que me mostraste' (65). The verb 'mostrar' suggests that it is the visual present-ation and bodily present-ness of the sculptures that connect them with the journalistic testimony, whose qualities of immediacy, directness and concreteness are exemplified in Laura's raw statement that 'de mi hija sólo me ofrecieron ver las manos cortadas de su cuerpo y puestas en un frasco' (67). Again, immediacy is paradoxically conjured up through incompleteness, through the synecdochic fragment, through absence. By presenting the reader with the hands, Laura makes violence palpable; absence, present; the distant, proximate. The resulting present-ness turns the space and time in which the characters read and view the respective objects into 'ese agujero en que estábamos como metidos los dos, esa duración que abarcaba una pieza de París y un barrio miserable de Buenos Aires, que abolía los calendarios y nos dejaba cara a cara frente a eso, frente a lo que solamente podíamos llamar eso' (66). The hole, like the 'hueco' in 'La noche boca arriba', is produced by the shock experience. As suggested by the repetition of the demonstrative shifter 'eso', the two media — the journalistic testimony and the sculptural art — abolish time by pointing to the unnameable, corporeal *Erlebnis* of violence. Linguistic and visual forms alike have a deictic quality that brings the reader and viewer face to face with a reality from which they are otherwise spatio-temporally detached.

These formal experiments are arguably connected to the ethics of memory under conditions of (post-)dictatorship that Cortázar outlines in 'Negación del olvido' (1981). Haunted by the thousands — perhaps ten, perhaps fifteen — of 'desaparecidos', whose disappearance is hushed by those responsible through the dual tactics of fear and hope, Argentina is depicted by Cortázar as a land of shadows.[90] His essay is a call to 'mantener en un obstinado presente, con toda su sangre y su ignominia, algo que ya se está queriendo hacer entrar en el cómodo país del olvido' (427). 'Recortes' is an artistic manifestation of the same desire to present — and by doing so, to make present — this reality, through all possible means and media. Hence the horrific image of the daughter's fragmented body turns into a kind of music, or poetry. The narrator walks down the street,

> marcando ese ritmo en el que la fatiga y las obsesiones insertan tantas veces una melodía que vuelve y vuelve, o una frase de un poema, sólo me ofrecieron ver sus manos cortadas de su cuerpo y puestas en un frasco, que lleva el número veinticuatro, sólo me ofrecieron ver sus manos cortadas de su cuerpo (71–72)

Laura's *Erlebnis*, the shocking sight of her daughter's severed hands, is mediated by the words into which she casts the experience, a sentence which in turn becomes a kind of musical phrase or poetic line that repeats itself time and again in the head of the narrator Noemí and in the body of Cortázar's story. The repeated fragment from Laura's testimony in this passage, and in the ensuing scene (76), is such that the prose text begins to communicate to the reader through effect and rhythm rather than through plot and meaning. Segmented and severed from the narrative to which it belongs, Laura's legalistic, journalistic phrase is transformed into a musical *ritornello*, a lyrical refrain. Given the excess of the experience of violence over representation, any medium is insufficient, hence the constant substitution or supplementation of one medium by another. The narrative, as we are beginning to see, constitutes a sustained search for new ways of present-ing violence, of sharing with the reader an ineffable, traumatic experience.

   In the convergent narrative strand, presentation and present-ness play a similarly structural role. On her walk away from the sculptor's house, Noemí encounters a little girl sobbing on a doorstep. When asked what is wrong, the child responds: 'Mi papá le hace cosas a mi mamá' (73). The raw language of the child, like that of the narrator in Rulfo's 'Es que somos muy pobres', places the unnameable *Erlebnis*, the thing-ness of traumatic experience, at the heart of the narrative. By filtering the scene initially through the child's eyes, the narrative resists explanation and rationality from the outset, presenting a situation without embedding it in a narrative fabric. Leading Noemí to the sadistic scene, the daughter does not say another word, but merely points: 'me mostraba algo con un dedo' (73); 'la nena me mostró [la puerta] con la mano' (74). Taking on the deictic quality of Laura's testimony, the narrative fabric is ruptured by the extra-verbal, material *Erlebnis*. It is the same rupture that turns the child's testimony, like Laura's, into a musical phrase that returns, with variations, throughout the torture scene: 'el papá de la nena le hacía cosas a la mamá' (74); 'ahora la mamá le hacía cosas al papá' (76). The single, isolated sentence thus returns, in all its materiality and thing-ness, to haunt the narrative as a poetic, musical refrain, paradoxically endowing the narrative with immediacy and directness through the medium of the lyric.

   Primacy is given to the visual in the scene that follows, linking this narrative passage with the sculptures encountered earlier. Lighting effects are highlighted from the start: before Noemí enters the room, 'una raya de luz se filtraba bajo la puerta del fondo' (74); when the child opens the door, Noemí 'recib[ió] en plena cara el rayo amarillento de la rendija que se ampliaba poco a poco, ol[ió] un olor a quemado, o[yó] algo como un alarido ahogado que volvía y volvía y se cortaba y volvía' (74). A connection is suggested between the single ray of light from which the violent torture scene bursts forth and the lamp with which the sculptor illuminates his works: 'las ponía bajo una luz bien pensada, me dejaba mirarlas despacio y después las hacía girar poco a poco' (64). The revolutions of the sculptures foreshadow the wails of the mother, which 'volvían y volvían ... y volvían', a circular motion that is reproduced in the text through rhythmic repetition. Given that this passage would become her text to accompany the sculptor's catalogue, Noemí has fulfilled her goal of writing 'un texto como esas piezas' (64) — not in content, but in form.

In addition, a significant link is formed between the way in which Noemí 'recibe en plena cara el rayo' and the way in which she is struck by the photograph in the second press clipping from *France-Soir*: everything is there, the shed, the vegetable garden, the wire fences, the high walls, 'todo ahí golpeándome la cara entre los pedazos de la noticia' (79). It is surely significant that the visual shock of the scene is echoed by the posthumous shock of the photograph, which jumps out from the fragmentary pieces of news. As in Cortázar's account of Brenda Rocha, whose striking smile is mediated and shared with the Nicaraguan collective through the newspapers' dissemination of her photograph, the experience of violence in 'Recortes' becomes a shared event through 'vías diagonales'. Whether the experience is engendered through the media — the posthumous redemption of the photograph and the physical impact of the sculptures — or the immediate experience takes on the qualities of these media when it is represented, Cortázar blurs the distinction between fantasy and reality, mediation and immediacy, in order to invoke the reader's participation and to pose the corresponding ethical challenge. Viewing artistic representations and technological reproductions entails a participation that re-actualizes and re-enacts the experience in question through snippets, fragments, clippings, and severed refrains. As in 'Las babas del diablo', the implication is that there is no such thing as detached spectatorship, whether of lived, present experience or reproduced, re-presented experience.

Alongside photography and sculpture, a variety of layers of mediation intersect during the torture scene, as indicated by Noemí's affirmation that 'pud[o] haberlo visto en una película o leído en un libro' (75). Though on the one hand, the technique is a straightforwardly self-reflexive one, highlighting the fictional quality of the scene and hinting at the final twist produced by the second newspaper clipping, on the other hand it points to the constant medial shifts enacted in the narrative. First, Noemí views her own actions from a moving position, as if through a cinematographic camera lens: 'arrancarle la toalla de la cara [de la mujer] y verla enderezarse en silencio, ahora perfectamente en silencio como si eso fuera necesario y hasta imprescindible, mirar el cuerpo en el suelo [...] mirarme a mí sin palabras' (75). The narrative becomes detached from the narrator as it is filtered through another gaze: that of the female victim (who is on the point of becoming the aggressor). Switching from gaze to gaze, the narrative turns into a series of silent cinematic shots. At this point, words are displaced by images, and then by an eerie vibration: 'ese silencio donde algo parecía vibrar y temblar y en un sonido ultrasónico' (75). The soundtrack accompanies, and adds tensions to, the images of violence, the close-up shots of the women's vengeful hands: first, the naked woman's two hands ripping the man's clothes, unbuttoning his trousers; then, four hands tearing off his jacket, shirt and underpants.

Second, this scene brings back 'otra cosa indeciblemente vivida pero no vista, un pasaje de un cuento de Jack London', a moment in which a tribe of women kill a trapper, in ways that are never told, 'cada nueva variante jamás descrita pero ahí' (76). The narrative not only takes on the fictional quality of this short story, but also its formal properties. Like Jack London, the narrative voice withholds the denouement, the description of the man's murder: 'lo que sigue no lo sé' (75), the narrator affirms. This prefigures — but perhaps also stems from — the fragmentary form of the press clipping from the sensationalist tabloid *France-Soir*, carelessly ripped by Noemí: 'el horrendo espectáculo que se ofreció a los, el recorte se interrumpía ahí, al fin y al cabo al mojar demasiado el cierre del sobre había hecho lo mismo que Jack London' (79). An explicit link is thus created between the different media: the short story, with its technique of narrative withdrawal, and the newspaper article, accidentally torn — a tear that turns sensationalist hyperbole into poetic understatement. Again, it is the fragmentation of narrative, whether artful or accidental, that at once demands and provides a bridge between different media, different ways of communicating the ultimately incommunicable experience of torture, violence, and murder.

During the climax of the torture scene, the different strands of the narrative come together through the multiple, interconnected media:

> pedazos de imágenes volviendo desde un recorte de diario, las manos cortadas de su cuerpo y puestas en un frasco que lleva el número 24, por informantes no oficiales nos hemos enterado que falleció súbitamente en los comienzos de la tortura, la toalla en la boca, los cigarrillos encendidos (76)

As is evident here, places, forms and media become entangled: Buenos Aires and Marseilles; prose fiction, testimonial letter and newspaper article; lyrical poetry, musical refrain and photographic image. Such transitions are necessitated by a fragmentary narrative whose core is the unknown, the incomprehensible, the indescribable. The inadequacy of any medium, whether linguistic or visual, realistic or fictional, demands a constant process of intermedial supplementation. Hence 'Recortes' experiments with different media, whether photography or cinema, sculpture or literature, music or journalism, each of which displace one another. Cortázar's wish is to blast open the four walls by which the writer is confined, and to turn the text into a collective process in which the reader is forced to participate; into a montage of acts and actions, of voices and images.

To finish, I shall turn to 'Graffiti', a story about a pair of individuals who, in defiance of state regulation and repression, exchange messages through abstract graffiti. Though, as the narrator asserts at the beginning, his graffiti are not political since they have no overt message at all, a political rhetoric underlies the artistic actions and medial movements in the story. As García Canclini affirms, the art of graffiti is inherently multi-material and transcultural, fusing word and image, private and public, popular iconography and student movements, daily life and politics.[91] In what follows, I shall examine the use of the public space of the city as the site of artistic intervention; the fleetingness of the urban artworks, in terms of production and reception; and the constant metamorphosis between verbal and visual forms.

As elsewhere in Cortázar's *oeuvre*, form and materiality take precedence over substance and message. The reader's attention is drawn throughout to the colour, texture, relief and shape of the graffiti: 'lo había hecho con tizas rojas y azules en una puerta de garaje, aprovechando la textura de las maderas carcomidas y las cabezas de los clavos' (127). Drawn on a dilapidated garage door, the picture's abstractness is the paradoxical result of its concreteness, its embeddedness in wood and metal. It is surely relevant, then, that this text was originally written to form part of the 1978 exhibition 'Tapias de Tàpies', which gathered works by the Catalan artist Antoni Tàpies — works that combine oil paint with other found materials, from cord and fabric to wood and cardboard. Like Tàpies' work, the graffiti in Cortázar's story emerges from the multimedial interaction between different shapes (the lines of the drawing, the heads of the nails), textures (the roughness of the worm-eaten wood, the smoothness of the nails) and reliefs (the two-dimensional line drawings, the protruding nails). As Martín-Barbero affirms, citing some manifestoes on Tepito, a neighbourhood in Mexico City,

> 'frescoes' are painted on the walls, not to cover up the cracks, but along the lines of the cracks, 'where the plaster is mouldy, is falling off and begins to reveal a popular memory, without preparing the surface for painting, without sketching out the design before, directly on the wall, integrating rhythms provided by the spatial elements of the neighbourhood'. (202)

The individual artistic act, in 'Graffiti' as in Martín-Barbero's account, is inscribed in a shared urban space, narrative and experience. It is not just the spatial elements of the neighbourhood, though, that characterize the graffiti in Cortázar's story. Because of the clandestine nature of the acts, they are also inextricable from speed and temporality: 'a veces una rápida composición abstracta en dos colores' (126); 'elegiste para tus dibujos esas calles que podías recorrer de un solo rápido itinerario' (127); 'un rápido paisaje con velas y tajamares' (127). Though the drawings have no overt content or narrative, their message lies partly in the urgency expressed through the haste of production. Moreover, the graffiti are not only drawn, but also viewed, at a fast pace: 'la gente que le echaba una ojeada al pasar, nadie se detenía por supuesto' (126); 'ella no se detendría después de ver tu dibujo' (127); 'volviste a [...] mirar fugitivamente las paredes' (129). This fleetingness endows them with movement, a rhythm which the narrative reproduces through the constant hesitation between shifting spatio-temporal perspectives, between 'diferentes puntos de mira' (128). The work of art, whose movement and vitality comes from the movement of its viewers, is thus upheld as a collective process rather than the fruit of a solitary experience.

In a sense, 'Graffiti' foreshadows Cortázar's 'Nuevo elogio de la locura' (1981), where he defends the supposed 'madness' of the *Madres de la Plaza de Mayo*, the Argentine women who demand explanations for the disappearance of their loved ones, gathering in the central square of Buenos Aires as an act of resistance and visibilization. The status quo of repression and oblivion, he affirms, is disturbed and collapsed not by a smooth historical process, but by the momentary irruption of 'lo irracional, lo inesperado, la bandada de palomas, las Madres de la Plaza de Mayo'.[92] Momentary, fleeting actions and enactions are thus accorded a vital political role. Similarly, in 'Graffiti', the momentary drawings open a 'space' for hope: 'el tiempo que transcurría hasta que llegaban los camiones de limpieza se abría para vos algo como un espacio más limpio donde casi cabía la esperanza' (126). Subverting what Levy sees as our 'presuppositions about what constitutes great art' — imperishability and permanence — the graffiti only stay on the wall for the brief spell before the authorities find and erase them. This element of delay and postponement brings temporality, normally associated with narrative art, into play with the spatiality of abstract pictorial art. It therefore adds an element of undecidability, indetermination and freedom which, as we have seen in relation to Rulfo's fiction, Bergson associates with retardation.[93]

The symbiotic relationship between narrative and image is made increasingly explicit in the story. According to the narrator herself, one of the drawings 'valía como un pedido o una interrogación, una manera de llamarte' (127). Pictorial signs, devoid of determinate meaning, turn into linguistic, grammatical structures; into demands, pleas or questions; into calls for action. Conversely the words the male character desires to say to her turn into another drawing: 'le hablaste le dijiste todo lo que te venía a la boca como otro dibujo sonoro, otro puerto con velas' (127). Language metamorphoses into image, turning the story into a Möbius strip in which media morph seamlessly into one another. Importantly, this intermedial movement is achieved not through the narrative, but through its withdrawal. Since we are not told what he says, content is displaced by form — by the manner in which he talks, or in which the words emerge, or even in which his mouth opens. It is the lack of actual knowledge, information or story that fuels intermedial relations. This becomes clear in the following passage:

> un esbozo en azul, los trazos de ese naranja que era como su nombre o su boca, ella ahí en ese dibujo truncado que los policías habían borroneado antes de llevársela; quedaba lo bastante para comprender que había querido responder a tu triángulo con otra figura, un círculo o acaso una espiral, una forma llena y hermosa, algo como un sí o un siempre o un ahora. (128)

The drawing is doubly fragmented: it is interrupted, and partially erased, by the police. Rupture and erasure lead to multiple levels of metamorphosis. First, the connotative colour conjures her name and her mouth, her identity and her voice: severed from its author, the line drawing functions as a container in which she remains even after she has been removed. Second, the residues of the drawing suggest different shapes: a circle or a spiral, or perhaps a different one altogether, thus producing formal indeterminacy and undecidability. Third, the uncertain, incomplete form suggests a complete form, which in turn evokes a word, leading to the metamorphosis between the suggestive pictorial form and the denotative linguistic form. Though these words denote completion and wholeness (yes, always, now), the sentence structure undermines that, through the repetition of the destabilizing 'o', which unleashes, once more, the logic of indeterminacy, postponement and supplementarity.

The supplementary relation between narrative and image carries on in the next passage, when he adds his drawing to the wall from which hers was erased: 'llenaste las maderas con un grito verde, una roja llamarada de reconocimiento y de amor, envolviste tu dibujo con un óvalo que era también tu boca y la suya y la esperanza' (129). Colours turn into expressions of anger, recognition and love, whose verbal, vocal quality is implied by the words 'grito' and 'boca', and even the verb 'llamar' that nestles within the noun 'llamarada'. The oval shape reminds us of the word 'o' that proliferates in the tale, and carries the same hesitation, employing what Martín-Barbero terms, in relation to graffiti art, the 'expressiveness and polysemy of the image' (202) to suggest his mouth, her mouth, and hope.

Her final picture — the point at which, as critics have often pointed out, the female character divulges her identity as the narrator — is a pictorial supplementation of the initial graffiti phrase, 'a mí también me duele'. From the barely visible purple stains of this final drawing, fragmented, paralysed maimed body parts seem to jump out and assail the viewer: 'una cara tumefacta, un ojo colgando, una boca aplastada' (130). The plot of the story, again, is reduced to a few forms; this time to fragmented, maimed, deformed body parts that suggest acts of violence and torture; violence that is inscribed on the human flesh. This is the female character's way of asking him to carry on by making her absence present, by displaying signs of repression that constitute calls to action. The wordless plea will also enable her (from her confined space, perhaps a hiding place or a prison cell) to persist in her task of imagination: 'así como había imaginado tu vida, imaginando que hacías otros dibujos, que salías por la noche para hacer otros dibujos' (130). The repetition of the verb 'imagine' is crucial here. What the reader has been presented with, it is implied, is her imagining his life (his story), imagining her life (her story). As highlighted by this self-reflexive disclosure, the fabric, or fabrication, of the narrative is constructed upon the drawings, the abstract-cum-material forms devoid of meaning. Invention and action, creation and resistance, suffering and rebellion, desires and furies thus come together in a narrative woven around fragmentary images, around what Hugo Assman terms the 'popular forms of hope'.[94]

Inconclusions and Addenda

In this chapter, then, we have seen how Cortázar's stories enclose the logic of non-literary, popular or mass media, moving between different forms in order to open up worlds. Broadening out this study, I would suggest that it is not just in Cortázar's short stories that intermediality is essential, but also in the short story as a genre. To a certain extent, all media are intermedial. According to McLuhan, 'the "content" of any medium is always another medium. The content of writing is speech, just as the written word is the content of print, and print is the content of the telegraph'.[95] Elleström, similarly, sees intermediality as constitutive of mediation, defining the former as 'the phenomenon whereby the properties of *all* media partially inter-sect' (my emphasis).[96] My contention, though, is that the short story develops as a 'strongly multimodal' form, to use Elleström's term (38), due to its particular aesthetics of fragmentation, and to the corresponding practical, social and political circumstances that fuelled its growth.

As Cortázar insists in 'Algunos aspectos',[97] the short story is a deliberate break from the oral storytelling tradition, detaching narrative from the human voice, from the embodied presence of the storyteller. Instead it seeks new forms of communication through different disembodied media, whether telephony or photography, cinematography or graffiti. More specifically, the growth of the short story, as its theorists have often argued, is closely connected to the explosion of the publishing industry.[98] First published in newspapers, journals and magazines, short stories appeared alongside not only different types of writing, but also drawings, photographs and advertisements. The journals in which Cortázar first published his work — including the three examined above, *Los Anales de Buenos Aires* (1946), *Confirmado* (1967) and perhaps most significantly *Visión* (1969) — are but one example of this phenomenon. Most relevant in this context is McLuhan's interest in what happens when several items are arranged in a mosaic on one sheet.[99] As he argues,

> the book is a private confessional form that provides a 'point of view.' The press is a group confessional form that provides communal participation. It can 'color' events by using them or by not using them at all. But it is the daily communal exposure of multiple items in juxtaposition that gives the press its complex dimension of human interest. (204)

Cortázar's short stories, from the very beginning, demand a radicalization of the promise of the media, laying the ground for what in *Rayuela* he would develop as a theory of the 'complicit reader'. The communal participation that, as we have seen, is inextricable from the forms and practices that characterize urban popular culture, should be viewed as a wider feature of the short story. As we are beginning to see, the genre not only stems from the disintegration of social relations, but also participates in their reintegration and reconfiguration.

By revisiting and destabilizing the oppositions constructed by short story theorists, Cortázar's critics, and Cortázar himself — between short story and novel/collage, closed form and open form, directness and indirectness, popular and literary — I have sought to shed light on the paradoxes of the short story, both within and beyond Latin America. As I have argued, the supplementary relationship between the enclosed frame of the short story and its outside leads simultaneously to the deconstruction of existing genres, arts and media, and to the construction of new forms. In a sense, all literature might be said to be intermedial insofar as it is composed of words and phrases which come from an archive that is culture-wide, and are infected and inflected by other art forms and media, whether linguistic or non-linguistic. In this work, though, I am seeking to highlight the particularly intermedial quality of the short story as a compositional form that is constituted and defined by limits. As I have demonstrated in the above chapter, Cortázar's short stories suggest and overspill into other forms and media due to the Derridean logic of parergonality identified by Moran, which produces the blurring between interior and exterior. This blurring — or 'rubbing' as Derrida calls it — of the very limits that underpin the short story form is such that it becomes inextricably linked to other genres (like the novel and the collage work) and media (like photography and cinema).

In the spirit of Cortázar's theory of the tunnel, the intermediality of his stories constitutes not only a destructive transgression of boundaries, but also a creation of new ways of seeing, experiencing and being; not only a rupture, but also a promise. This promise produces a two-way bond between Cortázar's work and his readers: his short stories break down medial boundaries in order to produce different forms of cultural, social and political contact; his readers are invoked as sites of passage, 'vías diagonales' through which his stories open onto ever-evolving worlds.

Notes to Chapter 2

1. Julio Cortázar, 'El escritor y su quehacer en América latina', in *Textos políticos* (Barcelona: Plaza & Janes, 1985), pp. 121–37 (p. 128).

2. *Media Borders, Multimodality and Intermediality*, ed. by Lars Elleström (Basingstoke; New York: Palgrave Macmillan, 2010), p. 27. The term *intermedia* was coined by Dick Higgins in his essay 'Intermedia', in *Something Else Newsletter*, vol. 1, no. 1, 1966. It referred to the conceptual fusion, as well as the mere juxtaposition, of different media. See also Marina Grishakova and Marie-Laure Ryan, *Intermediality and Storytelling* (Berlin; New York: Walter de Gruyter, 2010); Peter Wagner, *Icons, Texts, Iconotexts: Essays on Ekphrasis and Intermediality* (Berlin: Walter de Gruyter, 1996).

3. Cortázar, 'Teoría del túnel' (1947), in *Obra crítica 1* (Buenos Aires: Alfaguara, 1994), pp. 31–147 (p. 68).

4. Philip Swanson, *The New Novel in Latin America: Politics and Popular Culture after the Boom* (Manchester; New York: Manchester University Press, 1995), p. 3.

5. Charles May, *The Short Story: The Reality of Artifice* (New York: Routledge, 2002), p. 133.

6. Cortázar, *Rayuela*, chapter 79, p. 517.

7. David Trotter, *Cinema and Modernism* (Oxford: Blackwell, 2007), p. 11.

8. Cortázar, 'Algunos aspectos' (p. 513).

9. Cortázar, *La vuelta al día en ochenta mundos* (Madrid: Debate, 1994), pp. 39, 41.

10. Gustavo Pellón, 'Cortázar and the Idolatry of Origins', in *Julio Cortázar: New Readings*, ed. by Carlos J. Alonso (Cambridge: Cambridge University Press, 2011), pp. 110–29 (p. 127).

11. Saúl Yurkievich, *Julio Cortázar: mundos y modos* (Madrid: Anaya & Mario Muchnik, 1994), p. 11.

12. Marcy Schwartz, *Invenciones urbanas: ficción y ciudad latinoamericanas* (Buenos Aires: Corregidor, 2010), p. 157.

13. Saúl Sosnowski, *Julio Cortázar, una búsqueda mítica* (Buenos Aires: Noé, 1973), p. 2.

14. Jacques Derrida and Craig Owens, 'The Parergon', *October*, 9 (Summer 1979), 3–41 (p. 21).

15. Dominic Moran, *Questions of the Liminal in the Fiction of Julio Cortázar* (Oxford: Legenda, 2000), p. 93.

16. Derrida and Owens, 'The Parergon', p. 20.

17. Jacques Derrida, *Of Grammatology*, trans. by Gayatri Chakravorty Spivak (Baltimore, MD: Johns Hopkins University Press, 1998), pp. 144–45.

18. Steven Boldy, *The Novels of Julio Cortázar* (Cambridge: Cambridge University Press, 2010), p. 42.

19. Carmen de Mora Valcárcel, *Teoría y práctica del cuento en los relatos de Cortázar* (Seville: Escuela de estudios hispanoamericanos, 1982); Sosnowski, *Julio Cortázar: una búsqueda mítica*; Graciela de Sola, *Julio Cortázar y el hombre nuevo* (Buenos Aires: Editorial sudamericana, 1968); Keith Cohen, 'Cortázar and the Apparatus of Writing', *Contemporary Literature*, 25.1 (1984), 15–27; Valeria de los Ríos, 'Fotografía, cine y traducción en "Las babas del diablo"', *Revista Chilena de Literatura*, 72 (2008), 5–27; Terry J. Peavler, '*Blow-Up*: A Reconsideration of Antonioni's Infidelity to

Cortázar', *PMLA*, 94.5 (1979), 887–93; Dan Russek, 'Verbal/visual braids: The Photographic Medium in the Work of Julio Cortázar', *Mosaic: A Journal for the Interdisciplinary Study of Literature*, 37.4 (2004), 71–86; Adelaida López de Martínez, ' "Las Babas del Diablo": Teoría y práctica del cuento', *Hispania*, 67.4 (1984), 567–76; Maurice Hemingway and Frank McQuade, 'The Writer and Politics in Four Stories by Julio Cortázar', *Revista Canadiense de Estudios Hispánicos*, 13.1 (1988), 49–65.

20. Eva Valcárcel, 'El cuento: aproximación teórica', in *El cuento hispanoamericano del siglo XX*, pp. 21–29 (p. 21).

21. See Boldy, *The Novels of Julio Cortázar*, pp. 22–27.

22. Cortázar, *Rayuela*, pp. 13, 293.

23. Julio Cortázar, 'Del cuento breve y sus alrededores', in *Último round* (Mexico City; Barcelona: Editorial RM Verlag, 2010), pp. 34–45 (p. 37).

24. The term 'glocal' was popularized in the 1990s by the British sociologist Roland Robertson and the Canadian sociologists Keith Hampton and Barry Wellman.

25. *Cinematográfica Interamericana* advertisement, *Los Anales de Buenos Aires*, November 1946, No. 11.

26. *Televa* advertisement, *Confirmado*, 21 May 1962, No. 3, p. 4.

27. *Deneb* advertisement, *Confirmado*, 4 June 1965, No. 5.

28. *Siemens & Halske AG* advertisement, *Visión*, 20 April 1962.

29. *CADE* advertisement, *Los Anales de Buenos Aires*, July 1946, No. 7.

30. *Philips* advertisement, *Visión*, 9 March 1962.

31. *Esso* advertisement, *Confirmado*, 14 May 1962, No. 2, p. 21.

32. *Trans World Airlines* advertisement, *Visión*, 23 February 1962.

33. *Boeing* advertisement, *Visión*, 4 May 1962.

34. García Canclini, *Culturas híbridas*, p. 87.

35. García Canclini, *Culturas híbridas*, p. 85.

36. Sosnowski, *Julio Cortázar, una búsqueda mítica*, p. 45.

37. Roland Barthes, *Camera Lucida: Reflections on Photography*, trans. by Richard Howard (London: Vintage, 1993), p. 26.

38. Walter Benjamin, 'The Work of Art in the Age of Mechanical Reproduction', in *Illuminations*, pp. 222, 225.

39. Peter Standish, 'Another Glance at Marini's Island', *Neophilologus*, 60 (1976), 389–96 (p. 395).

40. Michel de Certeau, *The Practice of Everyday Life* (Berkeley; London: University of California Press, 2011), p. 112.

41. Alberto Paredes, *Abismos de papel: los cuentos de Julio Cortázar* (Mexico City: Universidad Nacional Autónoma de México, 1988), p. 59.

42. Manuel Benavides, 'La abolición del tiempo: análisis de "Todos los fuegos el fuego" ', *Cuadernos hispanoamericanos, Homenaje a Julio Cortázar* (1980), 484–94 (p. 486).

43. David Lagmanovich, 'Estructura de un cuento de Julio Cortázar: "Todos los fuegos el fuego", *Cuadernos hispanoamericanos, Homenaje a Julio Cortázar* (1980), 375–87 (pp. 385–86).

44. Joan Hartman, 'La búsqueda de las figuras en algunos cuentos de Cortázar', *Revista Iberoamericana*, vol. XXXV, no. 69 (1969), 539–49 (p. 549).

45. Cortázar, *Todos los fuegos el fuego* (Buenos Aires: Punto de Lectura, 2010), p. 137. Hereafter, all references to this edition will be made within the body of the text.

46. Lagmanovich, 'Estructura', p. 386.

47. Susan Hayward, *Cinema Studies: The Key Concepts* (London: Routledge, 2006), p. 96.

48. Cortázar, *Rayuela*, chapter 79, p. 518.

49. James Monaco, *How to Read a Film: The Art, Technology, Language, History, and Theory of Film and Media* (New York; Oxford: Oxford University Press, 1981), p. 323.

50. Cortázar, 'Algunos aspectos', pp. 516–19.

51. Sergei Eisenstein, *Montage of Attractions*, cited in Michael Payne and Jessica Rae Barbera, *A Dictionary of Cultural and Critical Theory* (Chichester: John Wiley and Sons, 2010), p. 223.

52. Cortázar, *Final del juego* (Mexico City: Punto de Lectura, 2008), pp. 170, 170, 176.

53. Cortázar, 'Algunos aspectos', p. 513.

54. Julio Cortázar, 'Del cuento breve y sus alrededores', pp. 34–45 (p. 38).

55. See David Kelman, 'The Afterlife of Storytelling: Julio Cortázar's Reading of Walter Benjamin and Edgar Allan Poe', *Comparative Literature*, 60.3 (Summer 2008), 244–60.

56. Defamiliarization or *ostranenie*, a means of forcing the reader or viewer of art to see the familiar as strange, is a term coined by the Russian formalist Viktor Shklovsky in 1917.

57. Ernst Bloch, *Spuren*, cited by Wolfgang Schivelbusch, in *The Railway Journey: The Industrialization of Time and Space in the 19th Century* (Berkeley; Los Angeles: University of California Press, 1987), pp. 130–31.

58. See Boldy; Sosnowski; Ilan Stavans, *Julio Cortázar: A Study of the Short Fiction* (New York: Twayne Publishers, 1996); Evelyn Picón-Garfield, *¿Es Julio Cortázar un surrealista?* (Madrid: Gredos, 1975); Sara Castro-Klarén, 'Cortázar, Surrealism, and "Pataphysics"', *Comparative Literature*, 27.3 (Summer, 1975), 218–36.

59. See 'Interview: Julio Cortázar', Lucille Kerr, Julio Cortázar, Roberto González Echevarría, David I. Grossvogel and Jonathan Tittler, *Diacritics*, 4.4 (Winter 1974), 35–40, where Cortázar affirms that surrealism has had 'a decisive and tremendous impact [on his work], by way of Antonin Artaud, Rene Crevel, and Aragon, not to mention the infinite Surrealistic cronopios avant la lettre, like Lichtenberg, Alfred Jarry and Lewis Carroll' (p. 39).

60. Hal Foster, *Compulsive Beauty* (Cambridge, MA; London: MIT Press, 1995), p. xi.

61. García Canclini, *Culturas híbridas*, p. 110.

62. Yurkievich, 'Julio Cortázar: al Unísono y al Dísono', *Revista Iberoamericana*, vol. xxxix, no. 84–85 (1973), 411–24 (p. 420).

63. Marshall McLuhan, *Understanding Media: The Extensions of Man* (London: Ark, 1987), p. 4.

64. Julio Cortázar, *Fantomas contra los vampiros multinacionales* (Buenos Aires: Ediciones Destino, 2002), p. 72.

65. Marshall McLuhan, *Understanding Media*, p. 5.

66. Schwartz, *Invenciones urbanas*, p. 79.

67. Jorge Rodríguez Padrón, 'Un itinerario cortazariano: "El otro cielo"', in *Cuadernos hispanoamericanos, Homenaje a Julio Cortázar* (1980), 495–509 (p. 509).

68. Paredes, *Abismos de papel*, p. 234.

69. See Martiń-Barbero, *Communication*, pp. 177–78.

70. The name Laurent, as Emir Rodríguez Monegal suggests in 'Le Fantôme de Lautréamont', is a reduction of the name Lautréamont, the pseudonym of the Montevidean writer Isidore Ducasse, whose works exerted a strong influence on the Surrealists. Indeed, the two epigraphs in the story belong to his narrative poem *Les Chants de Maldoror* (1868), to which 'El otro cielo' owes much inspiration, particularly in its setting (the neighbourhood of the galleries in which both Lautréamont and his protagonist Maldoror lived), and its use of doubles: the Argentine narrator and his Parisian other; Laurent and the 'sudamericano'. See Emir Rodríguez Monegal, 'Le Fantôme de Lautréamont', in *Narradores de esta América*, vol. 2 (Buenos Aires: Editorial Alfa Argentina, 1974), pp. 156–73.

71. Martiń-Barbero, *Communication*, p. 177.

72. Cited by Martiń-Barbero, *Communication*, p. 196.

73. Boldy, *The Novels of Julio Cortázar*, p. 41.

74. Benjamin, 'On Some Motifs in Baudelaire', in *Illuminations*, pp. 157–96 (p. 177).

75. Alicia d'Amico, Sara Facio, Julio Cortázar, *Buenos Aires Buenos Aires* (Buenos Aires: Editorial Sudamericana, 1968), p. 22.

76. Cortázar, 'La urna griega en la poesía de John Keats' (1946), in *Obra crítica 2*, pp. 31–100 (p. 88).

77. Practical considerations force me to narrow my focus to three stories, but this is not to say that these are the only texts in the collection that enclose strong intermedial properties. On the contrary, intermediality is overtly omnipresent in this collection. Key examples include the play on the idea of film editing and mechanical reproduction in 'Queremos tanto a Glenda'; the exploration of the mysterious, ominous Buenos Aires underground system in 'Texto en una libreta'; the use of the visual medium of the window frame and the trope of dance in 'Tango de vuelto'; the variations on the Baroque fragments of Bach's *Musical Offering* in 'Clone'; the use of jazz, visual image and filmic technique in 'Historias que me cuento'; and the various states through which the dying Janet passes in 'Anillo de Moebius' (geometrical shapes like cubes and polyhedrons; states like hot and cold, liquid and solid; media like musical scores; complex, modern systems like mathematical sets and computer circuits).

78. Aníbal González, ' "Press Clippings" and Cortázar's Ethics of Writing', in Maurice Hemingway and Frank McQuade, 'The Writer and Politics in Four Stories by Julio Cortázar'; Amanda Holmes, *City Fictions: Language, Body, and Spanish American Urban Space* (Lewisburg, PA: Bucknell University Press, 2007).

79. Swanson, *The New Novel*, p. 7.

80. Aníbal González, ' "Press Clippings" and Cortázar's Ethics of Writing', in *Julio Cortázar*, ed. by Alonso, pp. 237–57 (p. 238).

81. Cortázar, 'La literatura latinoamericana a la luz de la historia contemporánea' (1980), in *Obra crítica 3* (Buenos Aires: Editora Argentina, 2004), pp. 263–84 (pp. 270–71).

82. Roberto González Echevarría, '*Biografía de un cimarrón* and the Novel of the Cuban Revolution', *Novel: A Forum on Fiction*, 13 (1980), 249–63 (p. 250).

83. Cortázar, 'Discurso en la constitución del jurado del Premio Literario Casa de las Américas 1980', in *Obra crítica 3*, pp. 285–302 (p. 295).

84. Cortázar, 'Discurso en el Recibo del Orden Rubén Darío' (1983), in *Obra crítica 3*, pp. 475–90 (p. 480).

85. Cortázar, 'Nicaragua desde adentro' (1982), in *Obra crítica 3*, pp. 437–58 (p. 439).

86. García Canclini, *Culturas híbridas*, p. 42.

87. Amanda Holmes, *City Fictions*, pp. 70–71.

88. Holmes, *City Fictions*, p. 79.

89. Julio Cortázar, *Queremos tanto a Glenda* (Buenos Aires: Santillana, 2010), p. 64. Hereafter, all references to this edition will be made within the body of the text.

90. Cortázar, 'Negación del olvido' (1981), in *Obra crítica 3*, pp. 419–28 (p. 424).

91. García Canclini, *Culturas híbridas*, p. 316.

92. Cortázar, 'Nuevo elogio de la locura' (1981), in *Obra crítica 3*, pp. 429–36 (p. 432).

93. Henri Bergson, *The Creative Mind*, p. 93.

94. Cited by Martín-Barbero, *Communication*, p. 199.

95. McLuhan, *Understanding Media*, p. 8.

96. Elleström, p. 4. See also W. J. Thomas Mitchell, *Picture Theory: Essays on Verbal and Visual Representation* (Chicago, IL: University of Chicago Press, 1995), p. 5.

97. Cortázar, 'Algunos aspectos', p. 526.

98. See in particular Frederick Lewis Pattee, *The Development of the American Short Story* (New York: Harper & Bros., 1923); Andrew Levy, *The Culture and Commerce of the American Short Story* (Cambridge: Cambridge University Press, 1993); and Stuart Sillars, *Visualisation in Popular Fiction, 1860–1960: Graphic Narratives, Fictional Images* (London; New York: Routledge, 1995).

99. McLuhan, *Understanding Media*, p. 204.

CHAPTER 3

Augusto Monterroso, the Microwriter

Introduction: Hybrid Forms and Cultures

In the previous chapters, I explored Rulfo's and Cortázar's art of fragmentation. I challenged some of the conventional views of the Latin American short story, arguing that the oral, mythical or 'primitive' aspects of the form are dialectically intertwined with features of modern aesthetics and technological media. My contention is that the generic, spatio-temporal limits of the short story are connected not only with historical limits — the Benjaminian 'death of the storyteller', the decay of rural communities, the rupture from tradition — but also medial boundaries, the sites at which the short story form is infiltrated by other media, whether the fragmentary novel or the poem, the newspaper article or the photograph, the cinematic shot or the sculpture. The limits, therefore, are not just a symptom of loss and decay, but also positive points of departure, windows into different expressive, communicational possibilities.

In this final chapter, I shall add an important dimension to the study by analysing the work of a third, lesser known writer, Augusto Monterroso. Relating his work to that of his more famed and recognized friends and contemporaries, Rulfo and Cortázar, will enable me to fulfil several interrelated goals. The first is to place the work of this modest, cripplingly self-doubting writer in relation to broader aesthetic trends. By pointing to the dialogue between his work and that of his contemporaries, I will highlight his crucial contribution to the development of the short story genre — a genre to which his *oeuvre*, like that of Rulfo and Cortázar, both belongs and exceeds. This is not to reduce his work to simple definitions but rather to shed light on its complexities, on the way it explodes its own limits; not to restrict his idiosyncratic art to a classificatory corset, but rather to better understand it within a wider aesthetic and socio-cultural context.

The second purpose is to help unravel the intrinsic contradictions of the short story, a genre rooted in an oral, rural tradition and uprooted by print culture and urban modernity. His work will help to mediate the tensions, resulting partly from this inherent formal paradox, between the works of Rulfo and Cortázar, who fit uneasily under the same umbrella, associated as they are with nostalgia and celebration, tradition and modernity, country and city, respectively. As I have argued in the previous chapters, critics have reinforced, and to a certain extent constructed, these reductive oppositions, which I shall seek to problematize and dismantle through the work of Monterroso. This is not to say that this chapter will smooth over these tensions. Quite the contrary, I wish to be faithful to the contradictions inherent in the hybrid genre of the short story, and consequently between the works in my corpus. As Martín-Barbero insists, the aim must not be to avoid the contradictions inherent in *mestizaje*, but rather to 'move them out of their established schemas so that we can take a fresh look at them in the process of their composition and decomposition' (188). In so doing, I hope to do justice to an author for whom the denial of contradiction is a failure to embrace life and its complexities, as suggested by this self-reflexive, unpublished *microcuento* (1984): '— En su texto de ayer hay una contradicción. / — Fue la única que pude lograr.'[1] In what follows, I shall read Monterroso's work as a composition and decomposition of contradictory cultural forms, modes and media.

The contradiction between the seeming hermeticism of the short story, and its constant flirtation with other media, is apparent in Monterroso's reflections on his own writing, the short story and modern literature. In a fragment entitled 'El otro mundo' (*La letra e*), he affirms: 'Falta en lo que he hecho, en lo que hago, el mundo del cine, de la radio, del periodismo, de la televisión, eso de que me he mantenido alejado y que podría constituir en el futuro la expresión de nuestra época.'[2] In a typically Monterrosian manner, this text contradicts itself in order to provoke its reader. Monterroso claims that his literary writing excludes other modern, technological media, which belong to the titular other world and to the future. Yet by provocatively placing this 'other world' at the very centre of this fragment, Monterroso deliberately undermines his own claim, suggesting that these supposedly alien media in fact lie at the very heart of the production and reception of his literary texts. This suggestion is reinforced in his unpublished notes for a course on the modern short story, where he writes that

> El escritor de hoy no puede ser el mismo que era antes de los inventos de hoy: el teléfono, la radio, el cine, la televisión, los aviones, la electrónica. AUNQUE EL HOMBRE NO CAMBIA sí hay una cierta manera distinta de percibir las cosas y de comunicarlas. Hoy no se escribe una carta; se llama por teléfono. No se describe un paisaje, porque el lector ya lo ha visto en el cine, etc.[3] (Monterroso's capitals)

The modern writer, according to this assertive passage, is necessarily part of the 'other world', the world of modern communications: telephones, radios, cinema, television, planes, and computers. Written in the context of a class on the modern short story, this fragment is both relevant and revealing. The implication is that this supposedly independent, self-contained literary genre is heavily dependent on, and impacted by, the rise of other media; its internal characteristics respond to external changes and demands.

Monterroso's interest in the infiltration of extraneous media into modern literature is demonstrated further by an intertextual fragment entitled 'Marinetti' (*La letra e*), in which he translates a section from Giovanni Lista's catalogue *Le livre futuriste, de la libération du mot au poème tactile* (1984):

> La poesía buscó nuevas formas lingüísticas por medio de los grafismos abstractos, las láminas o planchas 'librepalabristas', los poemas táctiles, las composiciones plásticas, etcétera. El libro se convirtió así en 'libro-objeto' o 'libro de artista'

> y reencontró su materialidad o devino la base de una integración de la pintura
> y la escritura. (355)

Marinetti's futurist writing constitutes a fierce attempt to liberate the word from
the book, and vice-versa. Monterroso thus presents a particular reaction to the
threat posed to the written word by the explosion of modern artistic forms, like
photography, cinema, and other image-based media. Yet he also supplements this
quotation with the provocative comment that the futurist rebellion is in fact 'ni más
ni menos — habría que añadir — que lo que se hacía con los libros iluminados,
de oración y profanos, de antes de la invención de la imprenta' (356). By linking
this supposedly avant-garde movement to the Illuminations tradition, Monterroso
deconstructs the chronological opposition between future and past, modern and
medieval.

As we shall see, the deconstruction of dualistic reasoning is a constant aspect
of Monterroso's work. Particularly relevant to this examination of the short story
genre is the way in which Monterroso blurs the distinctions between spoken and
printed word. 'Premio Juan Rulfo' (*La vaca*, 1998) presents a metatextual storytelling scene. Gathered around the fire telling tales, 'el dulce acento brasileño de
Nélida [Piñón] nos hacía sentirnos vivamente unidos a la gran literatura de su
país'.[4] Monterroso therefore creates a dialectical interplay between an author, who
has won the titular literary prize for her novels and short stories, and a performer,
who enchants her listeners through the sensual musicality of her voice; whose oral
storytelling nonetheless produces a connection to the great literature of her country,
Brazil. Conversely, 'Los libros tienen su propia suerte' concerns the printed word.
Once printed, a book becomes an independent object, with its own fate, its own
life: 'el libro correrá su propia suerte y va a prosperar o a ser olvidado, o ambas cosas,
cada una a su tiempo. / No importa lo que hagas por él o con él.'[5] This might be
read as a kind of tongue-in-cheek response to, and extension of, Cortázar's 'Del
cuento breve', with which Monterroso was familiar:[6] severed from his literary
creation, the author is powerless, incapable of controlling its fate. The book is a
kind of autonomous body, which 'speaks' for itself, following its own trajectory,
whether through lofts or shop windows. Furthermore, an oral element is restored
to the printed text which may, the narrator suggests, spend a fleeting moment 'en
boca de todos' (9).

Critics have often fallen short of acknowledging the structural dialectical relations
that will be the principal concern of this chapter. As suggested by the very title of
her article, 'El decálogo del escritor de Augusto Monterroso: un ars poética singular',
Gloria Hernández focuses on his artistic idiosyncrasy.[7] José Miguel Oviedo points
out that his ironic humour is 'su modo personal de decir no, de burlarse de todo
lo establecido (la literatura, entre otras cosas) y de estimular gozosamente nuestra
propia rebeldía'.[8] Yet, as I shall argue, his personal brand of humour is formally
linked to broader aesthetic and social processes of fragmentation. The aim of this
chapter is to tie in his witty *ars poetica*, without detracting from its singularity, with
the web of dialectical relations that underpin the short story form.

Other critics have regarded Monterroso as a fundamental member of a
distinct group of writers, whose subgenre is called, variously, the *microcuento*, the

minicuento, the *cuento ultracorto*, or the *texto narrativo brevísimo*. Recent examples include Lauro Zavala's *La minificción bajo el microscopio* (2006), Guillermo Siles's book on the formation of the subgenre in the twentieth century (2007), and David Lagmanovich's article on the Spanish-American *microrrelato* (1994).[9] Others, like Juan Armando Epple in *Brevísima relación*, have anthologized his stories alongside other *microcuentos*.[10] The principal shortcoming of these critical works is that they often regard this subgenre as an exclusive formal product of the twentieth century rather than a complex mixture of traditional and modern elements. As suggested by his title, Siles's work focuses of the 'formation' of a modern genre. Under the same guiding conviction, Zavala opens his book with the affirmation that 'la minificción es el género más reciente de la historia literaria. Su nacimiento ocurrió a principios del siglo en México' (7). Yet these views omit the dual origins of Monterroso's brevity which, as the author affirms on several occasions, is not so much a new form as the renewal of a tradition. In a 1995 interview with Carlos Morales, for example, he is questioned on the nature of his aesthetics of brevity:

> C.M. — Usted buscaba la brevedad o fue un proceso natural?
> A.M. — Fue una cosa natural... Probablemente porque mis lecturas más comunes eran autores breves: poemas de autores latinos como Horacio, Catulo, Persio... De allí salté yo a los clásicos españoles, donde también me atrajeron los autores más breves, ¿no?, como Graciano y otros.[11]

Less than a deliberate rupture or a calculated choice as Rulfo and Cortázar affirm, Monterroso sees his aesthetics of brevity as a natural product of his readings, a continuation of tradition. The classical influences in Monterroso's fiction have been examined in specialist articles, such as that by José Miralles Maldonado, which indicates the multifarious presence of the classical fable (Phaedrus, Babrius, Aesop) in the themes, form and structure of Monterroso's work; and the points of contact between his *ars poetica* and that of Horace.[12]

By playing out the tensions that permeate Monterroso's minimalist aesthetics, I shall attempt to bridge the gap between the studies of the twentieth-century, modern aspects of his work on the one hand, and the classical, traditional elements on the other. In this sense, I shall align myself with Lauro Zavala, who considers him a postmodern writer because of his tendency to juxtapose contradictory cultural elements. Zavala, in seeking to map out the short story and the micro-story, distinguishes between three types of narrative forms: classical, modern and postmodern:

> Lo clásico es propiamente tradicional, mientras lo moderno, como ha señalado Octavio Paz, establece una *tradición de ruptura*. [...] La dimensión posmoderna de un texto o de una interpretación intertextual posmoderna consiste, precisamente, en la superposición de elementos clásicos y anti-clásicos.[13]

Monterroso's work can only be properly understood if it is regarded under the third umbrella, in all its contradictions and multiplicities. Its incorporation of classical traditions and modern phenomena has an effect not of return or rupture, but of renewal. This gesture is significant in the context of Latin American modernity. As García Canclini suggests in *Culturas híbridas*, postmodern relativism profoundly undermines any fundamentalism or evolutionism, and thus permits the elaboration of 'un pensamiento más abierto para abarcar las interacciones e integraciones entre los niveles, géneros y formas de la sensibilidad colectiva' (23). As we shall see, Monterroso's art destabilizes any perceived boundaries, creating artistic openings from heterogeneous forms and genres.

Indeed, another aspect of Monterroso's fiction that has received some critical attention is its generic hybridity, its cannibalistic ability to incorporate fables, short stories, essays, diary entries, parabola and aphorisms, as well as other ill-defined genres like quasi-philosophical reflections, humorous anecdotes and literary fragments.[14] Yet I wish to go beyond the scope of these studies to ask how *generic* hybridity relates more widely to *cultural* hybridity. For García Canclini, *historietas* and graffiti are products of, and contributions to, cultural hybridization: they constitute bridges between art and journalism, images and words, and different genres; they are consumed collectively, by different sectors of the public, different members of the family; they break down the divisions between *lo culto* and *lo popular* (316). Though the fate of Monterroso's stories is certainly not that of the popular *historietas* — the literature with the best sales and highest revenue in Mexico at the time that García Canclini writes *Culturas híbridas* — their generic hybridity suggests a desire to loosen up cultural distinctions, to unite different modes of production and consumption, different types of audiences and readers.

The point of departure for this chapter will be Wilfrido Corral's point of arrival: 'en la última instancia Monterroso y sus textos traducen los intersticios de varias culturas y la reacción humana a los secretos escondidos en ellos'.[15] In the first section, I shall examine the transcultural facets of his collage work *Movimiento perpetuo* (1972), which consists of short stories, essays and intertextual fragments. The fly — in the essay that opens the collection and in the quotations with which it is peppered — will provide a frame through which to look at the paradoxes that underlie two manifestations of his fragmentary aesthetics: the collection and the short story. In the second section, I shall turn back to look at his first — and only, in the strictest generic sense — short story collection, *Obras completas (y otros cuentos)* (1959). Here, I shall go beyond an examination of the generic hybridity of his fiction to examine in detail its medial and cultural hybridity which, though crucial to his aesthetics, has largely been overlooked by his critics.

Beware of Flying Objects: Structural Paradoxes in *Movimiento perpetuo*

> El ensayo del cuento del poema de
> la vida es un movimiento perpetuo
> (*Movimiento Perpetuo*, 7)

In the first chapter, I approached Rulfo's art of fragmentation through some of the recurring tropes that dominate his stories: bodies, corpses and ruins. A comparable figure around which Monterroso's writing revolves, and which revolves around his writing, is that of the fly. It appears fleetingly under multiple guises: a collectable object, an irritating presence, an aesthetico-philosophical concept, a god-like figure, a harbinger of death and an assurance of perpetual life, to name but a few. I shall argue that Monterroso's playful treatment of this complex, paradoxical and evasive creature is a highly self-reflexive one, a *mise en abyme* of his self-contradicting aesthetics. It stands at once for life and death, reproduction and decay, movement and stagnation, time and timelessness, finitude and infinity, particularity and universality, centrality and marginality. In this respect, it furnishes a deeper insight not only into Monterroso's own writing, but also into the dialectical relations that characterize — and indeed form the basis of — the short stories of his forebears and contemporaries. These complex interrelations far exceed the scope of this book, and indeed the literary genre of the short story. Nevertheless, by using Monterroso's flies as a way of unpacking the tensions within, and between, the works of Rulfo and Cortázar, we might — through the synecdochic logic that underpins the art of the short story — deepen our understanding of the complexities and contradictions that underpin the Latin American *cuento*.

In an interview with Jorge Ruffinelli, Monterroso insists that this collection is entirely lacking a single, organizing principle:

> Es un libro misceláneo: yo no 'quería' hacerlo desde un principio. Se fue haciendo con pequeños ensayos y cuentos de diverso carácter; algunos textos fueron escritos para él, otros estaban hechos sin saber que irían a parar allí. [...] Como de mis otros libros, espero que no tenga ninguna unicidad.[16]

This statement is surely enough to put any willing critic off attempting a sustained reading of this collection and might go some way to explaining the fact that critical attention to Monterroso's work has been relatively light — in length, quantity and spirit. Yet as I shall argue, a logical strand does underpin this work: its (disparate, dislocated) unity lies in its contradictions, its warring principles. It is the reader's task to (re)construct these tensions. Since Monterroso's warring principles are always dialectically intertwined, since his contradictions are invariably mutually dependent, the process of reading is one of simultaneous construction and deconstruction, building and dismantling, composition and decomposition. By approaching the unstable text through the fly, I shall seek to answer Margo Glantz's provocative question, '¿es su persistente zumbido el que unifica los distintos textos reunidos bajo el título de *Movimiento perpetuo*?'[17]

In what follows, I shall examine *Movimiento perpetuo* through the opening essay 'Las moscas', the intertextual fly quotations, and the stories and essays themselves. These will help untangle two principal, interconnected aspects of his aesthetics of fragmentation. The first is the art of the collection, which I shall unpack by attempting — while accepting the necessary vanity of this endeavour — to grasp Monterroso's fly in its incarnation as a material object, a collector's item. The second is the art of the short story, which I will examine through the ever-morphing form of the fly that bears a close relation with the perpetual motion of Monterroso's aesthetics. Since the collection is invariably the location in which the short story begins or ends its published life, it is inextricably bound to the form and aesthetics of the genre. Yet the link between the short story and the collection is not just a practical one: it is also a complex, formal, aesthetic-philosophical one.

The collector's mentality permeates Monterroso's literary production and personal habits — two domains that are closely intertwined, as suggested by his own description of *Movimiento perpetuo* as a 'personal anthology' (cited above). The

Fig. 10. Augusto Monterroso, Drawing, *Wine glasses*
Series 3: Drawings and Photographs; 1941–93; Augusto Monterroso Papers, Box 41–47;
Manuscripts Division, Department of Rare Books and Special Collections,
Princeton University Library

fly collection is symptomatic of an obsessive tendency displayed in many areas of his life: his mania for collecting books, satirized in 'Cómo me deshice de quinientos libros';[18] his tendency to hoard manifested in his unpublished papers (the dozens of files containing hundreds of letters, for example, amount to a collection); and even his series of drawings with repeated subjects — shoes, wine glasses, coffee cups, among many others (see Fig. 10).

It is the same cumulative principle that drives the fly collection: 'Hace años tuve la idea de reunir una antología universal de la mosca. La sigo teniendo. Sin embargo, pronto me di cuenta de que era una empresa prácticamente infinita' (11). Monterroso narrowly avoids turning into his character Leopoldo, whose obsession with acquiring complete knowledge of the two subjects of his story — the porcupine and the dog — ends in perpetual failure and postponement of the work in question.[19] As can be seen in the vast set of quotations preserved in the Augusto Monterroso Papers, which far exceeds those contained in the collage of *Movimiento perpetuo*, the search for textual flies became a habit for many years of his life.[20] A creature which revolves endlessly, and which is so hard to shake off, the fly is emblematic of this obsession.

Yet this cumulative, totalizing, and universalizing practice is in fact the underside of the short story's art of abbreviation, partiality and singularity. Roger Cardinal, in *The Culture of Collecting*, elaborates on the paradoxical quality of the collector:

> I see the collector as one caught in a constant vacillation, between the hankering for perfection and the need to tolerate imperfection, between an ideal of wholeness and the anxiety of incompleteness. Whatever the collection, its true history can never be an even one; its narrative is always informed by both design and accident, coverage and lack, permanence and impermanence, the unique and the redundant.[21]

A supplementary logic underpins the serial nature of the collection: the constant possibility of adding another piece betrays its inherent incompleteness. Monterroso displays an acute awareness of this dilemma from the outset. In a footnote in 'Las moscas', he notes that 'a lo largo de este libro verán una pequeña muestra, absolutamente insuficiente' (11). This helps explain the continuity underlying the seemingly opposing forms adopted by Cortázar, Rulfo and Monterroso: the (deceptively) unified, hermetic short stories on the one hand, and the heterogeneous, dispersed fragmentary novels and collage works on the other. In fact, both are governed by a shared formal logic of supplementation, by a dialectical interplay between limitation and boundlessness, perfection and imperfection.

The Fly and the Collection

'Las moscas', the prologue-like essay that opens *Movimiento perpetuo*, furnishes a maddeningly complex vantage point from which to approach the collection. Monterroso's fly is portrayed as a vessel through which culture is transported:

> Las moscas transportan, heredándose infinitamente la carga, las almas de nuestros muertos, de nuestros antepasados, que así continúan cerca de nosotros, empeñados en protegernos. Nuestras pequeñas almas transmigran a través de ellas y ellas acumulan sabiduría y conocen todo lo que nosotros no nos atrevemos

> a conocer. Quizá el último transmisor de nuestra torpe cultura occidental sea
> el cuerpo de esa mosca, que ha venido reproduciéndose sin enriquecerse a lo
> largo de los siglos. (12)

The bodies of flies, as depicted here, constitute an assurance of the continuity of tradition. As vessels of mediation and transmission, they link one generation to the next, passing down the burden of wisdom, the accumulated layers of knowledge that constitute culture. The buzzing fly belongs to an ancient lineage: 'La mosca que hoy se posó en [tu nariz] es descendiente directa de la que se paró en la de Cleopatra [...] La mosca quiere que la envuelvas en esa atmósfera de reyes, papas y emperadores. Y lo logra. Te domina. No puedes hablar de ella sin sentirte inclinado a la grandeza' (13). Because it is attached to the distant past and thus bears the weight of tradition, the fly is endowed with a regal, papal authority.

In the context of this connection between religion, authority and tradition, it seems fitting to compare Monterroso's 'Las moscas' with Benjamin's 'Unpacking my Library' (1931) — an essay about his book collection that might be regarded as a companion piece to 'The Storyteller'. Benjamin's collector, like his storyteller, is endowed with inherited, accumulated wisdom. Hence the concern with each object's original context: 'the period, the region, the craftsmanship, the former owner — for a true collector the whole background of an item adds up to a magic encyclopedia'.[22] The term 'encyclopedia' suggests that the practice of collecting, like that of storytelling, is embedded in a unity and totality of knowledge. Supplemented entry by entry, it is cumulative and continuous. This is confirmed by his later assertion that

> inheritance is the soundest way of acquiring a collection. For a collector's atti-
> tude toward his possessions stems from an owner's feeling responsibility toward
> his property. Thus it is, in the highest sense, the attitude of an heir, and the most
> distinguished trait of a collection will always be its transmissibility. (66)

As with the storyteller, the collector's attitude toward a cultural tradition is one of reverence; his responsibility is to preserve objects as they are received. Hence Benjamin prophesies the same fate for the collector as for the storyteller: 'time is running out for the type that I am discussing here', since 'the phenomenon of collecting loses its meaning as it loses its personal owner' (67). Just as the decay of authority and tradition entailed the death of the storyteller and storytelling, here it entails the death of the owner — as personal receptor and repository of knowledge — and of the collection.

Yet a significant divergence is apparent between Benjamin's book collection and Monterroso's fly collection. Whereas Benjamin's is a private collection, whose objects retain their connection to the past through their personal owner, Monterroso's is a public collection, by virtue of its publication, reproduction and dissemination. The flies are released from their owner, and therefore severed from their original contexts. One might say that the severance is twofold: first, as individual quotations, they are cut out from their original textual, authorial context; second, as a published collection, they are liberated from their 'owner', Monterroso, to meet their own fate. They are decidedly divorced from any 'whole background', severed from an over-arching narrative. In this sense, the relation between Benjamin and his books on the one hand, and Monterroso and his flies on the other, can be seen in Susan Stewart's terms as relations to two distinct objects: the souvenir and the collection.

> In contrast to the souvenir, [...] the collection does not displace attention to the past; rather, the past is at the service of the collection, for whereas the souvenir lends authenticity to the past, the past lends authenticity to the collection. The collection seeks a form of self-enclosure which is possible because of its ahistoricism.[23]

Whereas the souvenir is past-oriented, the collection is future-oriented, severing objects from their origin and placing them in new relations and configurations. In turn, this severance is multiplied *ad infinitum* by the process of mechanical reproduction. As García Canclini suggests, technologies of mechanical reproduction change the nature of the literary text: for example, photocopying (one of the ways in which Monterroso lifted his fly quotations from their original context[24]) creates a 'relación fragmentaria con los libros [que] lleva a perder la estructura en que se insertan los capítulos' (284). Texts and images are disarticulated from their contexts. Meanings are untied from unifying semantic and historical references. The fragmentation of the literary work is highlighted by Monterroso himself in 'Fe de erratas y advertencia final': 'el libro termina en esta página, la 151, sin que eso impida que también pueda comenzar de nuevo en ella' (151). Placed out of chronological time, the collection is reversible, and thus guarantees — like Schopenhauer's flies (77) — a never-ending cycle of regeneration and rebirth.

Monterroso's playful collector is crucially distinct from Benjamin's dutiful collector/storyteller. The latter, reverent toward cultural tradition, preserves the past by remembering and retelling; the former, jovially irreverent, reinvents it by forgetting and reappropriating. This is made evident by Monterroso in his prologue to *La letra e*, which begins with an ironic reference to Jorge Manrique's *Coplas por la muerte de su padre*:

> Nuestros libros son los ríos que van a dar en la mar que es el olvido.
> La primera versión de las líneas que siguen se halla en cuadernos, pedazos de papel, programas de teatro, cuentas de hoteles y hasta billetes de tren; la segunda, a manera de Diario, en un periódico mexicano; la tercera, en este libro. (229)

Preserving scraps of fleeting experiences scribbled down on trains, in hotels and at the theatre is a process that involves selecting and discarding. Keeping hold of memories requires them to be constantly displaced and disconnected, rather than fixed in any given context. Like *La letra e,* the fly collage is the remainder that has resisted a long process of gathering and discarding, decontextualizing and recontextualizing. Its flies survive not in spite of, but rather because of, the continual act of forgetting, which endows them with infinite afterlives. 'Las criadas' (*Movimiento perpetuo*) might therefore be regarded as a metatextual representation of the Monterrosian collector:

> [Leen] en los restos de las tazas de café o de las copas de vino, en las colillas, o sencillamente introduciendo sus miradas furtivas [...] debajo de las almohadas, o recogiendo los pedacitos de los papeles rotos y el eco de nuestros pleitos. (95)

The maids' territory and reality are built around the minimal remainder, the insignificant left-over, the faint echo; residues that form the basis of their own inventions and imaginings. As shown by their filched goods, their 'caja de Nescafé o de Kellog's llena de ropa y de peines y de mínimos espejos' (95), they encroach on the territory of others and repossess its minimal treasures. The story might be read as an allegory for the Latin American writer appropriating and reinventing Western cultural products, represented here by Nescafé and Kellogg's. Like the symbolic maids, Monterroso — as can also be seen in *La oveja negra*, which, for reasons of space, is not included in this study — collects bits and pieces from other cultures in order to produce liberating reconfigurations.

In that sense, his attitude toward the fly-object is closer to that which Benjamín manifests in his transition in the thirties from book collector to quotation collector, one which would eventually come into fruition in his *Arcades Project* — a work composed between 1927 and 1940 that, like Monterroso's fly collection, would remain unfinished. As Arendt notes, his study of German tragedy is a mark of this shift:

> The main work consisted in tearing fragments out of their context and arranging them afresh in such a way that they illustrated one another and were able to prove their *raison d'être* in a free-floating state, as it were. It definitely was a sort of surrealistic montage. (47)

Breaking the spell of tradition, here, becomes not a negative rupture, but a positive one. Instead of mourning the traditional storyteller or collector, who hands down the past as a continuous string of acquired knowledge, Benjamín embraces the notion of cutting the string into little pieces, loose strands that can be tied together anew. The transmissibility of the past through continuity is replaced by the notion of transmission through rupture; specifically, through fragmentary narrative, quotation and montage. It is with this stage of Benjamín's development that Monterroso's art of the fragment — his status as fly collector — resonates. Indeed, like Benjamín, Monterroso was influenced by surrealism. In a 1984 diary entry, he reflects upon a possible form for his weekly diary fragments for *El sábado* (which would end up published as a collection in *La letra e*):

> Cada día siento más el deseo de abandonar la tarea, pero me detiene la idea de encontrar mi propia forma, por ejemplo evitando absolutamente el estilo convencional del diario, ahora pienso en algo como 'anotaciones', pequeños ensayos sobre cualquier tema. Quizá una especie de escritura automática surrealista en la que entre todo lo que me pase por la cabeza, sin apelar a la razón, libre, libre como lo que comencé hoy en la mañana. Sí; esto podría tener algo de original: mezcla de recuerdos, titulares de periódicos, trozos de cartas, recibidas y por contestar...[25]

Notes, little essays, headlines, pieces of unwritten letters: the logic of collected fragments, which might 'prove their *raison d'être* in a free-floating state', drives Monterroso's experimentation with form. This surrealist sensibility arguably lurks behind *Movimiento perpetuo*, whose montage of collected fragments creates new worlds by cutting, tearing, and wrenching pieces of text from their context. It is one shared with Cortázar, whose character la Maga, as Sara Castro-Klarén points out, might be likened to Breton's 'modest registering machine': walking around Paris, 'she goes from window to window, scanning and recognizing all the exceptional objects they contain without submitting them to any laws of taxonomy, letting them find their own affinities and associations.'[26] Monterroso's 'collecting tendencies', like la Maga's, unite the ordinary with the exceptional, the common and the strange, the logical and the aleatory. Just as *Rayuela* foreshadows Cortázar's later collage works, *Movimiento perpetuo* prefigures the surrealist principle underlying Monterroso's diary fragments, which end up collected in *La letra e*. The seeds of the aesthetic trajectory that leads both these authors towards collective works are thus already present in their earlier works in the spirit of the collector.

To conclude this section on the collection, however, it must be pointed out that the art of collecting is not regarded by Monterroso as a solely positive tendency. In fact, Benjamin's 'Unpacking my Library' can be directly contrasted with Monterroso's story about book collecting: 'Cómo me deshice de quinientos libros'. Here, the narrator recounts his (failed) attempt to get rid of some of his books. Collecting, here, is not seen in its glory, but rather in ostensibly negative terms, in terms of hoarding ('el mero afán de acumular', 91) and fetishism (the books are referred to as 'esos fetiches', 92). In contrast to Benjamin's treasured objects, which he seeks to preserve in order to retain an attachment to his and their past, Monterroso's books are treated as piles of unredeemable rubbish. He is trying to part from them, but troubled by the dilemma that 'tirarlos uno por uno a la basura no era digno de mí, de los libros, ni del basurero' (91–92). In a sense, one might see this as a parodic self-reflection of *Movimiento perpetuo*: he gets rid of the flies by publishing them and passing them on. López Parada makes this connection in her suggestive question: '¿dónde se tiran quinientos cuerpos exánimes de moscas, dónde en el fondo, se abandonan quinientos libros?' (217) His deficient solution is to send them to friends, as an alternative to donating or burning them. Yet like James Joyce's ' "mosca pegajosa" ' (119) — the image of the annoying, intrusive pest — the books return (by mail, in some cases) to taunt him (92).

This story might be seen as a parody — whether deliberate or coincidental — of Benjamin's link between the book collection and the accumulation of tradition, wisdom and knowledge. Collected books, the narrator suggests, give one 'la sensación de ser más sabios e incluso la más falaz e inútil de ser los depositarios de un saber que en todo caso no es sino el repetido testimonio de la ignorancia o la ingenuidad humanas' (92). The notion of inherited wisdom creates a link between the collected books and the flies of 'Las moscas', which 'acumulan sabiduría' (cited above). This notion is belittled, derided, and even turned upside down, as the delusion of wisdom through cumulative, bookish knowledge is merely the 'repeated testimony of human ignorance'. Audible here is another echo of 'Las moscas', whose narrator mocks the 'frases mosca' that all writers, including him in his phrase 'en el principio fue la mosca', fall into adopting: 'las frases perseguidoras de que están llenos nuestros libros' (12). Literature, then, is ultimately a fly-catcher, a collection of set phrases, prefabricated expressions, and inherited clichés. Hence Monterroso's constant attempt not only to collect, to repeat and to quote, but also to discard, to transform and to reinvent.

The Fly and the Short Story

In the previous section, I explored the ways in which Monterroso's fly-objects shed light on the dual logic underpinning the collection, which corresponds to jarring attitudes towards cultural tradition: a simultaneous attachment and detachment; respect and irreverence; a desire both to preserve and to discard. These tensions amount to a complex game in which the reader is invited to participate.

I shall now move on to examine the relationship between the fly quotations and the aesthetics of the short story. My argument is that the quotations act as fireflies whose flashes illuminate, from particular angles, the complex art of brevity. Buzzing as they do between different countries, time periods and genres, they are self-reflexive embodiments of the cultural interstitiality of Monterroso's fragmentary art. Put differently, the common (in both senses of the term) subject of the fly creates a network of relations between the contradictory elements that underpin the Latin American short story. By tying Monterroso's anthologized flies to fly-related texts by Rulfo and Cortázar — some collected by him, others probably unknown to him — I shall attempt to (re)construct a dialogue between the three authors of my corpus.

As I have already pointed out, Monterroso insists on the lack of structural unity in *Movimiento perpetuo*. This insistence takes on an interesting character in an interview with Marco Antonio Campos:

> M.A.C. — ¿Siguió algún modelo para la estructura de *Movimiento perpetuo*?
> A.M. — No; ninguno.
> M.A.C. — ¿Qué, si no es un género determinado, rige y ordena el libro?
> A.M. — Los libros son simples depósitos. Son como cajas. Uno puede poner eñ un libro una novela o varios cuentos, varios poemas y varios ensayos. Uno tiene algo y lo coloca allí.[27]

Monterroso rejects the need for any determining order, be it generic or other: for him, a book is a box-like container, a paper warehouse in which different textual objects are temporarily stored before they continue their perpetual journey. Later, when pushed by Campos regarding a possible 'law' for the short story, he cedes thus: 'una buena ley sería que el cuento no sea novela ni poema ni ensayo, y que a la vez sea ensayo y novela y poema siempre que siga siendo esa cosa misteriosa que se llama cuento'.[28] Humorously nudging the reader, Monterroso underlines the self-contradictory form of the short story, which as we have seen is simultaneously well-defined and ill-defined, hermetic and open, resistant and porous. It follows that the short story itself is a kind of box, an uncontained container that is seemingly hermetically sealed, but in fact exceeds its own limits.

Before tying Monterroso's fly quotations to the form of the short story, I shall begin by examining the chaotic hybridity of the collection, whose combination and reconfiguration of fragments from a pre-existing signifying code constitutes a *bricolage*, to use a term developed by Claude Lévi-Strauss in the context of his discussion on myth.[29] Firstly, the fly quotations are borrowed, or stolen, from different types of text, most literary, some philosophical (Blaise Pascal, Ludwig

Wittgenstein, Arthur Schopenhauer). More importantly, the literary fragments belong to fluctuating genres: poetry (Rubén Bonifaz Nuño, Rupert Brook, Guillaume Apollinaire), novel (Marcel Proust's *A la recherche du temps perdu*, James Joyce's *Ulysses*), diary (Jules Renard, Otto Weininger), and fairy tale (the Brothers Grimm), among others. A hybrid textual montage, the collection of short stories and essays gestures towards multiple other genres. Notably, it contains multiple forms of brevity: Marcus Valerius Martialis's satirical epigram (52); Renard's reflective diary fragment (80); and the surrealist proverb from a collection by Benjamin Péret and Paul Éluard (108). Monterroso's hybrid art of the short story arguably 'contains' all these different genres and fragmentary forms, which belong to vastly different cultures, from ancient Rome to modern France.

Indeed, the formal, generic heterogeneity of the montage is compounded with cultural heterogeneity. Firstly, the perpetual movement of the texts allows them to cross national borders and fly over oceans. The collection includes excerpts of texts by authors from different Spanish-speaking countries, whether Peninsular Spain (Benito Jerónimo Feijóo), Mexico (Rubén Bonifaz Nuño) or Chile (Pablo Neruda). Moreover, Monterroso uses translations of fragments from books in different languages, including French (Blaise Pascal, Jean Jaurès, Jules Renard, Proust, Paul Éluard), German (Meister Eckhart, Brothers Grimm), British (W. B. Yeats, Rupert Brook, T. S. Eliot) and Quechuan (anonymous, 131). The quotations thus share the quality of the flies from Guillaume Apollinaire's *Bestiario*: 'Nuestras moscas saben canciones / que en Noruega les enseñaron / las moscas gánicas que son / las blancas diosas de la nieve' (114). By translating the texts, Monterroso takes them one step further from their original cultural context. These linguistic mutations alter the original text, as is overtly the case in the quotation from Swift's text, where the original flea morphs into a fly (124). Semantic movement is thus the by-product of geographical, linguistic, cultural movement.

Secondly, *Movimiento perpetuo* encloses fragments from a huge range of historical periods. Roman Antiquity is represented by the statesman and philosopher, Cicero (106–43 BCE) and the poet and satirical writer, Martial (40–c.102 CE). Ancient indigenous Indian traditions, in turn, are represented by the books of *Chilam Balam* — a set of Mayan Yucatec 'town books' containing Mayan mythology, chronicles and predictions, written after the Conquest, chiefly in the seventeenth and eighteenth centuries (50). *Sermo Beati pauperes spiritu* is a medieval theological work by Eckhart von Hochheim, and dates from the fourteenth century. Monterroso intersperses these with quotations from modern texts, in order to create a transcultural montage that defies any historical, chronological logic.

The fly's particular ability to defy spatio-temporal boundaries is encapsulated in a fragment by Cortázar, 'Progreso y retroceso' (*Historias de cronopios y de famas*, 1962), which is included in Monterroso's original fly collection:[30]

> Inventaron un cristal que dejaba pasar las moscas. La mosca venía, empujaba un poco con la cabeza y, pop, ya estaba del otro lado. Alegría enormísima de la mosca.
>
> Todo lo arruinó un sabio húngaro al descubrir que la mosca podía entrar pero no salir, o viceversa a causa de no se sabe que macana en la flexibilidad de las

> fibras de este cristal, que era muy fibroso. En seguida inventaron el cazamoscas
> con un terrón de azúcar dentro, y muchas moscas morían desesperadas. Así
> acabó toda posible confraternidad con estos animales dignos de mejor suerte.[31]

Cortázar's characterization of the fly provides a useful thread — a Cortazarian
'piolín'[32] — that helps establish a relation between Cortázar's fantastic literature
and Monterroso's disordered, if not chaotic, writing. Admittedly, this Cortazarian
text is a 'reject', excluded by Monterroso from his *Movimiento perpetuo* collection.
This is not to detract from its importance, though: the significance of the fly in
Monterroso's *oeuvre*, as in this short story, is precisely *as a reject*, an excess which
defies the boundaries between inside and outside, inclusion and exclusion.

'Progreso y retroceso' might be seen as a Monterrosian variation on the orders
of *el lado de acá* and *el lado de allá* that structure Cortázar's fiction. Playing on the
quotidian problem that flies seem at once easily to get inside, and impossible to get
out, it challenges attempts by humans to construct clean, sealed boundaries between
inside and outside. The fly is a tongue-in-cheek permutation of Cortazarian
otherness: as an invader that must be expelled or killed, it might be seen to fit into
the second structure of interference as outlined by Boldy, whereby the inside, the
civilized, the human (represented here by the 'sabio húngaro'), is passively possessed
by the outside, the monstrous, 'lo otro' (see Chapter 2).[33] Yet Cortázar dismantles
this duality by humanizing the fly, endowing it with human feelings of happiness
and despair; reclaiming it as a 'worthy' creature; and in turn recasting the 'wise'
human as barbaric killer.

Cortázar's flies might be compared to those of Rulfo's 'Talpa' (which Monterroso,
given his admiration of Rulfo, had no doubt read) and Monterroso's quotation of
José María Méndez:

> el cuerpo de Tanilo [estaba] lleno por dentro y por fuera de un hervidero de
> moscas azules que zumbaban como si fuera un gran ronquido que saliera de la
> boca de él; de aquella boca que no pudo cerrarse. (81)

> 'lo verdaderamente horrible [de las moscas] es ver cómo se posan en nuestros
> ojos abiertos que ya no podemos cerrar, cómo se meten en el hueco de nuestras
> narices, cómo entran en grupo en nuestra boca abierta que quisiéramos
> mantener cerrada.' (138)

Both in and on the corpses, the flies dissolve the barrier between inside and
outside, selfhood and otherness. They are disturbing, if not horrific, insofar as they
profoundly undermine the supremacy of human 'civilization' by breaking down
the boundaries between man and animal, *res cogitans* and *res extensa*. Fundamentally
ungrounded, Monterroso's flies are paradigmatic of this unstoppable contamination:
'nadie ha visto nunca una mosca a primera vista. Toda mosca ha sido vista *siempre*'
(12). Always-already there, the fly has no origins; it belongs nowhere and
everywhere; it simply *is*. A shared aesthetic thus becomes apparent in the works of
the three short story writers of my corpus: one that dissolves boundaries through
the minimal fragment; one whose hermetic containment unleashes uncontainable
forces; one in which spatio-temporal limits serve paradoxically to provoke cross-
contaminations and contradictions.

In this vein, Monterroso's fly can be likened to Borges's 'zahir', the exchangeable symbol that adopts different forms in different cultural contexts:

> En Buenos Aires el Zahir es una moneda común de veinte centavos [...] (En Guzerat, a fines del siglo XVIII, un tigre fue Zahir; en Java, un ciego de la mezquita de Surakarta, a quien lapidaron los fieles; en Persia, un astrolabio que Nadir Shah hizo arrojar al fondo del mar [...]; en la aljama de Córdoba, según Zotenberg, una veta en el mármol de uno de los mil doscientos pilares [...])[34]

Borges paints a vivid, detailed picture of the interplay between the universality of the coin, the symbol of common exchange par excellence, and its infinite particularities. These are displayed by the list of different animals, people or things (a tiger, a blind man, an astrolabe, a vein of marble in a column), combined with disparate times and places. As the narrator later affirms, 'no había criatura en el orbe que no propendiera a *Zaheer*, pero [...] el Todomisericordioso no deja que dos cosas lo sean a un tiempo, ya que una sola puede fascinar muchedumbres' (111). The same duality is true of Monterroso's fly. On the one hand, it is universal, a common creature that is capable of representing anything for anyone. On the other hand, it preserves its singularity even as every reinscription revives its meaning.

Hence it provides a shared literary motif that unites works that are otherwise culturally, geographically, and temporally separate. As Monterroso affirms in 'Las moscas', 'la mosca invade todas las literaturas y, claro, donde uno pone el ojo encuentra la mosca' (11). A 'transmisor de la nuestra torpe cultura occidental' and the meanings and symbols it produces (12), it is an affirmation of the universality of culture and the consequent freedom of the Latin American writer. Monterroso's *ars poetica* thus resonates with that of Borges, who in 'El escritor argentino y la tradición' insists that Argentine writers do not need to fill their works with 'color local': there are, he claims, no camels in the Koran. Instead, Latin Americans must think that 'nuestro patrimonio es el universo'.[35] For Monterroso, as for Borges, cultural objects are in perpetual movement; it is the particular treatment of a theme in a particular context that renders it unique, 'local'.

This explains the seemingly contradictory readings of Monterroso's work. For Juan Villoro, 'el animal monterrosiano carece de toda singularidad intrínseca'.[36] Likewise, Margo Glantz insists on the universality of *Movimiento perpetuo*, reflected in his flies: 'han sido siempre un tema universal [... han] existido desde siempre [...], son en realidad la quintaesencia de la eternidad' (64–65). In contrast, López Parada focuses on the contingency and shifting quality of the 'frases-mosca' which, she explains, are 'frases terrenas que para atrás no significan nunca lo mismo', and that 'no revela[n] sino su propia contingencia' (218). If we unite these two views, we have a more holistic representation of Monterroso's flies, which reflect and refract the paradoxical form of the short story, caught as it is between universality and contingency, mythical time and fleeting instants. Though ordinariness is certainly one aspect of the Monterrosian creature, we must also grapple with the complexity of the beast, a perpetually shifting figure whose rarity emerges from its normality, its singularity from its universality and its evasiveness from its invasiveness.

The cultural hybridity of the flies — their simultaneous belonging to different times and places, temporalities and spatialities — helps to understand the generic

hybridity of Monterroso's work. In 'La brevedad', the narrator affirms that

> Lo cierto es que el escritor de brevedades nada anhela más en el mundo que escribir interminablemente largos textos, largos textos en que la imaginación no tenga que trabajar, en que hechos, cosas, animales y hombres se crucen, se busquen, se huyen, vivan, convivan, se amen o derramen libremente su sangre sin sujeción al punto y coma, al punto.
> A ese punto que en este instante me ha sido impuesto por algo más fuerte que yo, que respeto y que odio. (149)

This passage encloses a series of characteristic paradoxes. By referring to prolix texts from which his aesthetic principles bar him, and including a multiplicity of novelistic plots within this fragment, the *texto breve* 'contains' the novel. The accumulation of commas creates a listing effect which contradicts his claim of an external subjection to the full stop. Moreover, the final, supplementary sentence — which in turn is supplemented by a dual clause — undermines his affirmation of necessary closure. This logic of supplementarity is echoed by a (mis)quotation from Jonathan Swift: 'una mosca tiene moscas más pequeñas que la devoran, y éstas tienen otras más pequeñas todavía que las muerden, y así *ad infinitum*' (124). The *texto breve*, like Swift's fly, is perpetually supplemented by other, absent-present texts, by ghostly subtexts or intertexts that render it infinite. Monterroso's drawing of wine glasses (Figure 11) might thus be seen as an illustration of the minimal artwork, the container that is uncontained insofar as it encloses multiple other vessels.

In 'Fecundidad', a similar supplementary structure is employed to connect the *microcuentista* with the novelist. The story consists of a single sentence:

> Hoy me siento bien, un Balzac; estoy terminando esta línea. (61)

The narrator self-reflexively compares his one-line text with the work of Honoré de Balzac, the prolific writer who wrote *La Comédie humaine*, a series of ninety-one novels and short stories. This connection between brevity and prolixity is a self-conscious reflection of Monterroso's own art, as underlined by the following assertion, in the speech he gave in 2000 upon receiving the Prince of Asturias Prize: 'aprendí a ser breve leyendo a Proust'.[37] A closer examination of the temporality of 'Fecundidad' explains this paradox. The present, the tense of the now, is off-set by the gerund, which indicates continuation, perpetuation and extension.[38] In narratological terms, the story time of 'Fecundidad' is much greater than its discourse time; that is to say, the fictional time taken up by the action, which could be months or years, far exceeds the few seconds it takes to read the text.

In turn, this paradox helps explain two conundrums: why Monterroso claims that 'El dinosaurio' is in fact a novel;[39] and why short story writers are also (fragmentary) novelists. Monterroso's shortest short story — 'Cuando despertó, el dinosaurio todavía estaba allí.'[40] — contains within it infinite novelistic strands. Hovering uneasily between the preterite and imperfect tenses, it simultaneously recounts a brief event and a lingering mystery. The single moment, the point at which the subject wakes up, expands infinitely into the inaccessible, prehistoric past and the unknown future through the dinosaur's lurking presence. It is the same logic that links the 'closed textuality' of Rulfo's, Cortázar's and Monterroso's short

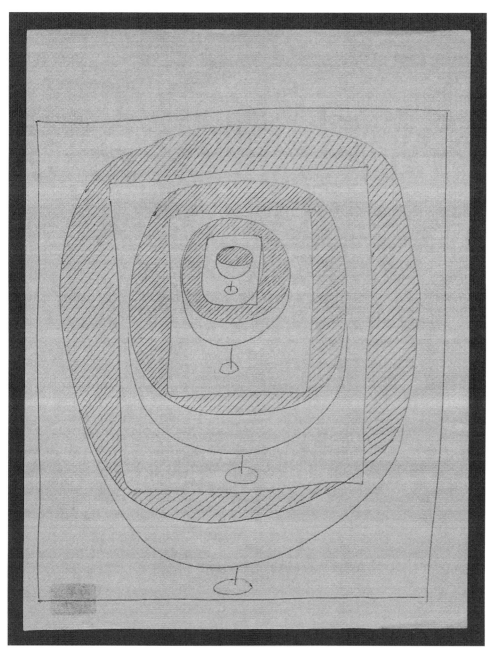

FIG. 11. Augusto Monterroso, Drawing, *Wine glasses within wine glasses*
Series 3: Drawings and Photographs; 1941–93; Augusto Monterroso Papers, Box 41–47;
Manuscripts Division, Department of Rare Books and Special Collections,
Princeton University Library

fiction with the 'open textuality' of their fragmentary novels and collage works. We might therefore re-evaluate May's claim (cited above) that short stories, in contrast to novels, aim not for truth, but for a moment of truth; not for general experience, conceptually created, but for *an* experience, directly and emotionally encountered. In fact, the temporal paradox of the short story creates an interplay between general concepts and particular experiences, exemplarity and singularity.

The story 'Movimiento perpetuo' is structured by the paradoxical relationship between fleetingness, change and singularity on the one hand, and permanence, repetition and universality on the other. Centring around a love triangle between Luis, Juan and Julia, the story opens *in medias res*, with Juan's question to Luis '¿Te acordaste?' This is followed by an absurd dialogue:

> — ¿Qué te pasó?
> — ¿Que qué me pasó?
> — Sí; cómo no te acordaste.
> No supo qué contestar. Un intento de contraataque:
> — Nada. Se me olvidó.
> — ¡Se me olvidó! ¿Y ahora?
> ¿Y ahora? (17)

By severing the preamble to the tale from the reader, the narrator conceals what was forgotten. The narrative thus continues with an exclusive focus on the 'ahora', on the ephemeral present: in front of the setting sun, the friends sit on an Acapulco beach drinking whisky — which, the narrator points out, would allow Luis to forget that he has something to remember — with ice that melts quickly in the summer heat. '— El hielo no dura nada — dijo Luis./ — Nada' (19). The setting prompts Juan to ponder: everything is changing, Acapulco is not the same anymore, and perhaps he himself has changed; only his wife is still the same. She, he reflects, would stay the same until the end of time, as he first saw her. Based on six years of repeated experiences, the second half of the story is Juan's conjecture about how the night would follow the usual sado-masochistic pattern: Julia would go off dancing and flirting with another man and incense her husband from a distance before returning home to possess him sexually. The story ends elliptically, as a local Mexican comes up and asks the predicted question, 'Me permite?', which suggests that the cycle will perpetuate itself. This circular pattern is formally replicated by the narrative ellipsis, which opens the text onto infinite future stories. Moreover, it is echoed in the intertextual flies:

> 'El misántropo: El sol no sirve más que para hacer revivir las moscas que me chupan la sangre.' (Jules Renard, 86)

> 'Al tiempo que vivo estás viviendo. / Mosca, mi dueña, ya colmada / por sus bodas obscenas; ya en el muro / Con su macho a la espalda. Y hierve y sube / un verano podrido, y ya prospera, / paño de larvas, la familia / a quien soy herencia desde ahora.' (Rúben Bonifaz Nuño, 38)

While Renard's aphorism succinctly conveys the mutually fuelling relationship between the human's blood and the fly's thirst, between mortality and re-birth, the fluctuating rhythm of Bonifaz Nuño's poem creates a lyrical counterpoint between reproduction and decay, growth and decline. In both cases, a dialectical relationship is created between the fleeting, short-lived creature and eternal, cyclical life. As suggested by the extension of the present tense through the gerund in Bonifaz Nuño's first line, these two temporalities are mediated by the enduring power of the present moment: infinity, the poem suggests, is always experienced 'desde ahora'.

In this context, the dialectic of the fly once again provides a significant point of contact between Monterroso's *Movimiento perpetuo* and the fragmentary aesthetics of Rulfo and Cortázar. In Rulfo's 'Talpa' (cited above), flies have a resurrecting function. As I examined extensively in the first chapter, the image of the swarming, buzzing flies on Tanilo's corpse shows life emerging from death, growth from decay, futurity from past-ness. The same paradox is displayed in a poem by Cortázar, entitled 'La mosca', which was published posthumously in *Papeles inesperados* (2009):

> Te tendré que matar de nuevo.
> Te maté tantas veces, en Casablanca, en Lima,
> en Cristianía,
> en Montparnasse, en una estancia del partido de Lobos,
> en el burdel, en la cocina, sobre un peine,
> en la oficina, en esta almohada
> te tendré que matar de nuevo,
> yo, con mi única vida.[41]

In 'La mosca', Cortázar creates an ambiguous relationship, an uncomfortable jarring, between supposed dualities. By addressing the fly in the second person singular, and listing its multiple incarnations through anaphoric repetition, the poem becomes a Möbius strip that links singularity and universality, specificity and generality, oneness and multiplicity, difference and repetition. The cyclicality of the poem, achieved through the repetition of the verse 'te tendré que matar de nuevo', formally recreates the connection implied in the poem between death and re-birth, between past, present and future. The fly is thus connected with the Cortazarian other, the ghostly figure that returns again and again to haunt the human subject in his single life.

Looking at Rulfo's and Cortázar's aesthetics through these Monterrosian flies, like looking through pinholes, clarifies the muddiness that results from jarring interpretations of their work. Crucially, it helps reconcile my reading of their art of the photographic, fleeting instant with those critics who regard their narratives as mythical, timeless and cyclical — whether Fuentes, Bartra and Sommers in the case of Rulfo, or Sosnowski, Benavides and Hartman in the case of Cortázar. As we have seen in this section, the short story is governed by two contradictory, yet coexisting, temporalities: the modern temporality of the ever-changing, fleeting moment and the 'primitive' temporality of the ever-repeated cycle. This temporal paradox is thus a reminder, and remainder, of the short story's dual cultural origins: the cyclical narrative tradition, whether that of Scheherazade, of Ulysses, or of *gauchos* gathered around the fire; the modern experience of the fleeting, whether through photographs or films, telegrams or newspapers, trains or planes.

Beyond Narrative: Forms of Transculturation in *Obras completas (y otros cuentos)*

I shall now return to Monterroso's first collection of short stories, *Obras completas (y otros cuentos)*, where the paradoxes that underlie the fly collection are already present, and indeed structural. Close readings of these stories will unveil a field of duelling contradictions between and within cultures. As Martín-Barbero insists, only once we take as the starting point of observation and analysis these *mestizajes*, 'in the sense of continuities in discontinuity and reconciliations between rhythms of life that are mutually exclusive, [can we] begin to understand the complex cultural forms and meanings that are coming into existence in Latin America' (188). In Monterroso's highly self-conscious works, culture is shown to be controlled not from above, through homogenizing structures and unifying institutions, but rather at ground level, through exchanges, transactions and negotiations between different people in different contexts. Contradictions are removed from the shells of abstract generalizations and seen, as Martín-Barbero suggests, 'in their processes of composition and decomposition' (188). Hence his works bring to the fore the complexities of what Martín-Barbero terms 'mediations', the transfers and articulations between different cultural sectors.

The stories that have received most critical attention are 'Mr Taylor' and 'Sinfonía concluida', which deal overtly, thematically and politically with the problem of mediation. Gloria González Zenteno reads 'Mr Taylor' as the depiction of 'un choque fatídico y profético entre los habitantes de dos mundos absolutamente distantes tanto en el espacio como en la historia.'[42] The Monterrosian jungle, from this perspective, is a site of intercultural clashes and conflicts. With a far more metaliterary object in mind, Mark Millington reads 'Sinfonía concluida' as 'a fable of certain aspects of crosscultural exchange'.[43] He uses this premise as a point of departure from which to consider the problem of reading transculturally, particularly 'that of academic critics in First World cultures and their work with Latin American literatures'. Bernard McGuirk, inspired by Millington's reading, proposes a significant deconstructive reading of Monterroso's 'Sinfonía concluida'. Behind this story, he argues, lurks the 'third term', the marginal excess which upsets and unsettles 'the provisional binaries in which we are locked'.[44] Broadening Millington's exploration of crosscultural exchanges, he offers a series of characterizations of 'Sinfonía concluida', all related to the workings of the 'third term':

* a fable of exchange, of intercultural transfer?
* a theory of transcultural reading?
* cultural production conceived of as property right? [...]
* Latin America reading Europe reading Latin America reading Europe — and so on?
* the story reading Vienna/Schubert reading the old man reading culture — and so on? [...]
* a complication *within* binary terms, the tracing of 'fault lines' in differences of economies, cultures, resources, interests?[45] (my ellipses)

Such locations and dislocations, as I shall argue, underlie the entire collection, whether explicitly or implicitly, fictionally or metafictionally. The stories are self-consciously structured around the mutual relations between writers and readers, artists and critics, actors and viewers, performers and listeners; relations which are invariably complicated by social, cultural and economic values. Trapped in the textual halls of mirrors, the complicit reader inevitably participates in these complex negotiations between individuals, societies, and cultures. In what follows, I shall concentrate less on the nature of these different exchanges and conflicts than on the different means, modes, and media by which the texts themselves operate in this field of cross-cultural negotiations and clashes; be it by performing or enacting transactions, challenging or subverting oppositions. My focus will therefore be on the form of the stories, often laid bare or problematized self-reflexively within the texts.

Another feature of this collection that has received much critical attention is its satirical quality.[46] Noguerol Jiménez suggests a crucial link between satirical humour and the short story form: 'el relato se constituye en uno de los formatos genéricos preferidos por el escritor satírico. Este hecho se explica por la esencial brevedad del género, que produce un efecto de concisión e inmediatez de gran valor para activar la denunciación.'[47] The restrictions and constrictions of the art of brevity, Noguerol Jiménez suggests, are crucial to the biting, incisive, or cutting effect of satire. Other literary critics, though, have suggested that satire relies on openness of form. Dustin Griffin, in his *Critical Reintroduction to Satire*, suggests that 'a rhetoric of inquiry and provocation enables us to see more clearly that satire is often an "open", rather than a "closed", form, that it is concerned rather to inquire, explore, or unsettle than to declare, sum up, or conclude.'[48] In the same vein, Northrop Frye observes that 'an extraordinary number of great satires are fragmentary, unfinished, or anonymous'.[49] From this point of view, suspense and digressiveness are essential to the art of provocation, which asks leading questions, but withdraws any answers or conclusions. Blanca Inés Gómez Buendía shares this perspective in her description of the fundamental role of satirical humour in Monterroso's work:

> [contribuye] al distanciamiento del lector haciendo propicia la percepción carna-valesca del mundo que impregna la palabra y la imagen en una nueva relación con la realidad. La alegre relatividad de la percepción debilita la univocidad de la mirada para entrar en el terreno de lo incierto y relativo y por supuesto de la percepción fragmentaria del mundo. (47)

Gómez Buendía highlights the distancing effect of humour, which serves to create cracks and openings that destabilize, fragment and relativize reality, producing new relations between existing objects. While Noguerol Jiménez argues that satirical humour is dependent upon unity, conciseness and denunciation, Gómez Buendía suggests that it results from fragmentation, dispersion and uncertainty. I shall situate myself between these two readings, arguing that we are once again faced with the formal paradoxes of constriction and freedom, closure and openness, reduction and complication that underpin the art of the short story.

One element that is suggested, but not elaborated, by Gómez Buendía is that Monterroso's humour is not only verbal, but also visual. As we shall see, the pictorial forms of caricature and cartoon lie at the centre of Monterroso's aesthetics.

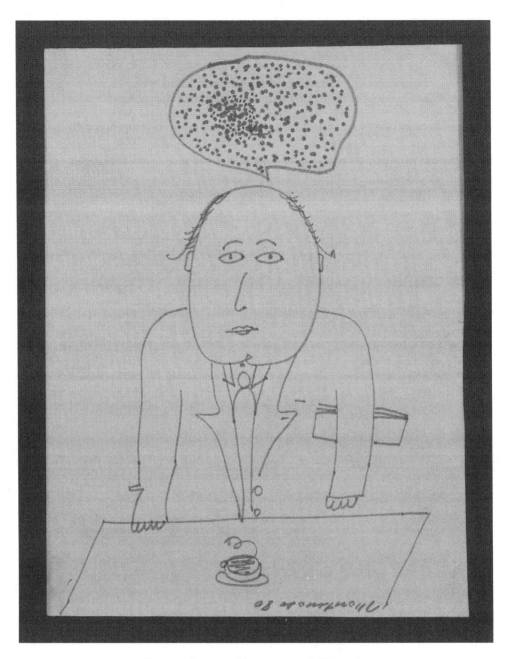

FIG. 12. Augusto Monterroso, *Self Portrait*
Series 3: Drawings and Photographs; 1941–93; Augusto Monterroso Papers, Box 41–47;
Manuscripts Division, Department of Rare Books and Special Collections,
Princeton University Library

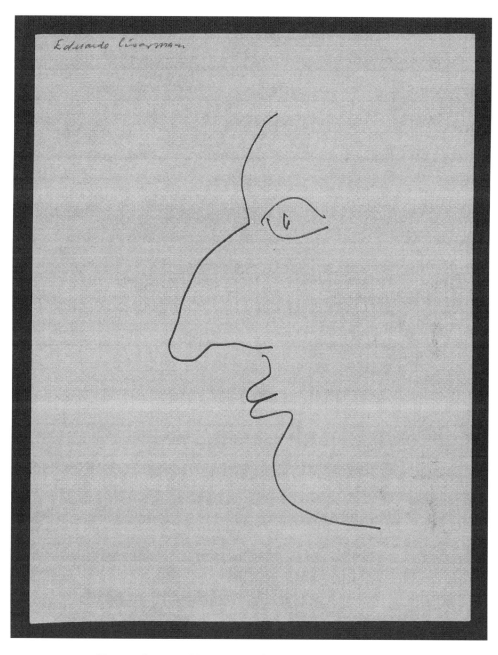

Fig. 13. Augusto Monterroso, drawing, *Eduardo Césarman*
Series 3: Drawings and Photographs; 1941–93; Augusto Monterroso Papers, Box 41–47;
Manuscripts Division, Department of Rare Books and Special Collections,
Princeton University Library

This influence is perhaps clearest in his drawings (Figs 12 and 13). As can be seen in the use of simple outlines to exaggerate certain features (stockiness in Monterroso's self-portrait, a large nose in that of Eduardo Césarman), as well as the speech bubble and the symbol (the squiggly line emerging from the coffee cup to represent heat), Monterroso employs techniques belonging to the art of the cartoon.

In what follows, I shall argue that the literary medium of Monterroso's short stories is constantly displaced, whether implicitly or explicitly, by line drawings, caricatures and cartoons; which are in turn supplemented by other metatextual media, whether photographs, films or newspaper articles. As with Cortázar, Monterroso's earliest short stories foreshadow the collage structure that underpins his later works, which combine essays, stories or biographical fragments with images: the animal-centred illustrations composed by Alba Rojo to accompany *La oveja negra (y demás fábulas)* (1969); the repeated, but ever-shifting, drawings of flies in *Movimiento perpetuo* (1972); and Monterroso's own drawings combined with reproductions of woodcuts, old maps and heraldic crests in Vicente Rojo's design of *La palabra mágica* (1983). Each story, as we shall see, is a Lévi-Straussian *bricolage*, a combination and reconfiguration of different, and sometimes mutually jarring or incompatible, forms from different socio-cultural contexts.[50] The logic of supplementarity of the collection — displayed ostentatiously in the tongue-in-cheek title, *Obras completas (y otros cuentos)* — is in fact at work in each individual story. The textual bodies, like Swift's flies, not only contain and transport words, messages and narratives, but also other vessels, which in turn undermine and 'bite' them.

Indeed, it was one of Monterroso's desires, voiced in a 1984 notebook entry, that his writing should take on the style of *The New Yorker* cartoonist, Saul Steinberg:

> El artista, pintor o dibujante de este siglo es Saul Steinberg. Cómo él dibuja me hubiera gustado, me gustaría escribir. ¿Cómo convertir sus líneas en palabras, sus palos en frases, sus cubos en párrafos, sus ideas en <u>mis</u> ideas? Todo está ahí: se ve, se toca, casi se oye; sólo falta pasarlo a <u>mi</u> papel y hacerlo oír, ver, y casi tocar.[51] (his emphases)

As revealed in this 1984 diary entry, Steinberg's use of form and shapes — his lines, sticks and cubes — have a profound effect on Monterroso. Since Steinberg started working with *The New Yorker* in 1942, it is possible that this influence dates back to the forties and fifties, when Monterroso was writing the stories that would later be published in *Obras completas* in 1959. Moreover, over the last two centuries, cartoon art has been an extremely popular form in Mexico, where Monterroso arrived as an exile from Guatemala City in 1944, and lived definitively from 1956: from the Hogarth-inspired cartoons that emerged around the time of the War of Independence (1810s); through the political cartoons of the satiric penny press in the years preceding the Revolution (1900s); the famous murals by Diego de Rivera, José Clemente Orozco and David Alfaro Siqueros in the first half of the twentieth century; and the social cartoons of Abel Quezada (1920–1999); to the comic strips that to this day are so avidly consumed by the Mexican population.[52] Yet the formal link between Monterroso's writing and cartoon art is a deep one that arguably transcends specific or national influences. For Randall Harrison,

> the cartoon is 'communication to the quick' — in several senses. It is fast; it

grabs the reader on the run. It is lively; it sorts the 'quick from the dead.' And it is penetrating; it can tickle the funny bone or 'hurt to the quick.' In an era when media are increasingly fast-paced and visual, the cartoon seems to capture the best — and perhaps the worst — of modern communication.[53]

In this sense, the cartoon shares many of the properties that, as we have seen, characterize both the short story and the photograph: as a fragmentary form, it communicates through speed and brevity, directness and immediacy; capturing the viewer in the present moment, it can amuse or hurt, tickle or injure. As Harrison goes on to explain, echoing Ernst Gombrich's famous essay on caricature,[54] the cartoonist employs two principal techniques to achieve this effect: exaggeration (the use of deformity to emphasize weakness, to provide insight into the essence of a character) and simplification (the use of the minimum of strokes to grasp a personality). Yet as we shall see, this seemingly simplifying art, as suggested by Gómez Buendía, also serves to complicate, to problematize and to reinvent: by cutting people or objects down to key salient features, and severing them from their normal contexts, the caricaturist creates new relations and reshapes the world around him. In this sense, the visual braids of the cartoon contribute to the complications within, and between, cultural binaries that underpin not only 'Mr Taylor' and 'Sinfonía concluida', but each of the stories.

As a deceptively simple *microcuento* that conceals a series of complexities, 'La vaca' is a good place to start:

> Cuando iba el otro día en el tren me erguí de pronto feliz sobre mis dos patas y empecé a manotear de alegría y a invitar a todos a ver el paisaje y a contemplar el crepúsculo que estaba de lo más bien. Las mujeres y los niños y unos señores que detuvieron su conversación me miraban sorprendidos y se reían de mí pero cuando me senté otra vez silencioso no podían imaginar que yo acababa de ver alejarse lentamente a la orilla del camino una vaca muerta muertita sin quien la enterrara ni quien le editara sus obras completas ni quien le dijera un sentido y lloroso discurso por lo buena que había sido y por todos los chorritos de humeante leche con que contribuyó a que la vida en general y el tren en particular siguieran su marcha. (129)

The juxtaposition of different perspectives and modes of mediation make this story extremely difficult to untangle. On the first level, the narrator presents his own view of the dead cow, but also the way in which he himself becomes an object of spectacle for the other passengers. Filtered through these two gazes, the narrative hovers bathetically between the serious and the ridiculous, the transcendental and the absurd. The fleeting view through the moving train window is counteracted by a filmic slow motion, an effect produced verbally through the adverb 'lentamente' and the incantatory repetition of 'muerta muertita'. The fast movement of the train is therefore counteracted by a suspended moment of quiet contemplation through an experience that Monterroso, in relation to the art of brevity, calls 'intensity': the amplification and extension of the instant.[55] At the same time, the other passengers become secondary viewers, stopping their conversations abruptly to stare at the narrator–viewer, who is waving his arms around gleefully. Their surprise produces a metatextual epiphany, one that is immediately undermined as their laughter turns the narrator into an object of ridicule — a figure that, as we shall see, recurs throughout the stories of *Obras completas*.

On the second, extradiegetic level, the intradiegetic humour is replicated through a cartoonish image, which reduces the narrator to a pair of flailing arms, which are in turn distorted into animal-like 'patas'. The window turns into a mirror, self-reflexively linking the image of the cow to that of the internal writer (the narrator). Underlying the tale is thus a pictorial imagination, as reinforced by a later drawing by Monterroso, which probably dates from his journey around North America in 1984.[56] Drawn on a train journey, on the reverse side of an Amtrak leaflet (Figure 14), the picture is fruit of the same experience that inspired Monterroso to write 'Vaca' many years earlier. What he plays on here is the visual relationship between the cow and the train, as suggested by the bottom images, which connect the cow's legs, spots and perhaps even smell (represented by the spiral figure above the cow), with the train's four wheels, windows and smoke (or steam, perhaps, in homage to the origins of the transport). In turn, the cow is connected, through the spiral figure traced by Monterroso's pen, with the stocky figure at the top which, given its similarity to Figure 12, is undoubtedly a caricatured self-portrait.

Indeed, digging further into the text, it becomes clear that an intricate web of relations is woven between the author, the train and the cow. The 'vaca muerta muertita' becomes a satirical image of the neglected author whose metatextual *obras completas*, like the cow's 'chorritos de leche', have (indirectly, partially) contributed to the running of the train. This is surely a comment on the place and standing of the writer under the conditions of capitalism. He is located not at the top of an ivory tower, nor at the centre of a lettered city, but at the base level of production and at the margins of social life. His status is that of a small cogwheel in a much larger capitalist machine, a minor by-product of a consumerist system. Dispossessed of any transcendental, spiritual 'aura', his artistic output is fragmented into consumable, disposable, material objects.

'La vida en general' is composed of multiple, hybrid parts: Monterroso's (in)complete works; the cow's modest trickle of milk; this particular train journey. Rather than contrasting modern, urban, industrial culture with traditional, rural, pre-industrial society, Monterroso's experience on the train brings them together. In a sense, this simultaneous fragmentariness and interconnectedness is an experiential phenomenon enabled by train travel which, as Robert Hughes suggests, implies 'the succession and superimposition of views, the unfolding of landscape in flickering surfaces as one [is] swiftly carried past it, and an exaggerated feeling of relative motion (the poplars nearby seeming to move faster than the church spire across the field) due to parallax'.[57] The fleeting view and relative motion produce disconnections and reconnections that fragment any cultural 'whole', rearticulating it through a series of separate, but interrelated parts.

These socio-cultural interconnections are developed into a tongue-in-cheek theory in a fragment in *La letra e*, entitled 'Tren Barcelona-París' (1984): 'Después del libro, probablemente lo mejor que ha inventado el hombre sean los trenes. Tengo una teoría: a partir de este invento, la economía, el estado general de un país corren paralelos a la velocidad y la organización de su sistema ferroviario' (244).

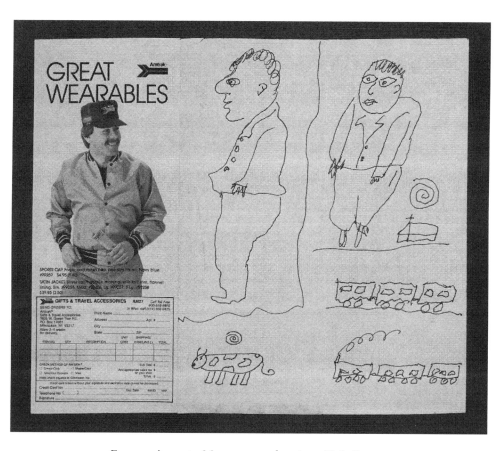

FIG. 14. Augusto Monterroso, drawing, *Train Journey*
Series 3: Drawings and Photographs; 1941–93; Augusto Monterroso Papers, Box 41–47;
Manuscripts Division, Department of Rare Books and Special Collections,
Princeton University Library

Monterroso thus connects the rail system, with its contingent factors of speed and organization, with the general state of the country. With a characteristic *guiño de ojo*, he undermines the idea of the nation as a set of intrinsic, essential properties, by emphasizing relativity, contingency and perpetual movement. Echoed in the reference to the book in this fragment, 'Vaca' places the literary work in the midst of a series of material exchanges within complex, socio-economic systems, industrial and agricultural, urban and rural.

As García Canclini insists, 'no hay producción de sentido que no esté inserta en las estructuras materiales'.[58] Culture and society do not belong to separate, autonomous spheres: philosophy, literature and art are influenced and transformed by technological, economic and social operations; in turn, they reproduce and transform relations of production, as well as inventing new ones (43). What García Canclini says of Latin American handicrafts under the conditions of capitalism is true of the metafictional *Obras completas* in 'Vaca': '[el capitalismo] los sacó de un sistema social en el que la producción y el intercambio eran regulados por la organización comunal, aun ritual, y los reubicó en un régimen de competencia intercultural' (144–45). Removed from the tradition of storytelling, a local community and a ritualistic role, the short stories' fate lies in the hands of national or international editors; their publication and diffusion depends on the perpetually shifting demands of a global market; their success is contingent on their ability to compete with similar products.

In 'Primera dama', it is a poem by Rubén Darío that becomes an object of transaction in another network of socio-economic connections. In this story, a headmaster complains to the President that children in his school are frequently fainting from malnutrition. The eponymous First Lady, under the pretext of charity, organizes a fundraising event that gives her the opportunity to place herself under the spotlight by performing, and in fact savaging, Rubén Darío's *Los motivos del lobo*. Her selfishness and egotism, thinly disguised as solidarity and generosity, are revealed through the satirical juxtaposition of her words and thoughts: when the headteacher tells her about the problem, for example, she exclaims 'pobres criaturas', while thinking 'qué bueno que haya esa oportunidad' (41). The headteacher's opening address, conveyed in reported speech, also belies a profound lack of solidarity:

> estábamos allí movidos por un alto espíritu de solidaridad humana. Que [...] como le había dicho personalmente el Presidente cuando le llamó para hacérselo ver hay que hacer algo por esos niños en interés de los altos destinos de la patria mueva usted las conciencias remueva cielo y tierra conmueva los corazones en favor de esa noble cruzada. (46)

In his grandiose, pompous speech, the headteacher borrows the nationalistic, religious rhetoric of the president to disguise the futility and spiritual emptiness of the fundraising event. His hyperbolic language echoes that of the state official in Rulfo's 'El día del derrumbe', a story with a shared theme of mock solidarity and deferred authority: the delegate, promising to provide support for a rural community after the titular landslide, in fact unites himself with the candidate to presidency, a higher authority whose democratic principles ironically uphold 'el supremo vínculo de unión con el pueblo' (see Chapter 1). In 'Primera dama', the president's discourse, reported by the headteacher, reveals the same hypocrisy: he asks that the audience be moved in the interest not of starving children, but of the lofty fate of the fatherland. Instead of talking from the perspective of the suffering children, the headteacher seeks to raise his own status by borrowing the authority of the President; of North America, 'esa noble y generosa nación que con justicia [podían] llamar la despensa del mundo'; and of the 'Primera Dama de la República cuyo arte exquisito [tendrían] el honor de apreciar' (47). The words 'noble', 'exquisite' and 'honour' elevate the headteacher through his (supposed) association with high social, artistic and moral status. As in Rulfo's story, the delegate to the presidential authority, under the pretence of serving a community, in fact maintains and bolsters social, economic barriers as a protective shield.

The ending of the First Lady's recital is equally revealing:

> Permaneció unos segundos con los brazos en alto. El sudor le corría en hilitos entre los pechos y por la espalda. Oyó que aplaudían. Bajó las manos. Se arregló con disimulo la falda y saludó modestamente. El público, después de todo, no era tan bruto. Pero buen esfuerzo le estaba costando hacerlo llegar a la poesía. Era lo que pensaba: poco a poco. Mientras estrechaba las manos de los que la felicitaban se sintió embargada por un dulce y suave sentimiento de superioridad. (50)

A bathetic effect is created through the juxtaposition of grand gestures and bodily functions: the First Lady's raised arms and physical elevation point synecdochically to her feelings (or delusions) of moral, artistic and social superiority; yet these lofty gestures are undercut by the grotesque physicality of the beads of sweat running down her chest and back, as well as her nervous movements as she readjusts her skirt. Just like the orator in 'El día del derrumbe', who is caricatured through excessive, bird-like movements, the First Lady is ridiculed through the stark depiction of her gestures. A visual image is summoned that might again be likened to Monterroso's own cartoonish drawing (Fig. 15). Here, Monterroso uses spiralling patterns and stark lines to inflate, and simultaneously deflate, the First Lady. While her vastly disproportionate coiffure blows her head up to the size of her body, her high-heeled shoes are reduced to tiny, laughable proportions. This deforming depiction through overstated biro-drawn shapes echoes Monterroso's bathetic characterization in 'Primera dama'.

In the story itself, though, her physical depiction is supplemented by the language of her internal thoughts — by 'speech bubbles'. Her patronising attitude toward her (supposedly) appreciative audience is revealed by her realization that people are not, after all, so ignorant — a condescension that merely reaffirms her internal conviction that 'la gente en general es muy ignorante y no sabe apreciar la poesía' (45). Culture is thus polarized, through the First Lady's internal thoughts, into the classification systems identified by Bourdieu in *Distinction* (1989): high and low, 'good taste' and 'bad taste', knowledge and ignorance, the 'happy few' and 'la gente en general'. For Bourdieu, there is an inextricable link between cultural practices and two social factors: education and family origin, measured by Bourdieu, respectively, using academic qualifications and the father's job.[59] According to

Fig. 15. Augusto Monterroso, drawing, *Primera Dama*
Series 3: Drawings and Photographs; 1941–93; Augusto Monterroso Papers, Box 41–47;
Manuscripts Division, Department of Rare Books and Special Collections,
Princeton University Library

Bourdieu, different 'zones of taste [...] roughly correspond to educational levels and social classes': legitimate taste 'is highest in those fractions of the dominant class that are richest in educational capital', while popular taste is most frequent among the working classes (16). As García Canclini suggests, these relations are accentuated in Latin America, where aesthetic modernism diverges from socio-economic modernization, where 'las élites cultivan la poesía y el arte de vanguardia, mientras las mayorías son analfabetas' (20). Poetry, in Monterroso's tale, is employed by the social elite as a mark of distinction and a means of alienation, as a means not of bridging gaps, but rather of widening them.

Yet Monterroso's narrative does what Bourdieu's analysis fails to do: it undermines these distinctions by filtering the poem through the First Lady's ill-judged perspective, with the effect of ridiculing not the allegedly ignorant public, but rather the star performer (proven ignorant). Notably, she lays bare her narrow-mindedness in her heartfelt reaction to the poem: 'verdaderamente se indignaba ante tantas canalladas que dejaban chiquitas las del lobo, que al fin y al cabo no era un ser racional' (50). She thus misses the point of the metatextual poem, in which Rubén Darío gives the wolf human qualities with the desired effect of disturbing the provisional oppositions between animal and human, barbaric and civilized, irrational and rational. Monterroso's incisive text, though, dismantles these dualities, by connecting the First Lady with the figure of the wolf, through her irrational behaviour, her bodily reactions, and her nasty, self-centred personality. By shattering her ivory tower, the text mixes different cultural territories and unleashes processes of hybridization.

The ending employs both satirical techniques identified by critics (outlined above): cutting brevity and suggestive ellipsis. On the one hand, her superiority is brought crashing down by a single, short, blunt sentence: 'El director le informó muy elaboradamente que tenían utilidades por $7.50' (51). This is the pinprick that decidedly deflates the over-blown grandeur of the event. After a hyperbolic build-up, they raised a derisible sum of money. On the other hand, the outcome is ultimately left undecided: the First Lady says to the head teacher, '"yo creo que poco a poco vamos a ir saliendo." / El dijo que claro; que poco a poco iban a ir saliendo' (52). These closing remarks make it an open-ended story, serving as a provocative nudge to the reader, a humorous question, a satirical inquiry into the possibility of charity given the self-serving nature of human beings; of mutually beneficial mediations between different social levels in a heterogeneous, uneven society.

'Primera dama', in both subject matter and visual form, begs comparison with 'El poeta al aire libre' (*Movimiento perpetuo*), a story that mocks a poet's futile attempt to convey his work to an indifferent crowd, distracted by the interfering noise of honking cars on a nearby road and an orchestra playing the William Tell Overture. Like the First Lady, the eponymous poet is a caricature of the performance artist: 'se ayudaba con el cuerpo y estiraba los brazos hacia adelante, como si de su boca lanzara al público en lugar de palabras, alguna otra casa, tal vez flores' (139). The poet's zeal is caricatured through exaggerated, hyperbolic gesture: as he flings his arms towards the audience, they extend and elongate; they hurl the verses from his mouth as if he were spitting out some material object, perhaps flowers. These flower-words are linked explicitly with the romantic cliché used in his poem which, as paraphrased by the narrator, is about 'una flor que alguna mujer llevaba en la mano iluminándolo todo' (140). The extradiegetic humour derives from a magic trick, the literalization of the metaphor that transforms the word into the thing, the signifier into the signified. Furthermore, the literary object is materialized by the audience, who use the programmes for the poetry reading as sunshields, another materialization of the literary object. As pointed out by the amused internal viewer, the three-year-old child, this practical solution renders the solemnity of the poetry reading ridiculous.

Similarly, the eponymous First Lady's words seem, from her own perspective this time (rather than the narrator's), to metamorphose into their object, as she imagines their visual incarnation:

> Pronto sintió que de su boca, a través de sus palabras, se iba asomando al mundo San Francisco de Asís, mínimo y dulce, hasta tomar la forma del ser más humilde de la tierra. Pero en seguida esa ilusión de humildad quedaba atrás porque otras palabras, encadenadas uno no sabía cómo con las primeras, cambiaban su aspecto hasta convertirlo en un hombre iracundo. (48)

Here, words take on the life of their objects, creating hyperbolic visual images in the reader's head that dissolve the false solemnity of the reading. Scales are exaggerated to add humour: because of the First Lady's lack of understanding of the poem's grammatical structures, the Saint metamorphoses suddenly from a tiny, humble creature to a man overflowing with rage.

Both stories, with their interplay of words and objects, resonate with Saul Steinberg's cartoons. In *The Labyrinth* (1960), for example, people utter flowers, animals, strings of beads, and so on (see Fig. 16); letters, words and signatures become materialized, substantial objects.[60] Monterroso and Steinberg alike play with the visualization of verbal forms and the literalization of metaphors. This not only renders the words absurd, but also turns them into malleable objects for the reader or viewer to play with, touch and distort. As Barthes says,

> Steinberg s'empare [des] énoncés insipides et qui ne valent que par leur signifié et en fait des meubles qu'un personnage transporte à bout de bras: le mot perd son usage, il devient un objet que l'on peut toucher, manier. Le signifié est la partie immatérielle du sens. Toucher un signifié est donc une opération magique: un miracle, en quelque sorte, dont la solennité est rendue dérisoire par l'imbécilité de l'objet transporté (comme sur un plateau).[61]

In Monterroso's stories as in Steinberg's cartoons, stale stereotypes — whether beautiful flowers, humble saints or barbaric wolves — are animated, turning immaterial concepts into material, base objects. Abstract concepts become concrete objects that are 'touched' and handled freely by the artist, woven into the texture of everyday life, moved and transported at will. Monterroso's purpose is not only to deride the solemnity of art and language, though, but also to make a serious point about the relation between literature and society. Cultural production, these texts suggest, is affected by material relations, by the ways in which objects are appropriated and misappropriated, transferred and transmuted. We thus return to García Canclini's point, cited above, that the production of meaning is conditioned by, and tied up

Fig. 16. Saul Steinberg, *Untitled*, 1959
Ink on paper, 69 × 59cm. Private collection. Originally published in
The New Yorker, 14 March 1959
© The Saul Steinberg Foundation/Artists' Rights Society (ARS), NY/DACS, London

in, other material structures, whether social, economic or technological.[62] Monter-roso's work is the tray ('le plateau') or container that passes these meanings around, transporting and 'serving' them to different users and consumers.

'Leopoldo (sus trabajos)' is another metafiction that combines words and images to dissolve the oppositions between civilization and barbarism, city and country upon which nineteenth-century discourses of modernity were constructed in Latin America, as exemplified by Domingo Faustino Sarmiento's *Facundo: civilización y barbarie* (1845). These were already significantly undermined in Mexico by the political and artistic movements of the 1920s and 1930s. As García Canclini affirms, the attempt to overcome the divisions of capitalist modernization was one of the programmes of nationalist-popular regimes: 'junto a la difusión educativa y cultural de los saberes occidentales en las clases populares, se quiso incorporar el arte y las artesanías mexicanas a un patrimonio que se deseaba común' (79). In the artistic world, Diego Rivera, David Alfaro Siqueiros and José Clemente Orozco offered iconographic syntheses of national identity inspired at once by Mayan and Aztec works, the designs and colours of local pottery and the experimental advances of the European avant-garde. In the literary world, Regionalist novels by Eustasio Rivera (*La vorágine*, 1924), Ricardo Güiraldes (*Don Segundo Sombra*, 1926) and Rómulo Gallegos (*Doña Bárbara*, 1929), though seeming to reinforce these oppositions, in fact problematized and undermined them. As Swanson points out with regard to Gallegos's novel, the plain and its human personification, Bárbara, are depicted as both beautiful and terrible; the city-educated Santos Luzardo only manages to triumph over his barbaric enemies by using their methods; and in his relationship with Marisela, he 'learns to bring out the positive qualities latent within her and the rural culture from which she hails'.[63] Monterroso's particularity, though, stems from his self-conscious humour, which places the writer in a complicit relation with the issues at stake, resulting in a deep destabilization of the very institution of literature — a light-hearted humour with profound effects.

On one level, 'Leopoldo' is a confessional self-parody that points to Monterroso's own dread of writing, affirmed in public and in private throughout his life. His notes for a discussion at the Centre for International Relations in 1981, for example, include the following statement: 'Yo sé lo que me mueve a no escribir: el miedo, el afán al perfeccionismo, el temor a no igualar los modelos'.[64] Likewise, Leopoldo's only defect as a writer, the narrator notes, is his dislike of writing: 'era presa de un profundo terror cuando se trataba de tomar la pluma' (83); 'aspiraba a que su obra fuera perfecta. Su deseo era abarcarlo todo con aquel sencillo tema' (102). His hankering for perfection leads to the constant postponement of, and digressions from, the act of writing. He has been writing a story about a dog and a porcupine for seven years, because his desire for perfection has led him to 'agotar, casi, la literatura existente sobre estos animales' (88). The word 'almost' undermines the desire for wholeness and universality, foreshadowing his later affirmation in 'Las moscas', in relation to his fly collection, that any attempt at gathering a universal anthology is futile: total knowledge is impossible.

A recurring, caricatural image is employed to depict the failing author: his tired eyes are 'circuidos por profundas ojeras azules que le daban un notorio aspecto intelectual' (88); as he loses sleep over his tale, 'sus amigos lo vieron preocupado y más ojeroso y pálido que nunca' (90); later, he senses the need to write 'cualquier cosa que justificara sus ojeras, su palidez' (96). Leopoldo's facial features are reminiscent of cartoon art: by focusing repeatedly and exclusively on the heavy bags under his eyes, the narrator communicates the plight of the frustrated writer, and the corresponding insomnia, tiredness and neurosis. The thick lines traced verbally by Monterroso to overstate his protagonist's weakness are reproduced in a *mise en abyme* of the internal author's pen, which 'trazaba los signos con firmeza y decisión' (88).

Furthermore, a bathetic effect is created by juxtaposing Leopoldo's 'triunfal entrada en la biblioteca' (81), his 'genio' (90) and his seven-yearly 'ciclos de esplendor' (91) with the tiny impact it has on the general public. A single sentence is all that his forthcoming short story collection warrants in the press: '"El escritor Leopoldo Ralón publicará en breve un libro de cuentos"' (90). This announcement is humorously overshadowed by the 'terrible news' about a cinema star with a broken foot and a dancer with a cold (90) — a comment on the 'exaggerated fascination with the stars of sports and entertainment' identified by Martín-Barbero in the popular press,[65] and a self-conscious reflection on the short story, whose verbal medium is displaced by visual media, whose literary form is permeated by popular and mass forms.

On another level, the focus in 'Leopoldo' is on the metatextual story about a porcupine and a dog, which the narrator outlines thus:

> Un pequeño perro de la ciudad se veía de repente trasladado al campo. Allí, por una serie de sucesos que Leopoldo tenía ya bien claros en la cabeza, la pobre bestia citadina se encontraba en la desdichada necesidad de enfrentarse en lucha a muerte con un puercoespín. (88)

The plot is founded on abstractions and generalizations, on the odd, aleatory opposition between the two anthropomorphized animals: the struggle to the death between dog and porcupine lays bare a black-and-white world view; the characterization of the 'poor' dog shows a one-sided bias; the clarity of the chronological sequence leads to simplification and reduction rather than suggestion and ambiguity.

Leopoldo's compositional dilemmas only underline his polarized vision. If the porcupine won, he reflects, the story might be seen to enclose 'una amarga crítica a la Civilización y el Progreso. Y entonces, ¿en qué quedaba la Ciencia? ¿En qué los ferrocarriles, el teatro, los museos, los libros y el estudio?' (89). If the dog won, it would demonstrate that 'la vida en las ciudades no menoscaba el valor, la fuerza, el deseo de lucha'; people might think that 'estaba abogando por una vida supercivilizada, alejada de todo contacto con la Madre Tierra' (89). His pained hesitations reveal not his sensitivity to different perspectives, but a bipolar vision. Whereas the dog is associated with urban life, civilization and progress, science and literature, museums and transport, the porcupine represents primitiveness and violence, strength and bravery. Later, the narrator connects the second creature provocatively with indigenous Indians: its spikes connote 'las sociedades de hombres, felizmente ya casi extinguidas, que durante milenios usaron las flechas para hacerse la guerra' (92). The dichotomy of city and country is thus linked in a chain of cultural reductions with those between civilization and barbarism, progress and backwardness, Europe and Latin America. Finally, Leopoldo opts for the dog's triumph:

> Viéndolo bien, si él mismo escribía sus obras con una estilográfica que no derramaba la tinta en los aviones; si con sólo dar unas cuantas vueltas en un disco podía comunicarse a través de tres mil millas de montañas y valles con un amigo querido; si a una simple orden suya la obra de alguien que había escrito en tablillas de cera dos mil años antes podía estar en sus manos, y todo eso le parecía perfecto, hubo un momento en que le resultó clarísimo que el perro tenía que triunfar. (91)

The dichotomies are thus set against one another in a struggle whose outcome reinforces the imperialistic cliché that civilization wins, that progress conquers primitiveness — a cliché that underpinned the ideology of developmentalism in Latin America (see Chapter 1). Yet the oppositions begin to unravel as pre-modern media (fountain pens and wax parchments) displace modern modes of transport and communication (aeroplanes and telephones). As in 'El eclipse', the oppositions are decidedly deflated by two satirical techniques. First, he discovers that dogs are not in fact as intelligent as is widely believed: 'Es verdad que el desarrollo de sus instintos era asombroso [...] Pero de inteligencia, señores, lo que se llama inteligencia, nada, absolutamente nada' (93). The cutting brevity of this realization brings the walls erected between two cultures, 'culto' and 'inculto', crashing down in one fell swoop. Second, he realizes that, since barely anything has been written about porcupines, 'apenas si sabía nada acerca de [ellos]. La de nunca acabar; hoy una duda, mañana un nuevo escrúpulo' (95). Ellipsis is not only used by the internal author as a tactic to postpone the dreaded act of writing, but also by the external author to relativize stark cultural binaries and ask the reader to participate in their dismantling.

In this way, Monterroso participates in what García Canclini calls 'la relativización posmoderna de todo fundamentalismo o evolucionismo', which 'facilita revisar la separación entre lo culto, lo popular y lo masivo sobre la que aún simula asentarse la modernidad, elaborar un pensamiento más abierto para abarcar las interacciones e integraciones entre los niveles, géneros y formas de la sensibilidad colectiva' (23). At the level of content and form, Monterroso's texts — with the participation of the cooperative reader — suggest, open or forge sensibilities that emerge from, and feed into, Latin America's hybrid cultures.

Before concluding this chapter, I shall turn to two texts in which power exchanges between perceived cultural poles — whether art and commerce in 'El concierto', insider or outsider in 'El centenario' — are carried out through the medium of money. Both these stories will be considered in the context of García Canclini's argument about the mutual relation between culture and money under the conditions of capitalism: 'cualquier hecho cultural — asistir a un concierto, preparar una conferencia — lleva siempre un nivel socioeconómico implícito'.[66]

This relation is fundamental in 'El concierto', where a girl's prowess as a pianist is entangled with her father's fortune. In this story, the narrator (the father) provocatively connects art with commercial competitiveness: 'Si hay un arte en acumular una fortuna y en ejercer el dominio del mercado mundial y en aplastar a los competidores, reclamo el primer lugar en ese arte' (108). By presenting the musical scene from the businessman's perspective, Monterroso formally replicates the intradiegetic situation: the filtering of the artwork through a financial channel. As in 'Primera dama', the reception and appreciation of the artwork, whether by friends or journalists, is conditioned by monetary relations: 'mis amigos más cercanos han aprendido en carne propia que la frialdad en el aplauso es peligrosa y puede arruinarlos. Si ella no hiciera una señal de que considera suficiente la ovación, seguirían aplaudiendo toda la noche' (108); 'claro que [los periodistas] me temen y con frecuencia puedo comprarlos' (109). The medium of music is therefore displaced by the media of money and journalism, suggesting the way in which art is caught up in a system of social hierarchies, power relations, and commercial exchanges. The expression 'in the flesh' is a nudge to the reader, suggesting a directness of reception, an immediate physical presence that is undermined by the multiple processes of mediation that stand between the performer and the audience. In fact, physical gestures — the performer's body signals and the public's applause alike — are connected with power exchanges.

Yet financial power is destabilized by Monterroso's narrative: 'Me pregunto cuál sería la opinión de la prensa si ella no fuera mi hija [...] Jamás podemos saber con certeza, ni ella ni yo, lo que en realidad es, lo que efectivamente vale' (109). Insecurity and self-doubt thus undermine financial security and confidence. The daughter's worth as a pianist, entangled as it is in economic values, will never be fully ascertained, instilling crippling uncertainty in the pianist and her father alike. Their shared 'incertidumbre e insomnio' undermines the seeming solidity of the father's power, who is ultimately shown to be as helpless and disempowered as his daughter (109). Extradiegetically, the temporal structure of the story, suspended in the sudden silence that announces the beginning of the performance, reproduces this sense of anxiety and uncertainty. By withdrawing the performance from the narrative, Monterroso forces the reader to receive the titular concert through these multiple, distorting media.

In 'El centenario', the social outsider — the giant Orest — is brought into the inside, but finally destroyed, by the lure of the titular coin. The protagonist's abnormality, his excessive, supernatural height of 2.47 metres, is used for comic effect:

> Imaginen. Como la debilidad de sus articulaciones no le permitía hacer ningún esfuerzo, para alimentarlo era preciso que algún familiar suyo se encaramara en las ramas de un árbol a ponerle en la boca bolitas especiales de carne molida, y pequeños trozos de azúcar de remolacha, como postre. Otro pariente le ataba las cintas de los zapatos. (113)

The reader's imagination is invoked to form a caricatural picture of the giant, to fill in the large gap between his mouth and shoes — a gap that elongates his body. An amusing image is conjured by extremes of scale: the altitude of the trees climbed by Orest's relatives to reach his mouth; the diminutive size of the sugar lumps and meatballs they feed him. The visual image is supplemented by journalistic language:

'Los periodistas, con la imaginación que los distingue, lo llamaban el hombre jirafa' (113). Three words thus supply a cartoonish caption: the giraffe man. The physical weakness caused by his frail joints becomes a literalization of his fatal flaw, an irresistible attraction towards money. His condition as a freak and an object of melodramatic sensation — of 'espectáculo lleno de gravitante peligro' (114) — leads him to raise money, first out of the 'charity' of his street viewers, second out of the curiosity of European kings. Finally, he dies a tragic death in Mexico during the celebrations of the Centenary of Independence, incurring twenty-five fractures in the attempt to pick up a centenary coin thrown by one of Porfirio Díaz's henchmen. He is thus killed by the coin and the authoritarian powers that control it.

This tale might be read as a satirical exploration of the connection between money and power: the relations between the characters, mediated by money and greed, become those between master and slave. At the start, the narrator points out that 'Orest atisbaba las nubes y se dejaba servir', both by his family and his servant Olaf (113). His status as master is reinforced by the reference to his 'espíritu aristocrático' (114). Over the years, he becomes powerful, famous, and (relatively) rich — 'uno de los gigantes más ricos del Continente' (115). At the end, though, he becomes slave to the dictator's henchman, as underlined by the visual image of his disastrous attempt to kneel down to pick up the *centenario*. The money-centred plot chimes with Rulfo's 'Anacleto Morones', where Anacleto uses his gift as a storyteller to do business and get rich. As with Orest, this commercialism eventually leads to his downfall, as he is murdered by his business partner, the narrator. Monterroso's and Rulfo's common concern with the alienating medium of money, and the master–slave relations it entails, recurs throughout their collections: whether in Rulfo's 'Es que somos' and 'Paso del Norte' or in Monterroso's 'El concierto' and 'Primera dama'. This shared theme must be viewed in the context of their shared aesthetics: both constitute a profound self-reflection on the relationship between the artist (or the artwork) and society; an implicit exploration of the ways in which the fragmentary form of the short story is caught up in the machinations of journalists, politicians and businessmen.

Another fruitful connection might be established between this story and the work of Julio Cortázar. Despite its setting in Mexico around the turn of the century, the tale is peppered with scattered references to Cortázar: Orest's gigantism; his depiction as an 'artista' whose international fame extends beyond Latin America, to Europe; his photographs alongside 'las más encumbradas personalidades' (115). Cortázar's relationship with Monterroso is also suggested in the following reflection: 'en el fondo de su corazón sentía especial envidia por los enanos, y se soñaba siempre tratando, sin éxito, de alcanzar los aldabones de las puertas' (114). Indeed, Monterroso's diminutive physical stature meant that he was often portrayed, by himself and others, as dwarf-like. In 'Estatua y poesía' (*Movimiento perpetuo*), Monterroso contrasts his stature with that of Cortázar: 'sin empinarme, mido fácilmente un metro sesenta. Desde pequeño fui pequeño' (125); later, he jokingly suggests that Cortázar is the one exception to the rule that all poets are small (127).

This caricatural exploitation of size links Monterroso's 'El centenario' with literary caricatures by Cortázar. Specifically, 'El centenario' might be compared to an early story by Cortázar, 'Las manos que crecen' (*La otra orilla*, 1945) which also uses deformation not only as its subject matter, but also as its formal technique. The plot revolves around the uncontrollable growth of the hands of the protagonist, Plack, following a fist fight with his friend Cary. Repeated focus on the swollen hands of the cartoon-like protagonist, onomatopoeically named Plack, produces a caricatured image of virile pride and violence. The story veers towards the grotesque as Plack's hands turn into 'gigantescas pantallas de carne arrastrando por el suelo', so large that he struggles to get through the door and into a taxi.[67] The hands provoke both hysterical laughter and horror in Plack, disgust and fear in his onlookers.

It is surely relevant that grotesquely inflated hands are also a recurrent subject in Monterroso's drawings (see Fig. 17). Whether or not these drawings were directly influenced by Cortázar's story, they demonstrate a formal impetus shared by the two artists, a common delight in comic caricature, grotesque exaggeration, and ugly deformation. The enormous hand, in Monterroso's drawings and Cortázar's story alike, lays bare the technique of the cartoonist, who characterizes not only through fragmentation — the synecdochic isolation of a single feature to portray the whole — but also through hyperbole and distortion. As Randall Harrison observes, 'the cartoon *deforms*. It not only simplifies, it exaggerates. Heads expand and bodies shrink, noses grow and brows disappear. Facial expressions telegraph emotion' (68). The need to transfer emotional, physical messages through formal concentration and intensification corresponds with the Cortazarian 'knock-out' (foreshadowed literally in this tale) and Monterroso's aesthetic principles of brevity, captured humorously in 'Aconsejar y hacer' (*La letra e*): 'Cuando vine a México tropezaba mucho con un anuncio que decía: *No escriba; telegrafíe*, que yo interpreté al pie de la letra' (299). For both authors, caricature is a formal technique that employs brevity, fragmentation and deformation as a means of achieving communicative immediacy.

Cortázar's pictorial aesthetic extends beyond this particular story, and beyond caricature. Cortázar's *La vuelta* (1967), *Último round* (1969) and *Fantomas* (1975) are flanked by drawings and comic strips, as well as photographs and reproductions of paintings. Anticipating these multimedial collages, the fragmentary novel *Rayuela* (1963) revolves around the motif of the chalk drawing on the ground, the *hopscotch* that is endowed with metaphysical power. It is peppered with references to drawing, principally in the 'capítulos prescindibles', which reveal the infiltration of pictorial art into the literary medium. The insufficiency of the linguistic medium is expressed in an argument between Étienne (who, incidentally, is an artist) and Oliveira regarding *porteño* bread: '— No tienen nada que ver [los panes de Italia con el pan francés de Buenos Aires]', Oliveira insists. 'Un día te voy a hacer un dibujo para que te des cuenta'.[68] A picture, Oliveira suggests, would allow him to communicate directly with Étienne and overcome the obscuring barrier of language.

Morelli expresses a similar desire to supplement language with pictures: 'Le gustaría *dibujar* ciertas ideas, pero es incapaz de hacerlo. Los diseños que aparecen al margen de sus notas son pésimos. Repetición obsesiva de una espiral temblorosa, con un ritmo semejante a las que adornan la *stupa* de Sanchi' (Chapter 66, 485).

FIG. 17. Augusto Monterroso, Drawing, *Disproportionate Hand*
Series 3: Drawings and Photographs; 1941–93; Augusto Monterroso Papers, Box 41–47;
Manuscripts Division, Department of Rare Books and Special Collections,
Princeton University Library

Like the repeated shapes and designs drawn by Monterroso, this reflection suggests a persistent desire to express concepts through the plastic arts. Moreover, it links the drawing with motion and emotion: the trembling spiral is the direct result of a bodily relation with the pen. This chimes with Monterroso's 'Leopoldo', in which the narrator foregrounds the physicality of tracing words. Drawing, for both internal writers, brings out the bodily aspect of writing that is lost with the print industry and mechanical reproduction. The physical materiality of pictorial art is highlighted in the following passages:

> La idea de que alguien tratara de matarlo no se le había ocurrido hasta ese momento a Oliveira, pero le bastó un dibujo instantáneo, un esbozo que tenía más de escalofrío que otra cosa, para darse cuenta de que no era una idea nueva. (Chapter 54, 419)

> Sobre el dolor físico como aguijón metafísico abunda la escritura [...] Si supiera dibujar mostraría alegóricamente el dolor ahuyentando al alma del cuerpo. (Chapter 83, 525)

In both passages, the art of drawing is connected with immediacy, presentation and present-ness. Whether in practice or in theory, it (re)produces the effect of physical pain or the possibility of being killed. Morelli's failed pictures, with their quivering curves, are foreshadowed by this 'instant picture' that has the quality of a shudder. This primitive pictorial art thus sustains an ambiguous relationship with the modern technology of photography: the line drawing has a physical immediacy that endows it with the power, strength and violence of the photographic *punctum*; the photograph and the drawing alike mediate between the artist, the viewer, and the object to (re)produce the sensation of direct experience.

It follows, then, that Cortázar's short stories — his art of 'knock-out' — contain a strong pictorial element, which is conjugated with their photographic and journalistic logic. Returning to 'Las manos que crecen', this connection is implied self-reflexively in the doctor's attempt to seize his singular patient for commercial purposes:

> Naturalmente, usted me permitía tomar algunas fotografías para el museo de rarezas de Pensilvania, ¿no es cierto? Además tengo un cuñado que trabaja en *The Shout*, un diario silencioso y reservado. [...] Un reportaje al hombre de las manos... digamos, de las manos extralimitadas, sería el triunfo para Korinkus. (86)

The caricature of violence is supplemented by photography and journalism, which both maximize on shock effect, whether through disturbing shots or the sensationalist language encapsulated in the newspaper's name, *The Shout*. This multimediality chimes with 'El centenario', where the cartoonish presentation of Orest by the narrator is complemented by the newspapers' high-impact term 'el hombre girafa' and the photographs in Rubén Darío's journal *Mundial*. In both cases, the popular forms of melodrama and sensationalism become entangled with the principles of caricature and exaggeration that underlie the literary texts.

Between Miniscule and Gigantic: The Short Story as Model Kit

Satirical form, as we have seen, breaks down social oppositions and relativizes culture through fragmentation, bathos and humour. In his caricatural portraits, Monterroso plays with the reader's perspectives through extremes of scale. The juxtaposition of the miniature and the gigantic creates bathetic effects: the diminutive cow, glimpsed from a distance through the train window, has a tremendous emotional, physical impact on the internal viewer; the aristocratic, noble giant is brought crashing down by a single coin, the titular *centenario*; the over-blown performance of the First Lady is contrasted with the tiny sum of money raised; the grand figure of the poet is ridiculed through the amused eyes of the small child. These spatial aspects of visual caricature are supplemented by the temporal dimension of narrative. Leopoldo's seven years of dedication to his story are juxtaposed with the single sentence announcing his forthcoming collection in the newspaper; the First Lady's hours of practice, and the narrative build-up to the climax, is contrasted bathetically with the brevity of the director's news that the event has raised seven and a half pesos. Spatio-temporal fragmentation thus produces humorous effects with serious consequences: the relativization and destabilization of socio-cultural categories, relations and systems.

Monterroso's playful handling of scale and duration in *Obras completas* foreshadows the paradoxical logic of the fly that, as I argued above, structures his collage work *Movimiento perpetuo*. This paradox is made explicit at the end of 'Las moscas':

> Oh, Melville, tenías que recorrer los mares para instalar al fin esa gran ballena blanca sobre tu escritorio de Pittsfield, Massachusetts, sin darte cuenta de que el Mal revoloteaba desde mucho antes alrededor de tu helado de fresa en las calurosas tardes de tu niñez y, pasados los años, sobre ti mismo cuando en el crepúsculo te arrancabas uno que otro pelo de la barba dorada leyendo a Cervantes y puliendo tu estilo. [...] Tú mira la mosca. Observa. Piensa. (13–14)

This self-reflexive comment on artistic, philosophical subjects exemplifies the fragmentation that is so structural in Monterroso's *ars poetica*. By juxtaposing the huge body of Melville's whale with the tiny figure of the fly, Monterroso creates dialectical relations between the two animals and literary motifs. By bringing together the daytime vision of the child and the night vision of the bearded old writer, he creates temporal connections that produce shifts in perspectives. Short circuits are thus produced between grandiose subjects and insignificant creatures, high-brow art and childish pleasures, literary sensibilities and culinary tastes — connections that demand the participation of the reader, who is asked to look at the fly, observe and think.

As we have seen, the same demand underlies the *Obras completas*, where fragmentary words and images require an active reader's mind and eye to produce perpetual movement. The short story, like the fly(ing) object, collapses cultural oppositions in that it produces constantly shifting relationships between different temporalities and spatialities: traditional and modern; timeless and fleeting; central and marginal; inside and outside. The eponymous cow is a prime example of the short story's paradoxical form. Spatially, it is both excluded and brought into the centre of 'life in general'. Temporally, its mortal remains are glimpsed fleetingly, yet also captured in slow motion thanks to an entrancing parallax view. Culturally, though its body is a disposable object that is left to rot, the narrator affirms its essential role in the smooth running of society. Historically, its 'chorritos de leche' represent a primitive rural economy, yet these are dialectically intertwined with modern, industrial forms, whether the productions of the publishing business or the systems of rail transport.

As with Rulfo, these transcultural processes are enabled by the short story's form as an uncontained container: like Monterroso's fly, it is a body that contains and transports a cultural tradition; yet like Swift's fly, it is also supplemented by other vessels, which undermine its wholeness, integrity and hermeticism. As with Rulfo too, fragments are reconstructed in ever-shifting configurations. Fixed objects, subjects and concepts, whether stale stereotypes, phrases or binaries, are treated in Monterroso's fiction as corpses — remainders from the past, residues of the present — on which the fly-stories feed in a continual process of decomposition and recomposition. To use Raymond Williams's terms, we might say that society and culture, which are already formed and fixed, are submitted to profound deformations, reformations and movements by 'the undeniable experience of the present': the present moment of reading the text.

Whereas Rulfo's readers are moved by the narrative-cum-photographic *punctum*, Monterroso's readers are tickled — amused, irritated or provoked — by a narrative which often veers into visual caricature. Whatever the effect on the reader/viewer, though, both authors use the paradoxical power of tiny objects to produce pinpricks, bites, stings, cuts, stabs or jabs. The physical, bodily quality of the micro-object is suggested by the Chilean writer José Donoso, in a letter to Monterroso in 1970: 'me gustaría tener una fábula "original" como objeto, son objetos, especialmente las cortas, a pesar de que parecería haberse olvidado de esto que es palmario, de tapa a tapa'.[69] Microfictions are material, portable objects that can be handled and grasped by the reader. The sensorial experience of reading encompasses vision and touch, which supplement and displace the oral/aural transmission of traditional stories. The 'aura' of the original artwork, which for Benjamin is dependent upon distance and uniqueness and lost in the age of mechanical reproduction, is from Donoso's perspective produced by the sensation of — or desire for — proximity created by Monterroso's microtexts.

As I have demonstrated in relation to the three authors in my corpus, the short story is not simply the product of a transition from 'relato popular' to 'cuento literario', as suggested by Eva Valcárcel (see Introduction). Rather it is a lively, complex response to emergent popular forms and sensibilities. Formally, Monterroso's literary works have strong resonances with cartoon art, and thus sustain indirect relations with mass-produced *historietas*. Metafictionally, they present different contexts in which cultural objects are used and abused by the public: in 'Primera dama', the 'high-brow' art of poetry is used (in vain) to raise money at a school fundraising event, where it is placed alongside the national anthem and patriotic music; in 'El poeta al aire libre', a poetry reading fails to entertain an urban crowd and the programmes are used as sunshields; a short story collection is publicized in a newspaper alongside news about a film star in 'Leopoldo'; in 'El centenario', press attention turns a Mexican giant into an object of spectacle and an international star. Cultural hierarchies dissolve into a hotchpotch of modes of producing and consuming, seeing and reading, experiencing and feeling. The literary form of the short story thus mediates between 'high-brow' tastes, popular *saberes* and mass media, participating in the formation of an ever-evolving collective *sensorium*.

As a final illustration of these intermedial movements, I shall turn to 'Uno de cada tres', in which the forms of letter and advertisement, oral tale and radio communication are playfully intertwined. On one level, the text is a letter offering its recipient a fifteen-minute slot on a radio channel designed for people to pour out their misfortunes. On another, it is an advert for 'una excelente radiodifusadora especializada' that would allow the paying participant to 'sostener a sus amistades ya no digamos al día, pero al minuto, de su apasionante caso' (25). Monterroso's playful mockery has as its target not only the technology of radio communication and the alienation of the modern individual, but also the universal human need to communicate, to tell stories, to share troubles.

The form and content of this story foreshadow the newspaper advert for the Neurotics Anonymous that kick starts Cortázar's *62/ Modelo para armar*: 'New Statesman: Are you sensitive, intelligent, anxious or a little lonely? Neurotics Anonymous are a lively, mixed group who believe that the individual is unique. Details s. a. e., Box 8662.'[70] This minimal advert is one of the points at which the fragmentary plots, unrelated characters and distant places join together. In 'Uno de cada tres', as in Cortázar's most radically experimental novel,[71] the narrative medium is displaced by other media: not only advertising and radio broadcasting, but also music (the 'ilustrativas selecciones de arias de ópera' incorporated into the fifteen-minute programmes) and sound effects ('los más increíbles ruidos que el hombre y la naturaleza producen') (26). Advanced technology is ironically put to the service of natural, human sounds, thus ridiculing the notion of progress and bringing together seemingly opposing cultures: primitive and civilized.

As I have argued in relation to collections by Rulfo, Cortázar and Monterroso, each short story combines disconnected fragments, residual and emergent forms, to produce a Lévi-Straussian *bricolage*. From this perspective, the modern Latin American short story might be regarded precisely as a model toolkit, a collection of disparate elements that are assembled by the complicit reader to create, in scaled-down form, a new version of reality.

Notes to Chapter 3

1. AMP, Subseries 1A, Box 1, Notebook, 1984.
2. Monterroso, *La letra e*, in *Tríptico: Movimiento perpetuo; La palabra mágica; La letra e* (Mexico City: Fondo de Cultura Económica, 1995), p. 379. All further references to this text are from this edition, and will be made within the body of the text.
3. AMP, Subseries 1A, Box 2, Folder 6.
4. Monterroso, *La vaca* (Mexico City: Alfaguara, 1999), p. 134.
5. Monterroso, *La palabra mágica*, p. 9.
6. Cortázar's essay 'Del cuento breve' is included in the reading lists prepared for a course on the short story in 1975, in AMP, Subseries 1A, Box 2, Folder 6.
7. In Gustavo Sánchez Zepeda, Gloria Hernández and Magda Fabiola Juárez Monterroso, *Los nuevos escritores y Augusto Monterroso* (Guatemala: Editorial Universitaria Universidad de San Carlos de Guatemala, 2004).
8. José Miguel Oviedo, 'Tres observaciones sobre Monterroso', in *Con Augusto Monterroso: en la selva literaria* (Mexico City: Ediciones del Ermitaño, 2000), pp. 12–18 (p. 13).
9. Lauro Zavala, *La minificción bajo el microscopio* (Mexico City: Universidad Autónoma de México, 2006); Guillermo Siles, *El microrrelato hispanoamericano: la formación de un género en el siglo XX* (Buenos Aires: Corregidor, 2007); David Lagmanovich, 'Márgenes de la narración: el microrrelato hispanoamericano', *Chasqui*, 23 (1994), 29–43.
10. Juan Armando Epple, *Brevísima relación: nueva antología del microcuento hispanoamericano* (Santiago: Mosquito, 1999).
11. Interview with Carlos Morales at a University Seminar (30 June 1995), in AMP, Subseries 4E, Box 51, Folder 9, p. 11. This notion is echoed in an interview with Ilan Stavans, 'On Brevity: A Conversation with Augusto Monterroso', *The Massachusetts Review*, 37 (1996), 393–405 (p. 396).
12. José Carlos Miralles Maldonado, 'La fábula clásica y Horacio en Augusto Monterroso: *Proprie Communia Dicere*', *Cuadernos de filología clásica: estudios latinos*, 23 (2003), 249–64.
13. Lauro Zavala, *Cartografías del cuento y la minificción* (Seville: Renacimiento, 2004), pp. 15–17.
14. Among others, Wilfrido Corral's *Lector, sociedad y género en Monterroso* (Xalapa: Centro de investigaciones lingüístico-literarias, Universidad Veracruzana, 1985); Francisca Noguerol Jiménez, *La trampa en la sonrisa: sátira en la narrativa de Augusto Monterroso* (Seville: Universidad de Sevilla, 2000); Juan Antonio Masoliver Ródenas, 'Un malabarista de los géneros literarios', *La Vanguardia* (Barcelona), 27 November 1992, p. 3; Ana Mercedes Patiño, 'Augusto Monterroso: el género como elemento lúdico', *Revista de literatura mexicana contemporánea*, 6.13 (2000), 47–63.
15. Wilfrido Corral, 'Sostiene Monterroso...: la traducción como autointerpretación', in *Con Augusto Monterroso*, pp. 75–90 (p. 85).
16. Monterroso, *Viaje al centro de la fábula* (Madrid: Alfaguara, 2001), p. 41.
17. Margo Glantz, 'Movimiento perpetuo: Augusto Monterroso', in *Con Augusto Monterroso*, pp. 61–69 (p. 62).
18. Monterroso, *Movimiento perpetuo* (Mexico City: Ediciones Era, 1991), pp. 87–92. Hereafter, all references to this edition will be made within the body of the text.
19. Monterroso, *Obras completas y otros cuentos* (Barcelona: Anagrama, 1998), pp. 79–104. Hereafter, all references to this edition will be made within the body of the text.
20. *Moscas*: Clippings and quotes, in AMP, Subseries 1E, Box 18, Folder 6.
21. Roger Cardinal, 'Collecting and Collage-making: The Case of Kurt Schwitters', in *The Cultures of Collecting*, ed. by John Elsner and Roger Cardinal (London: Reaktion Books, 1994), pp. 68–96 (p. 70).
22. Benjamin, 'Unpacking my Library: A Talk about Book Collecting' (1931), in *Illuminations*, pp. 59–67 (p. 60).
23. Susan Stewart, *On Longing: Narratives of the Miniature, the Gigantic, the Souvenir, the Collection* (Baltimore, MD: Johns Hopkins University Press, 1984).
24. *Moscas*: Clippings and quotes, in AMP, Subseries 1E, Box 18, Folder 6.
25. Diary entry (24 February 1984), in AMP, Subseries 1A, Box 2, 'febrero 84, Dia[rio]', pp. 19–20.
26. Sara Castro-Klarén, 'Cortázar, Surrealism, and "Pataphysics"', *Comparative Literature*, 27.3 (1975), 218–36 (p. 226).

27. Monterroso, *Viaje*, p. 86.
28. Monterroso, *Viaje*, p. 90.
29. Claude Lévi-Strauss, *The Savage Mind* (London: Weidenfeld and Nicolson, 1974), p. 16.
30. *Moscas*: Clippings and quotes, in AMP, Subseries 1E, Box 18, Folder 6.
31. Cortázar, *Historias de cronopios y de famas* (Madrid: Punto de lectura, 2007), p. 85.
32. Cortázar, *Rayuela*, chapter 56, p. 433.
33. Steven Boldy, *The Novels of Julio Cortázar* (Cambridge: Cambridge University Press, 2010), p. 42.
34. Borges, *El Aleph* (Buenos Aires: Emecé, 1972), p. 103.
35. Borges, 'El escritor argentino', pp. 196, 203.
36. Juan Villoro, 'El jardín razonado', in *Con Augusto Monterroso*, pp. 32–43 (p. 34).
37. 'Discurso de Augusto Monterroso al recibir el Premio Príncipe de Asturias de las Letras 2000' (Oviedo, 27 October 2000), in AMP, Box 20, Folder 14.
38. Rory O'Bryen, 'The Short Story 2: Augusto Monterroso', Lecture (Cambridge, 2008).
39. Monterroso, *Viaje*, p. 62.
40. Monterroso, *Obras completas*, p. 77.
41. Julio Cortázar, *Papeles inesperados*, ed. by Aurora Barnárdez and Carles Álvarez Garriga (Buenos Aires: Alfaguara, 2009), p. 473.
42. Gloria Estela González Zenteno, '"Mister Taylor" de Augusto Monterroso: de la América maravillosa a la ironía de la historia', *Romance Languages Annual* (1999), 470–77; available online at <http://tell.fll.purdue.edu/RLA-Archive/1999/Spanish/GONZALEZZ.HTM> [accessed 8 April 2014].
43. Mark Millington, 'On Location: The Question of Reading Crossculturally', *Siglo XX/20th Century*, 13.1–2 (1995), 13–39; online at <http://eprints.nottingham.ac.uk/28/0/millington2.txt> [accessed 22 May 2012].
44. Bernard McGuirk, *Latin American Literature: Symptoms, Risks, and Strategies of Poststructuralist Criticism* (London; New York: Routledge, 1996), p. 233.
45. McGuirk, *Latin American Literature*, p. 245.
46. Critics of Monterroso's satire include Francisca Noguerol Jiménez, *La trampa en la sonrisa: sátira en la narrativa de Augusto Monterroso* (Seville: Universidad de Sevilla, 2000); Blanca Inés Gómez Buendía, 'Monterroso, sátira y humor', *Cuento en red* (2000), 45–49; Saúl Sosnowski, 'Augusto Monterroso: la sátira del poder', *Zona Franca*, 3.19 (1980), 53–57.
47. Noguerol Jiménez, *La trampa*, p. 219.
48. Dustin H. Griffin, *Satire: A Critical Reintroduction* (Lexington: University Press of Kentucky, 1994), p. 95.
49. Northrop Frye, *Anatomy of Criticism: Four Essays* (Princeton, NJ: Princeton University Press, 1992), p. 234.
50. Claude Lévi-Strauss, *The Savage Mind*, p. 16.
51. Notebook entry (16th May 1985), notebook entitled '5 de noviembre 84, 1984–1985', in AMP, Subseries 1A, Box 3.
52. María Elena Díaz, 'The Satiric Penny Press for Workers in Mexico, 1900–1910: A Case Study in the Politicisation of Popular Culture', *Journal of Latin American Studies*, 22 (1990), 497–526; Victor Alba, 'The Mexican Revolution and the Cartoon', *Comparative Studies in Society and History*, 9 (1967), 121–36; Carlos Monsiváis, 'La cultura popular en el ámbito urbano', p. 139.
53. Randall Harrison, *The Cartoon: Communication to the Quick* (Beverly Hills, CA: Sage, 1981), p. 11.
54. Ernst Gombrich and Ernst Kris, 'The Principles of Caricature', *British Journal of Medical Psychology*, 17.3–4 (1938), 319–42.
55. Augusto Monterroso, 'Breve, brevísimo', in *Literatura y vida*, p. 106.
56. 'NY-Boston-Cambridge-Harvard-Filadelfia-Princeton', in AMP, Subseries 1A, Box 1, Notebook (1984).
57. Robert Hughes, *The Shock of the New: Art and the Century of Change* (London: British Broadcasting Corporation, 1980), p. 12.
58. Néstor García Canclini, *Las culturas populares*, p. 42.
59. Pierre Bourdieu, *Distinction: A Social Critique of the Judgement of Taste*, trans. by Richard Nice (Cambridge, MA: Harvard University Press, 1984), p. 13.

60. Harold Rosenberg, 'The Labyrinth of Saul Steinberg', in *The Anxious Object: Art Today and its Audience* (New York: Macmillan, 1973), pp. 163–66 (p. 163).

61. Roland Barthes and Saul Steinberg, *All Except You* (Paris: Galerie Maeght, 1983), p. 48.

62. García Canclini, *Las culturas populares*, p. 42.

63. Philip Swanson, 'Civilization and barbarism', in *The Companion to Latin American Studies*, ed. by Philip Swanson (London: Arnold, 2003), pp. 68–85 (pp. 77–78).

64. 'Plática de Augusto Monterroso en: Center for Interamerican Relations, New York' (12 Feb 1981) in AMP, Subseries 1F, Box 20, Folder 2.

65. Martín-Barbero, *Communication*, p. 177.

66. García Canclini, *Culturas populares*, p. 44.

67. Julio Cortázar, *La otra orilla* (Madrid: Santillana Ediciones Generales, 2008), p. 28.

68. Cortázar, *Rayuela*, chapter 100, p. 587.

69. José Donoso, letter (Barcelona, 30 September 1970), in AMP, Subseries 2A, Box 23, Folder 7.

70. Julio Cortázar, *62/ Modelo para armar* (Madrid: Punto de Lectura, 2007), p. 48.

71. Boldy, *The Novels of Julio Cortázar*, pp. 97–160.

CONCLUSION

Looking Forward:
After-lives, Adaptations and Legacies

Through close, comparative readings, intersected by different theoretical frameworks, I have explored the limits on which the Latin American short story dwells. On one level, this work adds depth to research on the three authors in my corpus. It departs from existing criticism by drawing connections between their short stories and the rest of their artistic output, whether fragmentary novels, photograph collections, collage works or drawings. This, in turn, has led me to suggest broader connections between the short story form and extra-literary media. On another level, I have suggested formal relationships between three bodies of work that supplement the social, intellectual, and even political relationships between their authors. Superficially and thematically, the works of Rulfo and Cortázar risk being polarized in terms of false dichotomies: local and cosmopolitan, traditional and modern, rural and urban. My contention, though, is that the Latin American short story is an intrinsically hybrid form which, far from erecting barriers, produces encounters between forms, media, and cultures. Monterroso's work, which self-consciously dissolves and dismantles the abstract cultural categories in which Latin American literature is entangled, serves to mediate between these two authors.

More broadly, my study fulfils a mediating role on a secondary, theoretical level, by playing out the clashes within individual theories and between different critical traditions through the frames of the short stories. Contradictions are not ironed out, but acknowledged, analysed and in part explained in relation to the internal paradoxes of the short story. I bring together different readings of the short story: literary studies by Terry Eagleton, Mary Rohrberger, Nadine Gordimer and Charles May, who contrast it with the realist novel and/or situate it in relation to broader aesthetico-philosophical movements; market-oriented studies by Walter Benjamin, Frederick Lewis Pattee, Andrew Levy and Stuart Sillars, who see it (whether positively or negatively) as a practical response to the demands of publishers and consumers. Furthermore, productive potential is found in the contradictions within Benjamin's work, which has been crucial for thinking about the broader historical processes inflected within these short stories: his nostalgia for the 'dying' figures of storyteller and collector, and for the corresponding structures of *Erfahrung* and tradition; his celebration of modern media, of the democratic, if not revolutionary, potential of mechanical reproduction, and of a fragmentary form of collecting that is (un)realized in the *Arcades Project*. The Latin American short story, I argue, articulates these contradictions in ways that respond to the complexities of the cultural contexts from which it emerges.

Using and extending Latin American studies of transculturation and hybridity, the short story is viewed at the limits, and as an intersection, between different (constructed) cultural categories. On one level, the Latin American short story sustains important relations with other literary genres and movements: essay, poetry, and novel; Fantastic literature, Surrealism and the 'nueva novela'. On another level, it owes some of its qualities to a relationship with 'lo popular': as critics like Pupo-Walker, González Echevarría and Rama have demonstrated, it cannot be fully separated from an oral, rural storytelling tradition, or rather a collection of native, African and European traditions. Finally — and to come to the principal contribution of the study — it draws much of its creative capacity from the media associated with the urban masses or, in other words, from emerging, contemporary forms of 'lo popular'. Journalism, photography, cinema, telephony, graffiti and cartoon art infiltrate the short stories both on thematic and formal levels, fuelling plots and furnishing structures. Simultaneously porous and resistant, the Latin American short story constitutes what Linda Hutcheon terms a 'complicitous critique':[1] its relationship with the mass media is one of simultaneous immersion and criticism, exploitation and denaturalization; whilst imitating and borrowing journalistic or cinematic techniques, it lays bare their concealed mechanisms.

As I have demonstrated, these different levels — *culto*, popular and mass — become tightly interconnected within the form and structure of the short story. Literary devices, whether suggestion, suspension, defamiliarization or immediacy, intersect with the principles of emerging mass media: photographic *puncta*, filmic *montages*, sensationalistic thrills, telephonic disjunctions, and cartoonish humour. These, in turn, supplement, displace or transform popular forms of communication: orality, dialogue, conversation, performance, and collective participation. The Latin American short story, in this way, is neither a purely literary phenomenon, nor an exclusive product of a popular tradition, nor a mere commodity in an emerging, globalized mass culture. Rather, its fragmentary form results from these interrelated cultures, from intersections and divergences, encounters and clashes, gatherings and dispersions.

By way of a conclusion, I shall now briefly turn to some of the after-lives of short stories by Rulfo, Cortázar and Monterroso: after-lives that bring out the internal features of the short stories; that actualize their productive potential. Within the body of the monograph, I analysed the hybrid, intermedial elements inscribed within the short stories themselves. An extension to this approach involves examining the varied fates of the short stories, the ways in which they are retold, or re-used, in different media: audio recordings, plays, films and even ballet. A detailed analysis of these after-lives and adaptations would warrant another project altogether. For the current purposes, though, a brief overview of the different media through which the short stories are revived will suffice to shed light on the relationship between the modes of production enclosed within the structure of the texts and the ways in which they are read and viewed, consumed and used.

All three authors have been recorded reading their short stories aloud. This

means that their dictations can be heard today through varied media, from tapes and CDs to internet sites[2] and You Tube.[3] Monterroso's and Cortázar's own reflections capture some of the effects of voice recording as a means of storage and transmission: fragmentation, dislocation, disconnection, and reconnection. In 'La voz humana' (*Literatura y vida*, 2003), Monterroso reflects on the inherent strangeness of voice recordings upon receiving a tape of forty fragments written and read by great European authors:

> Cuando escuchamos la propia voz en una grabación electrónica, nuestra primera reacción es de extrañeza y rechazo. [...] Sucede hasta con un simple contestador telefónico. En un rango parecido de cosas, creo que esa misma frustración sentimos con las fotografías.[4]

Listening to Leon Tolstoy, Jean-Paul Sartre and Thomas Mann, among others, he asks himself how they might have felt upon hearing their own voices captured on tape. He reflects on the distance between the original production and the mechanical reproduction, greater in earlier recordings, lesser in more recent recordings (53). When he listens to himself on recordings from La Havana, Madrid and Mexico City, he fears that 'los incesantes adelantos técnicos las hagan oír pronto como producto de otro planeta en que los años y aun la labora del minuto habrán de convertirlas' (53). Because of the dual effects of material decay (and the consequent deterioration of the recordings) and technological advances (which make early recordings sound other-worldly), time increases alienation and dislocation. Furthermore, the mechanical separation of the voice from the body produces an effect of dislocation, as Monterroso highlights by conjecturing that Sartre is 'probablemente en el Flore, su café parisino favorito' (52), and that Mann greets his audience 'desde un hotel de no sé qué ciudad' (53). As revealed by his hesitation, the technology for storing the spoken word — a modern form of orality — severs the voice from a known spatial context. These processes of spatio-temporal fragmentation and defamiliarization arguably replicate the internal techniques of the short story, which as we have seen is at least a partial product of the age of mechanical reproduction.

On a tape recording of some of his stories, Cortázar brings up similar concerns between two readings:

> Ahora que voy a completar este disco con otras lecturas, es curioso pensar como las cosas pueden ordenarse o desordenarse más allá de todo lo concebible. A lo mejor usted escuchó la primera cara y después se fue al cine, o estuvo seis meses estudiando matemáticas, o a lo mejor todavía no escuchó la primera cara porque no le gusta proceder metódicamente... y yo por mi parte grabé esos primeros textos hace ya cinco días y después estuve tan resfriado que no pude seguir porque mi voz parecía una foca pidiéndole pescados al domador... y a lo mejor usted está escuchándome en mangas de camisa y con las ventanas abiertas y en cambio aquí nevó anoche y yo me he puesto un polo abrigado y amarillo... Todo es distante y diferente y parece inconciliable... y a la vez todo se da simultáneamente en este momento, que todavía no existe para mí y que sin embargo es el momento en que usted escucha estas palabras que yo grabé en el pasado, es decir en un tiempo que para mí ahora es el futuro... [risa][5]

A number of levels of disconnection are made apparent within, and between, the processes of production and consumption. The tape recording allows both

listener and speaker to absent themselves, to intersperse fragments of the recording with other occupations and art forms, to return to it after several days or months. Moreover, the recorded voice is separated from the recording subject, detaching words from their original bodily source. Finally, the listener is temporally, spatially disconnected from the performer: they might be in different countries, climates, seasons, decades or indeed millennia. Yet Cortázar, rather than mourning the figure of a Benjaminian storyteller whose tale is rooted in his body, life and experience, turns the focus from disconnection to reconnection. He celebrates the present moment in which the stories are revived, the experience of listening that brings together past and future in a relation of simultaneity. The ability to pause, rewind and transport a recorded narrative already underlies the short story's paradoxical form as it is viewed in this study: severed from an embodied storyteller and reactivated in the instant of reading, it creates disconnections and reconnections, disorderings and reorderings.

One of the principal media to which short stories by Rulfo, Monterroso and Cortázar have been adapted, with varying degrees of success, is film. Most prominently, Cortázar's short stories have generated, since the 1960s, a consistent flow of adaptations from within, and outside, Argentina. Manuel Antín is the director who dedicated most films to Cortázar, with *La cifra impar* (1962, based on 'Cartas a mamá'), *Circe* (1964, adapted by Cortázar himself), and *Intimidad de los parques* (1965, based on 'Continuidad de los parques' and 'El ídolo de las Cícladas'). Internationally, the most popular productions are Michelangelo Antonioni's *Blow-Up*, a loose interpretation of 'Las babas del diablo' (1966); Jean-Luc Godard's *Weekend*, based on 'La autopista del sur'; and Walter Renaud's short film *La Fin du jeu* (1971), based on 'Final del juego'. Other examples include *Continuidad de los parques* (1972, a short film by Fabián Bielinsky), *Monsieur Bébé* (1974, a film by Claude Chabrol based on 'Los buenos servicios'), *L'Ingorgo* (1978, an Italian production by Luigi Comencini, based on 'La autopista del sur'), and *Sinfín* (1986, by Cristian Pauls, based loosely on 'Casa tomada'). Some more minor, scarcely diffused, versions ensued, like the North American *End of the Game* (1988), the Lithuanian *Autobús* (1994, based on 'Ómnibus'), the Australian *House Taken Over* (1997) and the Paraguayan *Sueños* (2006, based on 'La noche boca arriba'). *Mentiras piadosas*, Diego Sabanés's 2008 production (based on a combination of 'La salud de los enfermos' and 'Casa tomada') is the most recent attempt to adapt Cortázar's stories to the cinema.[6]

What is it, then, that makes the short story so adaptable to the cinematic medium? Monterroso himself provides a partial answer to this question in a 1975 notebook entry:

> Creo que contra lo que podría pensarse, es más bien de los cuentos de donde pueden hacerse buenas películas, siempre que el cuento sirva apenas de punto de partida, como en el caso de *Blow Up*, basada en el cuento de Cortázar: Por qué? Porque Antonioni no siguió para nada el cuento: se inspiró en él y ya.[7]

What makes a successful adaptation, for Monterroso, is the freedom of inspiration that privileges creative transformation over fidelity to the source text. The short story, an inherently suggestive, fragmentary and — from a Benjaminian perspective

— post-auratic form, invites participation, manipulation and reconfiguration. This is indeed the case in Eduardo Lizalde's adaptation of Monterroso's 'Sinfonía conclusa', a film that for financial reasons was never produced, which adds narrative, semantic and symbolic elements to the original story.[8] As Lizalde insists in his preamble to the synopsis, the short story contains 'la semilla de un amplio desarrollo anecdótico. En el cuento cada una de las frases implica y sugiere numerosos sucesos y movimientos — y diálogos — que es fácil deducir y desenvolver textualmente' (1). His adaptation merely follows the logic of supplementarity set in chain by the short story itself, a logic which for Derrida harbours two simultaneous significations: the addition of a 'surplus' to an already existing plenitude; the compensation for a lack, the filling of a void.[9]

It is not just the short story's formal aperture, though, but also its openness to different media that invites filmic supplementation: cinema, of course, is an intrinsically multimedial form. This can be seen, for example, in Pako González's 2005 short film entitled 'Graffiti', inspired by Cortázar's story.[10] Containing slices of music, radio, television, and two meta-films (*Raza*, by José Luis Sáenz de Heredia, 1941 and *Benito Mussolini*, a documentary by Pasquale Prunas, 1962), this film extends the story's internal intermediality. Interestingly, 'Graffiti' has also been adapted to the theatre by the Spanish director José Sanchis Sinistierra, in a recent production entitled *Cronopios rotos: variaciones sobre Cortázar* (October 2010). It is combined with a story from a different collection, 'Torito', through what the director sees as their shared quality: the dialogue with a real or imagined interlocutor. Sanchis Sinistierra himself reflects on the intermediality inherent in Cortázar's fiction: to justify his adaptation of these stories to the theatre, he explains that 'hay en su literatura una especie de oralidad latente que está muy cerca del teatro.'[11] The short story form, with its hybrid literary, oral elements, thus breaks its boundaries once again through the theatrical medium. The intermediality of the internal dialogue is thus perpetuated by the story's after-life.

As a final illustration, I shall turn to another performance art to which the short story form has — more surprisingly, perhaps — been adapted: ballet. Rulfo's story 'Talpa', for example, was transformed into a ballet by Rosa Reyna, with music by Blas Galindo, words by José Durand, and design by José Chávez Morado. Entitled *La Manda* and performed in Mexico City in 1951, this was a work of nationalist modern dance.[12] In an interview, Galindo explains that his music was inspired by the intersection of the story 'Talpa' with his own personal experience: in the Jaliscan village San Gabriel where he was brought up, he explains, pilgrimage and incestuous relationships were common currency.[13] Reyna, for very different reasons, draws from her personal engagement with the story: 'un año antes de *La Manda* estuve en el trance de vivir entre la vida y la muerte y después viví la experiencia del trío amoroso.'[14] In my chapter on Rulfo, I examined his short stories' capacity to be reinscribed in new contexts — to strike different chords with different people and to cause 'gut reactions' — in terms of photographic *puncta*. *La Manda* supplements the intermedial chain by bringing out the qualities of movement and fluidity that, as I have suggested, are paradoxically intertwined with the photographic stills in Rulfo's short fiction.

A final example is Arturo Garrido's dance production 'Todo es según el color del cristal con que se mira', which combined different fables from Monterroso's *La oveja negra*. Garrido describes the opening scene thus: 'como en el fondo de una fotografía todos los personajes se encuentran congelados (estáticos) a excepción del Mal y del Bien que deambulan acechando.'[15] The interplay between static image and balletic movement is an extension of the interplay between the permanent and the fleeting that, as we have seen, characterizes Monterroso's fragmentary art. In fact, the production brings together the isolated frames of the fables, juxtaposing the figures of the owl, frog, chameleon, cricket, dog, monkey, good and evil. These perform 'cambiantes caricaturas' (5), setting into motion the cartoonish figures of Monterroso's prose. Significantly, the music to which they perform is a hybrid composition of contemporary and Afro-American pieces. In turn, the ballet's openness to different media, narratives and cultures corresponds with Garrido's desire to open the artwork to a wider audience, expressed by his specification that the ballet is 'dirigida a todo público (niños, jóvenes y adultos)' (1). This desire is also expressed by Monterroso in a 1984 notebook, where he describes himself — with a typical touch of humour — as 'A. Monterroso, autor de literatura infantil'.[16] As we have seen, the attempt to make the work of art accessible to a wider public is one of the driving forces of the short story's internal intermediality.

In *A Theory of Adaptation*, Linda Hutcheon examines the permeability of different media, asking why modern culture is so bent on adaptation. She concludes by linking this tendency to the potentialities of narrative, of stories that can be told again and again: 'Because adaptations usually revisit stories', Hutcheon proposes, 'perhaps we should look to theories of narrative to explain the popularity of adaptations.'[17] Adaptation is therefore seen as a modern manifestation of storytelling, providing continuity and repetition as well as change and transformation by telling the 'same' stories over and over again. Aligning myself with Monterroso, though, I would argue that it is not only the continuity with, but also the departure from, the original story that enables the adaptations to take on their own after-lives. In Derridean terms, the adaptation is a supplement: it is not only added as a cumulating, culminating surplus, but also 'intervenes or insinuates itself *in-the-place-of*' the original version; it is a productive replacement, an active displacement.[18] In this vein, any adaptation is a vindication of the successful transfer of meaning-production from text to reader. It comes into fruition through the cooperation of the 'lector cómplice'.

My argument is that the short story's particular suitability to adaptation resides not only in its narrative core, but more importantly in its fragmentation of narrative and its consequent interpellation of the reader: the adaptor might be inspired by a single strand of the story which resonates with his or her own experience; might take the basic plot or premise as a point of departure; might combine different stories to form new correspondences. Hence adaptations like *la Manda* stem less from *Erfahrung* than from *Erlebnis*, less from continuous, shared experience than from fragmentary, singular, personal experience(s). The modern obsession with adaptation might therefore be explained less by the power of narrative, as Hutcheon would have it, than by its weakness (which is also its strength); by what it fails (or refuses) to say, capture, or express.

The lingering suggestiveness of Rulfo, Cortázar and Monterroso's narrative is such that it continues to experience posthumous redemptions in contemporary Latin American short fiction. To point to a few examples, Cristina Rivera Garza, from 2010 to 2011, wrote a collection of variations inspired by Rulfo's *Pedro Páramo* in a blog entitled *Mi Rulfo mío de mí*.[19] It takes the form of poetic and prose fragments interspersed with his photographs. Antonio Sonora's *Adiós a Rocamadour* (2011) is a series of nineteen short stories inspired by Cortázar's work.[20] As Alberto Chimal points out, Cortázar's influence can be found in multiple elements of Sonora's work, 'en el asunto subterráneo de los textos, así como en su brevedad, en el sentido casi poético de algunas ficciones, en los temas acerca de lo sobrenatural, en lo extraño y en la irreverencia que trató de imprimir en este libro'.[21] And Lauro Zavala highlights the literary repercussions of 'El dinosaurio' in *El dinosaurio anotado* (2002), which gathers microstories and poems by different authors (as well as a project for an opera) inspired by Monterroso's shortest short story.[22]

Moreover, their legacy is strongly felt in the ways in which current Latin American authors push back the limits of literature through emerging media, opening up new possibilities for production and consumption.[23] Rivera Garza, for example, publishes a monthly *fotonovela* on her blog *Historia de la increíblemente pequeña*, which combines fragmentary prose and poetry, illustrations, photographs and videoclips that together bring to life a character based on plastic figurines.[24] Alongside other writers, like her compatriots Mauricio Montiel Figueiras and Alberto Chimal, she has also used the social networking site Twitter as a literary medium, in a movement that has been termed *tuiteratura*; that replaces readers with followers; and that restricts the narrative to 140 characters.[25] The medium of Twitter opens literature up to a global community of readers, who are able to respond and participate. In Chimal's case, his tweets have led to a publication, *El viajero del tiempo* (2011), a collection of 123 minifictions about a time traveller.[26] His time traveller, appropriately, moves between different eras, confronting current Latinists with figures from classical Rome, Greek heroes with their film versions. Significantly, he acknowledges in an interview the influence of short story writers like Poe, Borges, Rulfo and Arreola on his writing.[27] Indeed, like the authors I have explored in this study, who use the limits of the short story as a point of departure from which limitless possibilities are opened up, Chimal produces encounters between different worlds *through* the constraints of Twitter.

The fragmentary form of short fiction, then, is at once a symptom and potentialization of changing conditions of production and consumption. Mourned pre-emptively by Benjamin, the storyteller is continually buried and revived in literary acts that adopt ever-evolving forms and demand new modes of participation. Rulfo's life-filled ruins and Monterroso's buzzing flies might be seen to emblematize the short story's obduracy, its ability to be reinvigorated precisely by that which seems bent on destroying it. The photographic reproduction, whose rising primacy competes with that of the printed word, is incorporated by Rulfo to revive the ghosts of decaying communities, to create close bonds with the distant reader, and to suggest openings in seeming dead-ends. The cartoon image, whose diffusion in comic books far exceeds that of the literary text in Mexico, is employed by Monterroso to create a particular brand of anti-authoritarian, anti-institutional humour. In Cortázar's case, multiple media are invoked to provide new forms of contact between seemingly separate realities and to cross spatio-temporal barriers. In all cases, the aesthetic configurations of the fragment gesture towards socio-cultural reconfigurations, towards ever new forms of cooperation and resistance, sociability and rebellion.

As García Canclini suggests, Latin America's cultural hybridity leads to artistic hybridity: 'hoy todas las culturas son de frontera. Todas las artes se desarrollan en relación con otras artes [...] Así las culturas pierden la relación exclusiva con su territorio, pero ganan en comunicación y conocimiento'.[28] The stakes of intermedial relations are high. The limits of narrative, points of intersection between forms, arts, media and cultures, are also sites of clashes and negotiations, conflicts and transactions. Hence Rulfo, whilst seeking a cooperative reader, communicates through the *punctum*; Cortázar demands a complicit reader whilst proceeding by 'knock-out'; Monterroso's texts, like his flies, bite and unite. At its limits, the short story produces, and is produced by, complex, conflicting relations that refuse to be resolved; relations that ensure its perpetual movement.

Notes to the Conclusion

1. Linda Hutcheon, *Politics of Postmodernism* (New York: Routledge, 2002), p. 13.
2. *A media voz* is the main collection of dictated works: <http://amediavoz.com/poetas.htm> [accessed 8 April 2014].
3. Two examples include Juan Rulfo's 'No oyes ladrar los perros', <http://www.youtube.com/watch?v=cewv7qyUpsA>; and Julio Cortázar's 'Me caigo y me levanto', <http://www.youtube.com/watch?v=PMWonO8jsdU> [accessed 8 April 2014].
4. Monterroso, *Literatura y vida* (Madrid: Alfaguara, 2004), p. 51.
5. Julio Cortázar, tape recording [n.d.].
6. Anon., 'Cortázar y el cine: una relación productiva', in *Página/12*, 6 January 2007, 'Espectáculos' section, <http://proyectoespartaco.wordpress.com/2007/01/15/cortazar-y-el-cine-una-relacion-productiva/> [accessed 8 April 2014].
7. Notebook, 1975, in AMP, Subseries 1A, Box 1.
8. AMP, Box 53, Folder 10: Miscellaneous.
9. Jacques Derrida, *Of Grammatology*, pp. 144–45.
10. Francisco 'Pako' González, 'Graffiti' (Napato Production, 2005, 20 mins), <http://www.youtube.com/watch?v=9IoYPIvMye4> [accessed 8 April 2014].
11. José Sanchis Sinisterra, cited by María Hernández Jesús, in 'Los cronopios de Julio Cortázar suben a las tablas de Galileo' (6 October 2010), <http://www.elmundo.es/elmundo/2010/10/06/ocio/1286373805.html>, [accessed 8 April 2014].
12. Patricia Seed, *José Limón and La Malinche: The Dancer and the Dance* (Austin: University of Texas Press, 2008), p. 140.
13. Roberto García Bonilla, *Visiones sonoras: entrevistas con compositores, solistas y directores* (Mexico City: Siglo XXI, 2001), p. 48.
14. Cited by Alberto Dallal, in 'Efemérides: recuerdo de Rosa Reyna', *Imágenes: revista electrónica del Instituto de Investigaciones Estéticas* (9 February 2007), <http://www.esteticas.unam.mx/revista_imagenes/efemerides/efe_rosareyna.html> [accessed 8 April 2014].
15. AMP, Subseries 1E, Box 19, Folder 6: Works in Progress.
16. Notebook, 1984, in AMP, Subseries 1A, Box 2.
17. Linda Hutcheon, *A Theory of Adaptation* (Abingdon; New York: Routledge, 2006), p. 175.
18. Derrida, *Of Grammatology*, p. 145.

19. Cristina Rivera Garza, *Mi Rulfo mío de mí* (blog, 2011–12), <http://mirulfomiodemi.wordpress.com/> [accessed 8 April 2014].
20. Antonio Sonora, *Adiós a Rocamadour* (Mexico: Atemporia/Museo Biblioteca Pape, 2011).
21. Cited in Anon., 'Adiós a Rocamadour, una introspección literaria inspirada en Cortázar' (12 April 2012), <http://www.conaculta.gob.mx/sala_prensa_detalle.php?id=20055> [accessed 8 April 2014].
22. *El dinosaurio anotado. Edición crítica de 'El dinosaurio' de Augusto Monterroso*, ed. by Lauro Zavala (Mexico City: Alfaguara/UAM, 2002).
23. Claire Taylor and Thea Pitman, *Latin American Identity in Online Cultural Production* (New York: Routledge, 2013).
24. Cristina Rivera Garza, *Las aventuras de la increíblemente pequeña* (2011), <http://increiblementepequena.tumblr.com/> [accessed 8 April 2014].
25. <http://twitter.com/albertochimal/>, <http://twitter.com/criveragarza>, <http://twitter.com/Elhombredetweed/> [accessed 8 April 2014].
26. Alberto Chimal, *El viajero del tiempo* (Monterrey: Ediciones Posdata, 2011).
27. Óscar Alarcón and Alberto Chimal, 'Entrevista a Alberto Chimal' (15 February 2010) <http://abartraba.blogspot.co.uk/2010/02/alberto-chimal.html> [accessed 8 April 2014].
28. García Canclini, *Culturas híbridas*, pp. 325–26.

BIBLIOGRAPHY

ALARCÓN, ÓSCAR, and ALBERTO CHIMAL, 'Entrevista a Alberto Chimal' (15 February 2010) <http://abartraba.blogspot.co.uk/2010/02/alberto-chimal.html> [accessed 8 April 2014]

ALBA, VICTOR, 'The Mexican Revolution and the Cartoon', *Comparative Studies in Society and History*, 9 (1967), 121–36

ALONSO, CARLOS J., ed., *Julio Cortázar: New Readings* (Cambridge: Cambridge University Press, 2011)

ANON., 'Adiós a Rocamadour, una introspección literaria inspirada en Cortázar' (12 April 2012), <http://www.conaculta.gob.mx/sala_prensa_detalle.php?id=20055> [accessed 8 April 2014]

——'Cortázar y el cine: una relación productiva', *Página/12* (6 January 2007), 'Espectáculos' section, <http://proyectoespartaco.wordpress.com/2007/01/15/cortazar-y-el-cine-una-relacion-productiva/> [accessed 8 April 2014]

ARONNE-AMESTOY, LIDA, *América en la encrucijada de mito y razón: introducción al cuento epifánico latinoamericano* (Buenos Aires: F. García Cambeiro, 1976)

BALDERSTON, DANIEL, 'The Twentieth-Century Short Story in Spanish America', in *The Cambridge History of Latin American Literature*, ed. by Roberto González Echevarría (Cambridge; New York: Cambridge University Press, 1996), pp. 465–96

BARTHES, ROLAND, and SAUL STEINBERG, *All Except You* (Paris: Galerie Maeght, 1983)

——*Camera Lucida: Reflections on Photography*, trans. by Richard Howard (London: Vintage, 1993)

——*S/Z*, trans. by Richard Miller (Oxford; New York: Wiley-Blackwell, 1990)

BARTRA, ROGER, *The Cage of Melancholy: Identity and Metamorphosis in the Mexican Character* (New Brunswick, NJ: Rutgers University Press, 1992)

BENAVIDES, MANUEL, 'La abolición del tiempo: análisis de "Todos los fuegos el fuego"', *Cuadernos hispanoamericanos, Homenaje a Julio Cortázar* (1980), 484–94

BELL, L. A. J., 'The Death of the Storyteller and the Poetics of (Un)Containment: Juan Rulfo's *El llano en llamas*', *Modern Language Review*, 107.3 (2012), pp. 815-836

——'Photography, Punctum and Shock: Re-Viewing Juan Rulfo's Short Stories', *Bulletin of Hispanic Studies*, 91.4 (2014), pp. 437–52

BENÍTEZ, FERNANDO, 'Conversaciones con Juan Rulfo', in Juan Rulfo, *Inframundo, El México de Juan Rulfo* ([Hanover, NH]: Ediciones del Norte, 1983), pp. 3–9

BENJAMIN, WALTER, *The Arcades Project*, trans. by Howard Eiland and Kevin McLaughlin (Cambridge, MA; London: Belknap Press of Harvard University Press: 1999)

——*Illuminations*, trans. by Harry Zohn (Glasgow: Fontana, 1982)

——*One-Way Street, and Other Writings*, trans. by Edmund Jephcott and Kingsley Shorter (London: NLB/Verso, 1979)

BERGSON, HENRI, *The Creative Mind: An Introduction to Metaphysics*, trans. by Mabelle L. Andison (New York: Wisdom Library, 1946)

BOLDY, STEVEN, *The Narrative of Carlos Fuentes: Family, Text, Nation*, Durham Modern Languages Series (Durham: University of Durham, 2001)

——*The Novels of Julio Cortázar* (Cambridge: Cambridge University Press, 2010)

BONILLA, ROBERTO GARCÍA, *Visiones sonoras: Entrevistas con compositores, solistas y directores* (Mexico City: Siglo XXI, 2001)

BORGES, JORGE LUIS, *El Aleph* (Buenos Aires: Emecé, 1972)

——'El arte narrativo y la magia' (1932), in *Discusión* (Madrid: Alianza, 1997), pp. 102–15

——'El escritor argentino y la tradición' (1951), in *Discusión* (Madrid: Alianza, 1997), pp. 188–203

——'La muralla y los libros' (1950), in *Otras inquisiciones* (Madrid: Alianza, 1997), pp. 9–13

BOURDIEU, PIERRE, *Distinction: A Social Critique of the Judgement of Taste*, trans. by Richard Nice (Cambridge, MA: Harvard University Press, 1984)

CARDINAL, ROGER, 'Collecting and Collage-making: The Case of Kurt Schwitters', in *The Cultures of Collecting*, ed. by John Elsner and Roger Cardinal (London: Reaktion Books, 1994), pp. 68–96

CARTIER-BRESSON, HENRI, *Henri Cartier-Bresson: Mexican Notebooks, 1934–1964* (London; New York: Thames and Hudson, 1995)

CASTRO-KLARÉN, SARA, 'Cortázar, Surrealism, and Pataphysics', *Comparative Literature*, 27.3 (1975), 218–36

CERTEAU, MICHEL DE, *The Practice of Everyday Life* (Berkeley; London: University of California Press, 2011)

CHIMAL, ALBERTO, *El viajero del tiempo* (Monterrey: Ediciones Posdata, 2011)

COHEN, KEITH, 'Cortázar and the Apparatus of Writing', *Contemporary Literature*, 25.1 (1984), 15–27

COMAY, REBECCA, 'Benjamin and the Ambiguities of Romanticism, in *The Cambridge Companion to Walter Benjamin*, ed. by David Ferris (Cambridge: Cambridge University Press, 2004), pp. 134–51

CORRAL, WILFRIDO, *Lector, sociedad y género en Monterroso* (Xalapa: Centro de investigaciones lingüístico-literarias, Universidad Veracruzana, 1985)

CORTÁZAR, JULIO, *62: modelo para armar* (Madrid: Punto de Lectura, 2007)

——'Algunos aspectos del cuento' (1962), in *Obra crítica 2*, pp. 505–34

——'Del cuento breve y sus alrededores', in *Último round* (Mexico City; Barcelona: Editorial RM Verlag, 2010), pp. 34–45

——'Discurso en el Recibo del Orden Rubén Darío' (1983), in *Obra crítica 3*, pp. 475–90

——'Discurso en la constitución del jurado del Premio Literario Casa de las Américas 1980', in *Obra crítica 3*, pp. 285–302

——*Fantomas contra los vampiros multinacionales* (Buenos Aires: Ediciones Destino, 2002)

——*Final del juego* (Mexico City: Punto de Lectura, 2008)

——*Historias de cronopios y de famas* (Madrid: Punto de lectura, 2007)

——'La literatura latinoamericana a la luz de la historia contemporánea' (1980), in *Obra crítica 3*, pp. 263–84

——'Negación del olvido' (1981), in *Obra crítica 3*, pp. 419–28

——'Nicaragua desde adentro' (1982), in *Obra crítica 3*, pp. 437–58

——'Nuevo elogio de la locura' (1981), in *Obra crítica 3*, pp. 429–36

——*Obra crítica 1* (Buenos Aires: Alfaguara, 1994)

——*Obra crítica 2* (Buenos Aires: Suma de Letras Argentina, 2004)

——*Obra crítica 3* (Buenos Aires: Editora Argentina, 2004)

——*La otra orilla* (Madrid: Santillana Ediciones Generales, 2008)

——*Papeles inesperados*, ed. by Aurora Bernárdez and Carles Álvarez Garriga (Buenos Aires: Alfaguara, 2009)

——*Queremos tanto a Glenda* (Buenos Aires: Santillana, 2010)

——*Rayuela* (Madrid: Cátedra, 2006)

——'Teoría del túnel' (1947), in *Obra crítica 1*, pp. 31–147

——— *Textos políticos* (Barcelona: Plaza & Janes, 1985)

——— *Todos los fuegos el fuego* (Buenos Aires: Punto de Lectura, 2009)

——— 'La urna griega en la poesía de John Keats' (1946), in *Obra crítica 2*, pp. 31–100

——— *La vuelta al día en ochenta mundos* (Madrid: Debate, 1994)

DALLAL, ALBERTO, 'Efemérides: recuerdo de Rosa Reyna', *Imágenes: revista electrónica del Instituto de Investigaciones Estéticas* (9 February 2007), <http://www.esteticas.unam.mx/revista_imagenes/efemerides/efe_rosareyna.html> [accessed 8 April 2014]

D'AMICO, ALICIA, SARA FACIO, and JULIO CORTÁZAR, *Buenos Aires Buenos Aires* (Buenos Aires: Editorial Sudamericana, 1968)

DE LOS RÍOS, VALERIA, 'Fotografía, cine y traducción en "Las babas del diablo"', *Revista Chilena de Literatura*, 72 (2008), 5–27

DERRIDA, JACQUES, *Of Grammatology*, trans. by Gayatri Chakravorty Spivak (Baltimore, MD: Johns Hopkins University Press, 1998)

DERRIDA, JACQUES, and CRAIG OWENS, 'The Parergon', *October*, 9 (Summer 1979), 3–41

DÍAZ, MARÍA ELENA, 'The Satiric Penny Press for Workers in Mexico, 1900–1910: A Case Study in the Politicisation of Popular Culture', *Journal of Latin American Studies*, 22 (1990), 497–526

DURÁN, MANUEL, 'La obra de Juan Rulfo vista a través de Mircea Eliade', *Inti: Revista de literatura hispánica*, 13–14 (1981), 25–33

EAGLETON, TERRY, *Heathcliff and the Great Hunger* (London: Verso, 1995)

ECHEVERRÍA, ESTEBAN, *El matadero*, in *Revista del Río de la Plata, periódico mensual de historia y literatura de América* (Buenos Aires), 1 (1871), 556–85

ELLESTRÖM, LARS, ed., *Media Borders, Multimodality and Intermediality* (Basingstoke; New York: Palgrave Macmillan, 2010)

ELSNER, JOHN, and ROGER CARDINAL, eds, *The Cultures of Collecting* (London: Reaktion Books, 1994)

EPPLE, JUAN ARMANDO, *Brevísima relación: nueva antología del microcuento hispanoamericano* (Santiago: Mosquito Comunicaciones, 1999)

ESCALANTE, EVODIO, 'Texto histórico y texto social en la obra de Rulfo', in *Juan Rulfo, Toda la obra*, ed. by Claude Fell, pp. 561–81

FERRIS, DAVID, ed., *The Cambridge Companion to Walter Benjamin* (Cambridge: Cambridge University Press, 2004)

FOSTER, HAL, *Compulsive Beauty* (Cambridge, MA; London: MIT Press, 1995)

FRANCO, JEAN, 'El viaje al país de los muertos', in *Juan Rulfo, Toda la obra*, ed. by Claude Fell, pp. 763–74

FRASER, HOWARD M., '*Inframundo*: Juan Rulfo's Photographic Companion to *El Llano en llamas*', *Chasqui*, 17 (1988), 56–74

FRYE, NORTHROP, *Anatomy of Criticism: Four Essays* (Princeton, NJ: Princeton University Press, 1992)

FUENTES, CARLOS, 'Juan Rulfo: el tiempo del mito', in *Juan Rulfo, Toda la obra*, ed. by Claude Fell, pp. 825–33

FUENTES, CARLOS, MARGO GLANTZ, JORGE ALBERTO LOZOYA, and OTHERS, *México: Juan Rulfo fotógrafo* (Barcelona: Lunwerg Editores, 2001)

GARCÍA CANCLINI, NÉSTOR, *Culturas híbridas: estrategias para entrar y salir de la modernidad* (Buenos Aires: Editorial Sudamericana, 1995)

——— *Las culturas populares en el capitalismo* (Mexico City: Nueva Imagen, 1986)

——— 'Noticias recientes sobre la hibridación', *TRANS/Revista transcultural de música*, 7 (2003), <http://www.sibetrans.com/trans/a209/noticias-recientes-sobre-la-hibridacion> [accessed 6 April 2014]

GARZA, GUSTAVO, *La urbanización de México en el siglo XX* (Mexico City: El Colegio de México, Centro de Estudios Demográficos y de Desarrollo Urbano, 2003)

GIMÉNEZ CACHO, MARISA, 'Juan Rulfo, fotógrafo', *Luna Cornea*, 6 (1995), pp. 50–58 (p. 51). Available online at <http://issuu.com/c_imagen/docs/lunacornea_6/53> [accessed 6 April 2014]

GLANTZ, MARGO, 'Movimiento perpetuo: Augusto Monterroso', in *Con Augusto Monterroso: en la selva literaria* (Mexico City: Ediciones del Ermitaño, 2000), pp. 61–69

GOMBRICH, ERNST, and ERNST KRIS, 'The Principles of Caricature', *British Journal of Medical Psychology*, 17.3–4 (1938), 319–42

GÓMEZ BUENDÍA, BLANCA INÉS, 'Monterroso, sátira y humor', *Cuento en red* (2000), 45–49

GONZÁLEZ, ANÍBAL, *Journalism and the Development of Spanish American Narrative* (Cambridge: Cambridge University Press, 1993)

—— '"Press Clippings" and Cortázar's Ethics of Writing', in Carlos Alonso (ed.), *Julio Cortázar: New Readings* (Cambridge: Cambridge University Press, 2011), pp. 237–58

GONZÁLEZ, FRANCISCO, 'Pako', director, 'Graffiti' (Napato Production, 2005, 20 mins), <http://www.youtube.com/watch?v=9IoYPIvMye4>, [accessed 8 April 2014]

GONZÁLEZ ECHEVARRÍA, ROBERTO, '*Biografía de un cimarrón* and the Novel of the Cuban Revolution', *NOVEL: A Forum on Fiction*, 13 (1980), 249–63

—— *The Cambridge History of Latin American Literature* (Cambridge; New York: Cambridge University Press, 1996)

—— ed., *The Oxford Book of Latin American Short Stories* (New York: Oxford University Press, 1997)

GONZÁLEZ ZENTENO, GLORIA ESTELA, '"Mister Taylor" de Augusto Monterroso: de la América maravillosa a la ironía de la historia', *Romance Languages Annual* (1999), 470–77

GRIFFIN, DUSTIN H., *Satire: A Critical Reintroduction* (Lexington: University Press of Kentucky, 1994)

GRISHAKOVA, MARINA, and MARIE-LAURE RYAN, *Intermediality and Storytelling* (Berlin; New York: Walter de Gruyter, 2010)

HARRISON, RANDALL, *The Cartoon: Communication to the Quick* (Beverly Hills, CA: Sage, 1981)

HART, STEPHEN, '"El oficio de escribir": Some Notes on Literary Print Culture in Spanish America in the Twentieth Century', *Neophilogus*, 83 (1999), 387–409

HARTMAN, JOAN, 'La búsqueda de las figuras en algunos cuentos de Cortázar', *Revista Iberoamericana*, vol. XXXV, no. 69 (1969), 539–49

HASSAN, IHAB H., 'Baudelaire's "Correspondances": The Dialectic of a Poetic Affinity', *The French Review*, 27 (1954), 437–45

HAYWARD, SUSAN, *Cinema Studies: The Key Concepts* (London: Routledge, 2006)

HEMINGWAY, MAURICE, and FRANK McQUADE, 'The Writer and Politics in Four Stories by Julio Cortázar', *Revista Canadiense de Estudios Hispánicos*, 13.1 (1988), 49–65

HERNÁNDEZ JESÚS, MARÍA, 'Los cronopios de Julio Cortázar suben a las tablas de Galileo', <http://www.elmundo.es/elmundo/2010/10/06/ocio/1286373805.html>, [accessed 8 April 2014]

HIGGINS, DICK, 'Intermedia', *Something Else Newsletter*, 1.1 (1966)

HOLMES, AMANDA, *City Fictions: Language, Body, and Spanish American Urban Space* (Lewisburg, PA: Bucknell University Press, 2007)

HUGHES, ROBERT, *The Shock of the New: Art and the Century of Change* (London: British Broadcasting Corporation, 1980)

HUTCHEON, LINDA, *Politics of Postmodernism* (New York: Routledge, 2002)

—— *A Theory of Adaptation* (Abingdon; New York: Routledge, 2006)

JIMÉNEZ, FRANCISCA NOGUEROL, *La trampa en la sonrisa: sátira en la narrativa de Augusto Monterroso* (Seville: Universidad de Sevilla, 2000)

JIMÉNEZ DE BÁEZ, YVETTE, 'Historia y sentido en la obra de Juan Rulfo', in Juan Rulfo, *Toda la obra*, ed. by Claude Fell, pp. 583–608

KELMAN, DAVID, 'The Afterlife of Storytelling: Julio Cortázar's Reading of Walter Benjamin and Edgar Allan Poe', *Comparative Literature*, 60.3 (Summer 2008), 244–60

KERR, LUCILLE, JULIO CORTÁZAR, ROBERTO GONZÁLEZ ECHEVARRÍA, DAVID I. GROSSVOGEL and JONATHAN TITTLER, 'Interview: Julio Cortázar', *Diacritics*, 4.4 (Winter 1974), 35–40

LAGMANOVICH, DAVID, 'Estructura de un cuento de Julio Cortázar: "Todos los fuegos el fuego"', *Cuadernos hispanoamericanos*, Homenaje a Julio Cortázar (1980), 375–87

—— 'Márgenes de la narración: el microrrelato hispanoamericano', *Chasqui*, 23 (1994), 29–43

LÉVI-STRAUSS, CLAUDE, *The Savage Mind* (London: Weidenfeld and Nicolson, 1974)

LEVY, ANDREW, *The Culture and Commerce of the American Short Story* (Cambridge: Cambridge University Press, 1993)

LÓPEZ DE MARTÍNEZ, ADELAIDA, '"Las Babas del Diablo": Teoría y práctica del cuento', *Hispania*, 67.4 (1984), 567–76

MARTÍN-BARBERO, JESÚS, *Communication, Culture and Hegemony: From the Media to Mediations*, trans. by E. Fox and R. White (London; Newbury Park, CA: Sage Publications, 1993)

MASOLIVER RÓDENAS, JUAN ANTONIO, 'Un malabarista de los géneros literarios', *La Vanguardia* (Barcelona), 27 November 1992, p. 3

MAY, CHARLES, *The New Short Story Theories* (Athens: Ohio University Press, 1994)

—— *The Short Story: The Reality of Artifice* (New York: Routledge, 2002)

—— 'Why Short Stories are Essential and Why They Are Seldom Read', in *The Art of Brevity*, ed. by Per Winther, Jakob Lothe and Hans H. Skei (Columbia: University of South Carolina Press, 2004), pp. 14–25

McGUIRK, BERNARD, *Latin American Literature: Symptoms, Risks, and Strategies of Poststructuralist Criticism* (London; New York: Routledge, 1996)

McLUHAN, MARSHALL, *Understanding Media: The Extensions of Man* (London: Ark, 1987)

MIGNOLO, WALTER, 'Escribir la oralidad: la obra de Juan Rulfo en el contexto de las literaturas del "Tercer Mundo"', in Juan Rulfo, *Toda la obra*, ed. by Claude Fell, pp. 429–45

MILLINGTON, MARK, 'On Location: The Question of Reading Crossculturally', *Siglo XX/ 20th Century*, 13.1–2 (1995), 13–39

MIRALLES MALDONADO, JOSÉ CARLOS, 'La fábula clásica y Horacio en Augusto Monterroso: *Proprie Communia Dicere*', *Cuadernos de filología clásica: estudios latinos*, 23 (2003), 249–64

MITCHELL, W. J. THOMAS, *Picture Theory: Essays on Verbal and Visual Representation* (Chicago, IL: University of Chicago Press, 1995)

MONACO, JAMES, *How to Read a Film: The Art, Technology, Language, History, and Theory of Film and Media* (New York; Oxford: Oxford University Press, 1981)

MONSIVÁIS, CARLOS, 'La cultura popular en el ámbito urbano: el caso de México', in *Posmodernidad en la periferia: enfoques latinoamericanos de la nueva teoría cultural*, ed. by Hermann Herlinghaus and Monika Walter (Berlin: Langer Verlag, 1994), pp. 134–58

—— 'Sí, tampoco los muertos retoñan, desgraciadamente', in Juan Rulfo, *Toda la obra*, ed. by Claude Fell, pp. 833–42

MONTERROSO, AUGUSTO, *Augusto Monterroso Papers* (1921–2003), Princeton University Library, Department of Rare Books and Special Collections, Manuscripts Division

—— *Con Augusto Monterroso: en la selva literaria* (Mexico City: Ediciones del Ermitaño, 2000)

—— *Literatura y vida* (Madrid: Alfaguara, 2004)

—— *Movimiento perpetuo* (Mexico City: Ediciones Era, 1991)

—— *Obras completas y otros cuentos* (Barcelona: Anagrama, 1998)

—— *La oveja negra y demás fábulas* (Mexico City: Ediciones Era, 1990)

—— *La palabra mágica* (Mexico City: Ediciones Era, 1983)

—— *Tríptico* (Mexico City: Fondo de Cultura Económica, 1995)

——*La vaca* (Madrid: Alfaguara, 1999)

—— *Viaje al centro de la fábula* (Madrid: Alfaguara, 2001)

MORAN, DOMINIC, *Questions of the Liminal in the Fiction of Julio Cortázar* (Oxford: Legenda, 2000)

MUNGUÍA ZATARAIN, MARTHA ELENA, *Elementos de poética histórica: el cuento hispanoamericano* (Mexico City: El Colegio de México, 2002)

O'BRYEN, RORY, 'The Short Story 2: Augusto Monterroso', Lecture (Cambridge, 2008)

ORTIZ, FERNANDO, *Contrapunteo cubano del tabaco y azúcar (Advertencia de sus contrastes agrarios, económicos, históricos y sociales, su etnografía y su transculturación)* (Madrid: Cátedra, 2002)

OVIEDO, JOSÉ MIGUEL, 'Tres observaciones sobre Monterroso', in *Con Augusto Monterroso: en la selva literaria* (Mexico City: Ediciones del Ermitaño, 2000), pp. 12–18

PAREDES, ALBERTO, *Abismos de papel: los cuentos de Julio Cortázar* (Mexico City: Universidad Nacional Autónoma de México, 1988)

PATIÑO, ANA MERCEDES, 'Augusto Monterroso: el género como elemento lúdico', *Revista de literatura mexicana contemporánea*, 6.13 (2000), 47–63

PATTEE, FREDERICK LEWIS, 'The Present Stage of the Short Story', *English Journal*, 12 (1923), 439–49

—— *The Development of the American Short Story* (New York: Harper & Bros., 1923)

PAYNE, MICHAEL, and JESSICA RAE BARBERA, *A Dictionary of Cultural and Critical Theory* (Chichester: John Wiley and Sons, 2010)

PEAVLER, TERRY J., '*Blow-Up*: A Reconsideration of Antonioni's Infidelity to Cortázar', *PMLA*, 94.5 (1979), 887–93

PELLÓN, GUSTAVO, 'Cortázar and the Idolatry of Origins', in *Julio Cortázar: New Readings*, ed. by Carlos J. Alonso (Cambridge: Cambridge University Press, 2011), pp. 110–29

PERUS, FRANÇOISE, 'Algunas consideraciones histórico-teóricos para el estudio del cuento', *Plural*, 189 (1987), 37–39

PICÓN-GARFIELD, EVELYN, *¿Es Julio Cortázar un surrealista?* (Madrid: Gredos, 1975)

PUPO-WALKER, ENRIQUE, *El cuento hispanoamericano* (Madrid: Editorial Castalia, 1995)

QUIROGA, HORACIO, *Todos los cuentos* (Madrid; Paris; Mexico City; Sao Paolo; Rio de Janeiro: Colección Archivos, 1996)

—— 'La crisis del cuento nacional' (1928), in *Cuento terciario y otros cuentos*, vol. xii (Montevideo: Claudio Garcia, 1945), pp. 35–40

RABB, JANE MARJORIE, ed., *The Short Story and Photography, 1880's–1980's: A Critical Anthology* (Albuquerque: University of New Mexico Press, 1998)

RAMA, ÁNGEL, *Ciudad letrada* (Hanover, NH: Ediciones del norte, 1984)

—— 'Una primera lectura de "No oyes ladrar los perros"', in Juan Rulfo, *Toda la obra*, ed. by Claude Fell, pp. 790–99

—— *Transculturación narrativa en América Latina* (Mexico City: Siglo XXI, 2004)

RAMÍREZ, SERGIO, and HUGO NIÑO, *Queremos tanto a Julio: 20 autores para Cortázar* (Managua: Nueva Nicaragua, 1986)

REVUELTAS, JOSÉ, 'Lugar del cine en el arte', *Anthropos*, 1 (1947), 2–10

RIVERA GARZA, CRISTINA, *Las aventuras de la increíblemente pequeña* (2011), <http://increiblementepequena.tumblr.com/> [accessed 8 April 2014]

—— *Mi Rulfo mío de mí* (blog, 2011–12), <http://mirulfomiodemi.wordpress.com/> [accessed 8 April 2014]

RIVERO, EDUARDO, 'Juan Rulfo, escritura de la luz y fotografía del verbo', in Carlos Fuentes and others, *México: Juan Rulfo fotógrafo* (Barcelona: Lunwerg Editores, 2001), pp. 27–32

RODRÍGUEZ MONEGAL, EMIR, 'Le Fantôme de Lautréamont', in *Narradores de esta América*, Vol. 2 (Buenos Aires: Editorial Alfa Argentina, 1974), pp. 156–73

RODRÍGUEZ PADRÓN, JORGE, 'Un itinerario cortazariano: "El otro cielo"', *Cuadernos hispanoamericanos, Homenaje a Julio Cortázar* (1980), 495–509

ROHRBERGER, MARY, *Hawthorne and the Modern Short Story* (The Hague; Paris: Mouton, 1966)

ROSENBERG, HAROLD, *The Anxious Object: Art Today and Its Audience* (New York: Macmillan, 1973)

ROWE, WILLIAM, *Rulfo: El Llano en llamas* (London: Grant and Cutler, 1987)

RULFO, JUAN, *Los cuadernos de Juan Rulfo* (Mexico City: Era, 1994)

—— *Inframundo, El México de Juan Rulfo* ([Hanover, NH]: Ediciones del Norte, 1983)

—— *El Llano en llamas* (Madrid: Cátedra, 1985)

—— *Toda la obra*, ed. by Claude Fell (Paris: Colección archivos, 1992)

—— 'El desafío de la creación' (1986), in Juan Rulfo, *Toda la obra*, ed. by Claude Fell, pp. 383–85

—— 'Situación actual de la novela contemporánea' (1965), in Juan Rulfo, *Toda la obra*, ed. by Claude Fell, pp. 371–79

RUSSEK, DAN, 'Verbal/visual braids: The Photographic Medium in the Work of Julio Cortázar', *Mosaic: A Journal for the Interdisciplinary Study of Literature*, 37.4 (2004), 71–86

SARLO, BEATRIZ, *Una modernidad periférica: Buenos Aires, 1920 y 1930* (Buenos Aires: Ediciones Nueva Visión, 1999)

SCHIVELBUSCH, WOLFGANG, *The Railway Journey: The Industrialization of Time and Space in the 19th Century* (Berkeley; Los Angeles: University of California Press, 1987)

SCHWARTZ, MARCY, *Invenciones urbanas: ficción y ciudad latinoamericanas* (Buenos Aires: Corregidor, 2010)

SCHWARTZ, MARCY, and MARY BETH TIERNEY-TELLO, *Photography and Writing in Latin America: Double Exposures* (Albuquerque: University of New Mexico Press, 2006)

SEED, PATRICIA, *José Limón and La Malinche: The Dancer and the Dance* (Austin: University of Texas Press, 2008)

SEGRE, ERICA, *Intersected Identities* (New York; Oxford: Berghahn Books, 2007)

SHARMAN, ADAM, *Tradition and Modernity in Spanish American Literature: From Darío to Carpentier* (New York: Palgrave Macmillan, 2006)

SILES, GUILLERMO, *El microrrelato hispanoamericano: la formación de un género en el siglo XX* (Buenos Aires: Corregidor, 2007)

SILLARS, STUART, *Visualisation in Popular Fiction, 1860–1960: Graphic Narratives, Fictional Images* (London; New York: Routledge, 1995)

—— 'The Illustrated Short Story', in Per Winther, Jakob Lothe, and Hans H. Skei (eds), *The Art of Brevity: Excursions in Short Fiction Theory and Analysis* (Columbia: University of South Carolina Press, 2004), pp. 70–80

SOLA, GRACIELA DE, and JULIO CORTÁZAR, *Julio Cortázar y el hombre nuevo* (Buenos Aires: Editorial sudamericana, 1968)

SOMMERS, JOSEPH, 'A través de la ventana de la sepultura', in Juan Rulfo, *Toda la obra*, ed. by Claude Fell, pp. 728–40

SONORA, ANTONIO, *Adiós a Rocamadour* (Mexico: Atemporia/Museo Biblioteca Pape, 2011)

SONTAG, SUSAN, *On Photography* (London: Penguin, 1979)

SOSNOWSKI, SAÚL, 'Augusto Monterroso: la sátira del poder', *Zona Franca*, 3.19, (1980), 53–57

—— *Julio Cortázar, una búsqueda mítica* (Buenos Aires: Noé, 1973)

STANDISH, PETER, 'Another Glance at Marini's Island', *Neophilologus*, 60 (1976), 389–96

STAVANS, ILAN, *Julio Cortázar: A Study of the Short Fiction* (New York: Twayne Publishers, 1996)

STAVANS, ILAN, and AUGUSTO MONTERROSO, 'On Brevity: A Conversation with Augusto Monterroso', *The Massachusetts Review*, 37 (1996), 393–405

STEINBERG, SAUL, *The Labyrinth* (New York: Harper and Brothers, 1960)

STEWART, SUSAN, *On Longing: Narratives of the Miniature, the Gigantic, the Souvenir, the Collection* (Baltimore, MD: Johns Hopkins University Press, 1984)

SWANSON, PHILIP, 'Civilization and Barbarism', in *The Companion to Latin American Studies*, ed. by Philip Swanson (London: Arnold, 2003), pp. 68–85

——'Introduction: Background to the Boom', in *Landmarks in Modern Latin American Fiction*, ed. by Philip Swanson (London; New York: Routledge, 1990), pp. 1–26

——*The New Novel in Latin America: Politics and Popular Culture after the Boom* (Manchester; New York: Manchester University Press, 1995)

SZARKOWSKI, JOHN, ed., *Looking at Photographs: 100 Pictures from the Collection of the Museum of Modern Art* (New York: Museum of Modern Art, 2009)

SZURMUK, MÓNICA and ROBERT MCKEE IRWIN, *Diccionario de estudios culturales latinoamericanos* (Mexico City: Siglo XXI, 2009)

TAYLOR, CLAIRE, and PITMAN, THEA, *Latin American Identity in Online Cultural Production* (New York: Routledge, 2013).

TROTTER, DAVID, *Cinema and Modernism* (Oxford: Blackwell, 2007)

VALCÁRCEL, CARMEN DE MORA, *Teoría y práctica del cuento en los relatos de Cortázar* (Seville: Escuela de estudios hispanoamericanos, 1982)

VALCÁRCEL LÓPEZ, EVA, ed., *El cuento hispanoamericano del siglo XX: teoría y práctica* (A Coruña: Universidade da Coruña, Servicio de Publicaciones, 1997)

VILLORO, JUAN, 'El jardín razonado', in *Con Augusto Monterroso: en la selva literaria* (Mexico City: Ediciones del Ermitaño, 2000), pp. 32–43

WAGNER, PETER, *Icons, Texts, Iconotexts: Essays on Ekphrasis and Intermediality* (Berlin: Walter de Gruyter, 1996)

WILLIAMS, RAYMOND, *Marxism and Literature* (Oxford: Oxford University Press, 1977)

WINTHER, PER, JAKOB LOTHE, and HANS H. SKEI, *The Art of Brevity* (Columbia: University of South Carolina Press, 2004)

WOLIN, RICHARD, *Walter Benjamin: An Aesthetic of Redemption* (Berkeley and Los Angeles; London: University of California Press, 1994)

YURKIEVICH, SAÚL, 'Julio Cortázar: al Unísono y al Dísono', *Revista Iberoamericana*, 39.84–85 (1973), 411–24

——*Julio Cortázar: mundos y modos* (Madrid: Anaya & Mario Muchnik, 1994)

ZAVALA, LAURO, *Cartografías del cuento y la minificción* (Seville: Renacimiento, 2004)

——*El dinosaurio anotado. Edición crítica de 'El dinosaurio' de Augusto Monterroso* (Mexico City: Alfaguara/UAM, 2002)

——*La minificción bajo el microscopio* (Mexico City: Universidad Autónoma de México, 2006)

ZEPEDA, GUSTAVO SÁNCHEZ, GLORIA HERNÁNDEZ and MAGDA FABIOLA JUÁREZ MONTERROSO, *Los nuevos escritores y Augusto Monterroso* (Guatemala: Editorial Universitaria Universidad de San Carlos de Guatemala, 2004)

INDEX

adaptation 63, 159–63
advertisements 71–80, 87–90, 105, 154
Alarcón, Óscar 166 n. 27
Alba, Victor 156 n. 52
Alegría, Ciro 67
alienation 43–46, 151, 164, 170
Alonso, Carlos J. 106 n. 10
Apollinaire, Guillaume 17, 123
Arlt, Roberto 17
Aronne-Amestoy, Lida 2
aura 14, 153, 162
authority 3, 6, 14, 29, 32–37, 45, 63 n. 13, 118, 138–39

Balderston, Daniel 25 n. 44
ballet 159, 162–63
Barthes, Roland 23, 32, 46–47, 52–54, 56, 58, 62,
    64–65, 77, 142
Bartra, Roger 22, 28, 60–62, 129
Baudelaire, Charles 14, 39, 42, 52
Benavides, Manuel 81, 129
Benítez, Fernando 29–31
Benjamin, Walter 5–6, 10, 15, 21, 32, 47, 52, 158
    The Arcades Project 24, 120, 158
    'On Some Motifs in Baudelaire' 13–14, 52–54,
        56–58, 62, 84, 93
    'A Short History of Photography' 46
    'The Storyteller' 3, 7, 13–14, 22–23, 29–30, 32–33,
        35–36, 40, 42, 52, 61, 63 n. 13, 110, 161, 164
    'Unpacking my Library' 24, 118–19, 121
    'The Work of Art in the Age of Mechanical
        Reproduction' 13–14, 17, 80, 153
Bergson, Henri 41, 103
blow-up 56, 77
body 23, 39–43, 45, 99, 104, 112, 139, 147, 152–53,
    160–61
Boldy, Steven 65 n. 58, 69–70, 86, 92
Borges, Jorge Luis 2, 5, 7, 39, 43, 47, 125, 164
Bourdieu, Pierre 139, 141
Breton, Henri 85, 121
brevity 5, 8, 10, 12–14, 16–17, 39, 52–53, 60, 113,
    122–23, 126, 131, 135, 141, 146, 149, 152
bricolage 19, 24, 122, 134, 154

Calvino, Italo 5–6
camera 14, 31, 61, 71–72, 76
    flash 15, 20
    lens 55–56, 80, 84, 100
capitalism 20, 33, 36, 136, 138, 146

Cardinal, Roger 117
caricature 47, 131, 135–36, 139–41, 149–53
Cartier-Bresson, Henri 60–61
cartoon 17–18, 22, 24, 131–35, 139, 142, 145, 148–51,
    153, 159, 163–64
Castro-Klarén, Sara 120–21
Certeau, Michel de 80–81
Cervantes, Miguel de 6–7, 152
Chekhov, Anton 2
child 35, 40–41, 99–100, 138–39, 142, 152
Chimal, Alberto 164
cinema 11, 13, 18, 20–21, 23, 52, 65 n. 58, 66–67,
    70–71, 73, 81–83, 87, 89, 96, 100–01, 105–06,
    110–12, 145, 159, 161–62
civilization, and barbarism 144, 146
Cohen, Keith 70
collection, art of the 115–22
Comay, Rebecca 61
comics 18, 23, 87, 134, 149, 164
consumption 12–13, 17, 20, 52, 54, 73, 114, 160, 164
containment 10, 36–47, 63, 124
contamination 17, 20, 46, 68, 124
corpse 23, 41–42, 45–46, 58–59, 114, 124, 129, 153
Corral, Wilfrido 114
Cortázar, Julio:
    62: modelo para armar 154
    'Algunos aspectos del cuento' 7–8, 38, 67, 69, 105
    Buenos Aires Buenos Aires 23, 71, 93
    'Del cuento breve y sus alrededores' 8, 84
    'Discurso en el Recibo del Orden Rubén Darío' 95
    'Discurso en la constitución del jurado del Premio
        Literario Casa de las Américas 1980' 95
    'El escritor y su quehacer en América latina' 66
    Fantomas contra los vampiros multinacionales 23, 71,
        87, 89
    Historias de cronopios y de famas 123–24
    'La literatura latinoamericana a la luz de la historia
        contemporánea' 95
    'Negación del olvido' 98–99
    'Nicaragua desde adentro' 96
    'Nuevo elogio de la locura' 102–03
    La otra orilla 149
    Papeles inesperados 129
    Queremos tanto a Glenda 94–104
    Rayuela 67, 69, 105, 121, 149, 151
    'Teoría del túnel' 66–67
    Todos los fuegos el fuego 76–94
    La vuelta al día en ochenta mundos 67, 70

craft 7, 20, 30, 53
crime 18, 21, 89, 92, 97

Dallal, Alberto 165 n. 14
D'Amico, Alicia 93
dance 43, 96, 108 n. 77, 162–63
Darío, Rubén 17, 138, 141, 151
Day of the Dead 45
De los Ríos, Valeria 70
death:
    in short stories 35, 41–43, 45, 47, 50, 59–61, 76,
        82–83, 87, 114–15, 129, 148
    of the community 3, 32–35
    of the novel 12
    of the storyteller 3, 22, 29, 32, 35, 118
decay, see death
defamiliarization 13, 15, 40, 84–87, 159–60
delay, see postponement
Derrida, Jacques 69–70, 106, 162
desarrollismo 20, 33, 146
desire 40–41, 77, 80, 85, 92, 102–03
developmentalism, see desarrollismo
dictatorship 4, 98–99
didacticism 2, 30, 33–35, 61
dream 80–81, 85–86
duality 53, 124–25, 129, 141
Durán, Manuel 29

Eagleton, Terry 12–13, 40, 56, 158
Echeverría, Esteban 16
Eisenstein, Sergei 83
Elleström, Lars 104–05
epigram 6, 123
Epple, Juan Armando 113
Erlebnis 14–15, 52–53, 56–57, 98–99, 163
Escalante, Evodio 22, 27, 29, 63
ethics 94, 98–99
excess 46, 86, 99, 124, 130
eyes 42, 46, 55, 59, 83–84, 92, 99, 144–45, 152

fable 6, 10, 113–14, 163
Facio, Sara 93
father 33, 35–36, 146–47
fleetingness 11, 15, 47, 53, 58, 102, 128
Foster, Hal 85
Franco, Jean 32–33, 36
Fraser, Howard M. 31, 50
Frye, Northrop 131
Fuentes, Carlos 22, 60–61, 129
futurity 41–47, 56, 129

Gallegos, Rómulo 67, 144
García Canclini, Néstor:
    Culturas híbridas: estrategias para entrar y salir de la
        modernidad 20, 52, 73, 76, 86, 97, 102, 113–14
    Las culturas populares en el capitalismo 20, 138, 142–44, 146
    'Noticias recientes sobre la hibridación' 19–20

García Márquez, Gabriel 2
Garza, Gustavo 33
gaze 41, 46, 77, 83, 100–01, 135
ghosts 28, 37–38, 46, 50, 70, 129, 164
Giménez Cacho, Marisa 30
Glantz, Margo 115, 125
Gombrich, Ernst 135
Gómez Buendía, Blanca Inés 131, 135
González, Aníbal 16–17, 94
González, Francisco 'Pako' 162
González Echevarría, Roberto 1, 60, 95, 159
González Zenteno, Gloria Estela 130
graffiti 22–23, 62, 71, 101–04
Griffin, Dustin H. 131
Güiraldes, Ricardo 7

Habermas, Jürgen 16
Harrison, Randall 134–35
Hart, Stephen 16, 18
Hartman, Joan 81, 129
Hassan, Ihab H. 42
haunting 58–60, 69, 82, 99, 129
Hayward, Susan 82–83
Hemingway, Maurice 94
Hernández, Gloria 112
Higgins, Dick 106 n. 2
Holmes, Amanda 94, 97
Hughes, Robert 136
Huidobro, Vicente 17
Hutcheon, Linda 159, 163
hybridity 19–22, 24, 40, 62, 96, 111, 114, 122–23,
    125–26, 136, 141, 146, 158–59, 163, 165

identity 87, 91, 103–04, 144
illusion 5, 44, 89
immediacy 3, 17, 23, 52, 67, 89–90, 98–100, 135, 149,
    151, 159
instant 12, 15, 23, 38, 46–47, 50–63, 76–77, 80–85,
    92–93, 125–26, 129, 135, 151, 161
intensity 12, 15, 32, 52–53, 58, 84–85, 92–93, 135, 149
interference 69–70, 81, 86–87, 124, 141
intermediality 66–67, 70–71, 94–98, 101–06, 108 n. 77,
    154, 159, 162–63, 165
intertextuality 111–15, 126, 128
irrationality 27, 40, 56, 60, 76, 141
irreverence 34, 119, 122, 164

Jiménez de Báez, Yvette 30–31
journalism 13, 16–18, 23–24, 59, 66, 70, 75–76, 87, 91,
    93, 96–101, 114, 147–48, 151, 159
journey 54, 80, 86–87, 89, 92, 122, 136–37
Joyce, James 2, 28, 121, 123

Kafka, Franz 2, 61
Kelman, David 84
knock-out 8–9, 15, 23, 32, 45, 52–53, 55, 59, 61–62, 84,
    149, 151, 165

Lagmanovich, David 81–82, 113
Lévi-Strauss, Claude 19, 21, 24, 122, 134, 154
Levy, Andrew 11, 14, 20–21, 103, 158
Lynch, Benito 7

mark 14, 19, 30, 53, 58–59, 86
Martí, José 17
Martín-Barbero, Jesús 10, 18, 21–22, 28, 71, 76, 90–91,
    102, 104, 111, 130, 145
mass media 16, 18, 21, 68, 76, 104, 159
May, Charles 12, 67, 90, 128
McGuirk, Bernard 130–31
McLuhan, Marshall 21, 73, 87, 89–90, 104–05
McQuade, Frank 94
mediation 31–33, 42, 67, 89–94, 96–97, 100, 104, 118,
    130, 135, 141, 147
memory 8, 43–44, 58–61, 62, 90–91, 96, 98, 102
microcuento 111–13, 126, 135, 153, 164
Mignolo, Walter 22, 27, 30
Millington, Mark 130
Miralles Maldonado, José Carlos 113
mirror 46, 91, 120, 131, 136
Mitchell, W. J. Thomas 109 n. 96
modernity 2, 5–6, 14–16, 18–22, 27–28, 52, 57, 84,
    110, 113, 144
Monsiváis, Carlos 18, 21, 36, 91
montage 15, 82–84, 93, 101, 120, 123, 159
Monterroso, Augusto:
    La letra e 8, 111, 119–21, 136, 149
    Literatura y vida 5, 135, 160
    Movimiento perpetuo 114–29
    Obras completas (y otros cuentos) 130–52
    La oveja negra y demás fábulas 10, 120, 134, 163
    La palabra mágica 112, 134
    La vaca 112
    Viaje al centro de la fábula 115
Moran, Dominic 69, 106
Munguía Zatarain, Martha Elena 1
music 20, 35, 50, 73, 94, 96, 98–99, 101, 112, 146–47,
    153–54, 162–63
myth 1–2, 5, 20–22, 28, 45, 60–61, 69, 76, 81, 110,
    122–23, 125, 129

nationalism 28, 36, 138, 144, 162
Noguerol Jiménez, Francisca 131

O'Bryen, Rory 156 n. 38
orality 1–7, 13–16, 19–28, 30, 39, 62, 105, 110, 112,
    153–54
Ortiz, Fernando 19
Oviedo, José Miguel 112

Paredes, Alberto 81, 89
parergon 69, 106
Pattee, Frederick Lewis 10–11, 14, 20, 59–60, 158
Peavler, Terry J. 70
Pellón, Gustavo 67

perfection 67, 117, 144, 146
Perus, Françoise 1
photography 7–8, 13–15, 22–23, 30–32, 46–47, 50–63,
    66, 69–72, 76–77, 80–82, 87, 89, 91–93, 96, 98,
    100–01, 105–06, 110, 112, 129, 134–35, 148–49,
    151, 153, 158–59, 162, 164
Poe, Edgar Allen 5, 10–11, 14, 39, 55, 164
politics 4, 18, 23, 29, 32, 36–37, 67, 94–98, 101–06, 144
postponement 8, 41, 103, 117, 144, 146
present-ness 31, 41–43, 51, 54, 59, 61–63, 67, 82,
    98–99, 151
progress 19, 33, 36, 145–46, 154
punctum 23, 32, 53, 56–57, 59–62, 77, 151, 153, 165
Pupo-Walker, Enrique 2, 159

Quiroga, Horacio 2, 7, 16

radio 18, 21–22, 24, 63, 96, 111, 154, 162
Rama, Ángel 19–22, 27–28, 30, 45, 54–55, 62, 159
realism 10–12, 66–67, 89, 158
Regionalism 7, 67, 144
remainder, *see* residuality
reproduction, mechanical 11–17, 20, 22, 58, 67, 73, 77,
    80, 91–93, 100, 118–19, 151, 153, 158, 160, 164
residuality 19, 22, 27–29, 32, 40, 46, 53, 63, 103,
    119–20, 129, 153–54
revolution:
    aesthetic 7, 14
    Cuban 7, 94–95
    Mexican 16, 21, 28, 33, 36–37, 44, 65 n. 58, 134
    Sandinista 4, 95–96
    technological 89, 158
Revueltas, José 50
ritual 20, 22, 45, 83, 138
Rivera, Eustasio 144
Rivera Garza, Cristina 164
Rivero, Eduardo 31–32, 59
Rodó, José Enrique 17
Rodríguez Monegal, Emir 108 n. 70
Rodríguez Padrón, Jorge 89
Rohrberger, Mary 12–13, 158
Romanticism 10, 12, 47
Rowe, William 28–29, 33–34, 36, 40, 45–46, 62
ruin 23, 29, 31–32, 38, 42–48, 50, 61–63, 114, 164
Rulfo, Juan:
    Los cuadernos de Juan Rulfo 52
    'El desafío de la creación' 38–39, 42
    Inframundo, El México de Juan Rulfo 30–31, 47, 50
    El Llano en llamas 27–63
    'Situación actual de la novela contemporánea' 39
Russek, Dan 70

Sarlo, Beatriz 10, 17–19, 54, 71–72
satire 22, 37, 91, 117, 123, 131, 134–36, 138, 141,
    146–48, 152
Schwartz, Marcy 68, 89
sculpture 71, 98–101

Segre, Erica 50–52

Sharman, Adam 27–28, 63 n. 13

shock 14–15, 18, 23, 32, 42, 52–54, 58–62, 71, 83–86, 93, 98–100, 151

Siles, Guillermo 113

Sillars, Stuart 11, 14, 17, 20–21, 54, 158

Sola, Graciela de 70

Sommers, Joseph 22, 60, 129

Sonora, Antonio 164

Sontag, Susan 53, 58, 62, 87, 89

Sosnowski, Saúl 68–70, 76, 81, 129

speed 5, 17, 53, 72, 85, 102, 135, 138

Standish, Peter 80

Steinberg, Saul 134, 142–44

Stewart, Susan 119

suggestion 22, 29, 43, 81, 145, 159

supplementarity 69–70, 86, 91, 94–99, 104–05, 117, 163

Surrealism 85–86, 97, 108 n. 59 & 70, 120–21, 123, 159

Swanson, Philip 29–30, 66–67, 94, 144

Szarkowski, John 62

telephone 23, 66, 71, 81, 83, 86–89, 93, 105, 111, 146, 159

television 18, 20, 71, 73, 96, 111, 162

temporality 8, 11–15, 20, 22–24, 27, 31, 38–41, 44–47, 50, 53–63, 66–69, 71, 76–77, 80, 82–86, 92–93, 98, 102–03, 110, 123–29, 147, 152–53, 160–61, 165

theatre 21, 37, 91, 96, 119, 162

totalization 12, 54, 60–61, 69, 81, 85, 117

touch 142, 153

tourism 20

trace *see* mark

transculturation 19–20, 22, 24, 28–29, 36, 45–46, 62, 102, 114, 123, 130–51, 159

transport:

aeroplane 76–77, 79–81, 129, 146

car 141

motorbike 83–85

train 11, 54, 58, 119, 129, 135–38, 152

trauma 58–60, 83–85, 99

trope 23, 43–45, 58–59, 114

Trotter, David 67

truth 3, 6, 59, 82, 128

Twitter 164

unity 3, 24, 37, 55, 68–69, 81, 115, 118, 122, 131

urbanization 15, 29–30, 33

Valcárcel, Carmen de Mora 70

Valcárcel López, Eva 22, 71, 153

Villoro, Juan 125

violence 23, 45, 47, 52–57, 60, 62, 77, 80, 85, 91–93, 97–101, 104, 145, 149, 151

Williams, Raymond 22, 29, 38, 41, 46, 63, 153

window (as frame) 80–81, 108 n. 77, 135–36, 152

wisdom 3, 6, 29, 35, 42, 56, 62, 118, 121

Wolin, Richard 56

wound 32, 42, 53, 58–61, 77, 85

Yurkievich, Saúl 67–68, 81, 86, 94

Zavala, Lauro 113, 164

zoom 77